AF207207

PAUL METCALF

COLLECTED WORKS, VOLUME THREE, 1987-1997

PAUL METCALF

COLLECTED WORKS, VOLUME THREE, 1987-1997

COFFEE HOUSE PRESS :: MINNEAPOLIS

Dustwrapper photograph by Steven Trubitt. Dustjacket design by Jinger Peissig. Book design by Allan Kornblum. Text preparation by Becky Weinberg, Abby Pelham, and Kelly Kofron.

Where Do You Put The Horse? was first published by Dalkey Archive Press. *Louis the Torch* was first published by CrossCountry Press. *Golden Delicious* was first published by Chax Press, and later reprinted by Membrane Press. *Firebird* was first published by Chax Press in association with Granary Books, and later reprinted by Membrane Press. *Three Plays* was first published by North Carolina Wesleyan College Press. *Mountaineers Are Always Free!* was first published by Bamberger Books. *". . . and nobody objected."* was first published by Paradigm Press. *Araminta and the Coyotes* was first published by the Jargon Society. Coffee House salutes the editors of these small independent presses for having presented these visionary works.

This project was made possible by major funding from the Lannan Foundation. Coffee House Press receives general operating support from the Minnesota State Arts Board, through an appropriation by the Minnesota State Legislature and the National Endowment for the Arts, a federal agency; The McKnight Foundation; Target Stores, Dayton's, and Mervyn's by the Dayton Hudson Foundation; General Mills Foundation; St. Paul Companies; Honeywell Foundation; Star Tribune/Cowles Media Company; James R. Thorpe Foundation; and the Butler Family Foundation.

Coffee House Press books are available to the trade through our primary distributor, Consortium Book Sales & Distribution, 1045 Westgate Drive, Saint Paul, MN 55114. For personal orders, catalogs, or other information, write to Coffee House Press, 27 North Fourth Street, Suite 400, Minneapolis, MN 55401.

Library of Congress CIP Data
Metcalf, Paul C.
  [Works. 1997]
  Collected Works, 1987-1997 / Paul Metcalf.
    v. <III> cm.
    Contents: v. III.
    ISBN 1-56689-062-4 (HC: V. III)
    I. Title.
PS3563.E83   1997   97-277
818'.5409—DC20   CIP

10   9   8   7   6   5   4   3   2   1

CONTENTS

for Adrienne

WHERE DO YOU PUT THE HORSE?

THE CATEGORIES

It is strange that, at all visible levels, American literature is so neatly organized into exclusive territories, Poetry and Fiction. Poets and Writers, Inc., has published two separate directories: American Fiction Writers and American Poets. Most universities hire a poet-in-residence and a fiction-writer-in-residence. Editors accept one or the other, poetry or fiction, and there is never a question as to which is which.

In practice, there are two warring tyrannies at work here: fiction writers make money . . . poets have class, or status, or altitude. As a fiction writer, I have a trade, a profession, I sell my wares, just about as fast as I can manufacture them . . . as a poet, I may have a job (poet-in-residence), but I'm above the marketplace, my gems are beyond price, and I look more than a little down on you.

All of this is more than a little ridiculous . . . particularly in view of the subliminal drive in two of our major forebears—Poe and Melville—to violate the questionable boundary between the two genres.

Poe and Melville wrote both poetry and prose. Poe's poetry was rhythmical and glittering, and, to the modern ear, too musical-mechanical to command respect. Melville wrote heavy-handed, laboring poetry. But both Poe and Melville wrote a prose that reached passionately toward the borders, prose full of feeling (both inward and outward), full of music, with the "higher sense," whatever you want to call it . . . Poe's and Melville's prose, almost without exception, is prose-poetry.

There are other examples, I'm sure, in our nineteenth-century heritage. Doesn't *The Red Badge of Courage* have that kind of passion? And Whitman, God knows, had to invent a poetry, a verse of his own—the raw goods of which were linsey-woolsey.

Perhaps this is what I'm after: that the reach in our literature, our tradition (and we have an example of this in as recent a writer as Carl Sauer), originates in prose, a dirt-prose, that in the power and energy of its own passion forces the gates of poetry. No wooden horse, no gimmicks—just sheer force.

In the face of this tradition—which, to me, has the force of an avalanche—it seems strange to see our official, functional world falling back into the little inherited European boxes that so antedate what is happening today and what has been happening for so many years.

—1977

BLAST-OFF

The first encounter in *Tropic of Cancer* involves Miller and a girl in an impatience of passion: they try it sitting down, they try it standing up, and the heat is too intense—he infuriates her by coming all over her dress while dancing, and this is the tipoff: the Whitman, the exhibitionist, the spraying of semen over exteriors, for the glitter of it—semen in place of ink, as the liquid of literature.

Everything, latterly, about the placing of European seed in virginal American soil has been external, exploited, public, the shoot-'em-ups are ever with us, we love nothing so much as exposé. Because they couldn't get into it, they had to get out to it: the West. (Latterly, that is, as opposed to the early West, the forested Appalachians that Jefferson contemplated at Monticello—this was a land to be penetrated privately, as Boone penetrated it.)

This is the problem, what Pound recognized as our failure to distinguish between the public and the private: the most private act being the placing of seed exactly, goddammit, where it belongs.

Now . . . with the conquest of the West, the Cowboy—the hero of the shoot-'em-ups—has been replaced by the Astronaut, who embodies for the American male the old dream of perpetual ejaculation, a fountain, one's own, a fountainhead, Old Faithful . . .

> (peripheral,
> off target,
> dispersed & exposed,
> [solo,
> hetero, homo])

shooting up into space!

—1973

PLAY IT AGAIN, SAM

Following is a reconstruction of a conversation I held May 7, 1976, with my daughter Adrienne.

ADRIENNE—I think I know what your problem is. You know, everybody has a problem.

PAUL—Oh?

ADRIENNE—You're a frustrated musician. I think if you'd been brought up in a musical household you'd have become a musician or composer, but because it was a literary household you turned to writing.

PAUL—You've been reading some of my books?

ADRIENNE—Yes. *Apalache.*

PAUL—That's funny. Because as a child I was forced to take piano lessons. I hated it, wouldn't practice. They tried me on a clarinet and that didn't take either.

* * *

PAUL—Perhaps you can say I've brought music to literature.

ADRIENNE—Uh-uh. You've got it backwards. You've brought literature to music.

* * *

ADRIENNE—You know, I really can't handle it. When I think that you're my father—and you wrote this book—and you're this guy I know—and I'm so moved by the book—all this, all together, I can't handle it, it's more than I can take.

* * *

ADRIENNE—I think the reason some people have difficulty reading your writing, they're looking for a beginning and an end, and there isn't any. It's like listening to a piece of music, it's what's happening right now. . . . I'm not musically inclined, but music has been a part of some of the most important things in my life.

—N.D.

THE POET AND HISTORY

The following was prepared as a lecture for a class at the University of Massachusetts.

The late poet Charles Olson could at times become absolutely obsessed with some given period of history. It has been said of him that he could read Herodotus like a daily newspaper.

I can understand this because I have had similar experiences myself when I have become immersed—I think of it as just short of drowning—in, say, the pre-Columbian Indians of Peru, the early Michigan days of Henry Ford, the life of Christopher Columbus or of Herman Melville. Some time ago I wrote a documentary history of the Potomac River watershed, everything, from the Indians—John Smith—Lords Delaware, Calvert, and Fairfax—the early adventurers, explorers, and surveyors—George Washington and the Federal City—John Brown, the Civil War, John Wilkes Booth—the flora and fauna—on up to the latest disastrous report from the Environmental Protection Agency. I was, for a year of my life, swimming in the Potomac. The book is just now being prepared for publication, and as I go back to it, to any given point in it, touching again the results of my research, when I was soaked in it, and combining this with my sense of the area from various visits I have made there, I can enter an ethos, a precise local quality, that may include the people, the past, the landscape, the geography, the geology, the climate, the natural ecology, the innumerable human and man-made changes, with the dynamics of each—so that I see it, feel it, think it, sense it, today, as a totality of *was/is*. And I think the success of the writing, insofar as there is success, is the result of this permeation.

Perhaps because of my own ancestry and upbringing, I was set up for these attitudes and methods. As a great-grandson of Herman Melville and the son of his literary executrix, I was exposed early to an atmosphere of both literature and history, the past. For many years, as a youngster, I rebelled against all this, refused to have anything to do with it. The Boston Red Sox certainly had a greater place in history than *Moby-Dick*. I think this was all very healthy. It was only later that I discovered that rebellion is a form of love.

The uses of history are not without danger. It's an easy trap. We're all familiar with the stodgy professor-type who retreated thirty years ago into, let's say, the eighteenth century and hasn't been heard from since. The retreat was okay, but the dynamics, the will, the energy, perhaps simply the imagination, were lacking to bring it all back to the here and now.

Of course the present may also become a trap: the man or woman, the newspaper reader, victimized by the topical; the person for whom language becomes a blunt instrument, who responds like Pavlov's dogs to the emotional and visceral, so that meretricious appetite and irritation spring from him when he is beaten with words like *communist, ecology, energy, Watergate*.

I would think of history—and the varieties of language that ride with it—as a vast resource into which one plunges with energy, comparable to sexual energy, demanding and focusing all one's vitalities. Following this, there is the second phase, which I learned absolutely from Charles Olson: History is important only insofar as it impinges on the present. First, the plunge, the descent into hell, the near-drowning, if you wish; then the return to the surface. Because, if you drown, who cares? And if you don't plunge, who cares?

For many of you, as students, it is a matter of conscience to study history. You are not "educated" unless you know history. But the words *conscience* and *consciousness* are close in sound, and in my sense of history, particularly as matter for the poets, the barrier between these words is shattered and they become one.

The plunge, and the return. This uniting of history and the present makes the historian himself, as a physical being living in the present, an integral element of the material he is handling. What material is pertinent (or, in that ugly word, "relevant")? The answer: *anything*—anything with which the poet-historian, by the dynamics of his presence, by the intensity and authenticity of his researches, by the passion of his caring, can so engross us in his periods of history as to make them at least twenty times more powerful than today's newspaper—by making them more *present.*

Einstein tells us that time is circular—and Marshall McLuhan explicates what we already know, that, thanks to the marvels of electronics, all information, past and present, is now instantly and ubiquitously available. All this would seem to make history illusory or superfluous—if time is circular, then old-fashioned linear time, historical time, evolutionary time cannot be important. This is a great temptation, and today there is a vast world—I find it a weird world—inhabited by scientologists and science fictioneers, UFO seekers and Brooklyn Buddhists, evangelical Christians and homestudy astrologers—an odd lot, to be sure—God knows what Einstein would make of them—but all of them, in this uncertain and corrupt world, escaping into constructs that avoid the hard and/or glorious realities of their own genetic and cultural heritage. History and evolution may appear to disappear—and it may be comforting to believe in the imminent end of the world. But the world, manifestly, does not end. And all that you are, past and present, once more comes into focus, every morning, when you awaken.

So you awaken. You've left college, gone into the world, taken a job, and you come home at the end of the day, tired. On the coffee table are *Playboy, Time, The Enquirer* and *The Springfield Republican.* On TV, Walter Cronkite, and Sonny and Cher. In the bookshelves—those impressive floor-to-ceiling mausoleums (above-ground burial)—are Literature and History. What do you pick up?

Some years ago the poet Jonathan Williams was given a short-term teaching assignment at the University of Illinois. He had a free hand to do as he pleased, so in preparation he began to think about downstate Illinois, rural Illinois: what is it that characterized the area? And the answer, obvious and everywhere, was corn. Illinois is the damnedest corn-growing area anywhere in the world. So he generated this enterprise on corn, involving students from any number of disciplines: poets, historians, plant biologists, agronomists, anthropologists, ethnologists, dancers, artists. A whole segment of the university just went sort of corn-crazy for a while. They found out about themselves, their place, their history, their inherited and

current culture, their *was/is*. I imagine he must have given them—
and they themselves—a terrific experience.

It's all there—all these endless and fascinating determinants in
your lives.

It's just a question of what *you* do with them.

—1975

BUTTING HEADS WITH
THE TRANSCENDENTALISTS

I have difficulty dealing with philosophy because I view it as conclusions, or distillations, derived from experience—and, for purposes of philosophy, I am too directly involved with experience itself.

Whenever I find myself reaching a conclusion, or a meaning, or a philosophic concept, I instinctively plunge it back into the day-by-day, rebury it.

Answer a question not with an answer, nor with a question, but with an unthinking, demanding physical activity.

That too is a philosophy—*mens sana in corpore sano*—but I don't view it as such: I view it as the Head blotted out, at least for a time, in the sweat of the Body (and that, too, is a false dichotomy, Head and Body: the two are one).

The head ignites, produces its illuminations, and then reburies, not just questioning itself, but incarcerating, risking itself, totally.

This is one of the dangers of the Age of Literacy in which we live: the Head can escape, live a life of its own (the Age of Literate Affluence or Affluent Literacy)—the Head in orbit, circuiting the Earth of the Body.

Hitherto, this has been a luxury of the aristocracy: the priesthood of primitive cultures, and the first true philosophers of ancient Greece—a slave-supported society.

Now, everyone has a Philosophy of Life, and if he doesn't, he can go out and get one.

But I find myself thrown back, or throwing myself back, into pre-thought, into plain experience. Which is why I dismiss Emerson—and am suspicious of Thoreau (I don't believe in transcending *anything*)—the Head will always rise, the world is full of Heads—what's difficult is the Body: Whitman's persistent lists, Melville's cetological details . . . it's difficult to hold onto that, to persist in that, when the Head wants to talk—as, God knows, it always does.

If ours is an agnostic age, it is because God has grown tired of listening. He's wearing a set of those ear protectors worn in noisy factories. He lives in a factory of philosophers.

—1977

HENRY DAVID! HENRY DAVID!
WHERE ARE YOU, HENRY DAVID?

Stanley Cavell writes in *The Senses of Walden:*

> Here is another underlying perception, or paradox, of *Walden* as a whole—that what is most intimate is what is furthest away . . .
>
> * * *
>
> The writer has secrets to tell which can only be told to strangers.
>
> * * *
>
> The more deeply he [Thoreau] searches for independence from the Puritans, the more deeply, in every step and every word, he identifies with them—not only in their wild hopes, but in their wild denunciations of their betrayals of those hopes, in what has come to be called their jeremiads. (This is a standing difficulty for America's critics, as for Christianity's; Americans and Christians are prepared to say worse things about their own behavior than an outsider can readily imagine.)
>
> * * *
>
> America's best writers have offered one another the shock of recognition but not the faith of friendship, not daily belief. Perhaps this is why, or it is because, their voices seem to destroy one another. So they destroy one another for us. How is a tradition to come out of that?

Thoreau, in making himself a Neighbor, first makes himself a Stranger. A Neighbor is always a Stranger, this is essential—should a Neighbor become a Friend, then he is no longer either Stranger or Neighbor, he is Friend, and has dropped out of or risen above the formula. Thoreau was always and to the end a Neighbor, a Stranger.

"I have traveled a good deal in Concord" . . . as Melville traveled the South Seas, anticipating the modern world, where the South Seas are a neighborhood.

As Thoreau was Neighbor and Stranger to Concord, so he was Neighbor and Stranger to Thoreau: that narrow but inviolate distance between the man and Concord, between the man and Thoreau. He could only get at himself through the year at Walden, the bridge . . . the book is a record of that attempt.

It is the nature of bridges to celebrate traffic—and separation.

—1979

INCORPORATION: THE NEXT FRONTIER

I have heard of some recent medical researches into the aging process. Among other subjects studied was the behavior of cancerous cells, and according to these researches, once a human cell becomes cancerous, it ceases to age.

This suggests wonderful possibilities to the imagination. It has always seemed to me that the philosophical approach to cancer—as a pathology, something evil, to be cut out, burned out, smashed, was questionable. This kind of thinking, behind most medical approaches to cancer, is suspiciously in harmony with the traditional American approach to Nature, the Landscape, Woodlands, etc.: if it's in the way, cut it down, burn it, get rid of it. Cut the trees, shoot the wildlife, level the land.

It has seemed to me for some time that no disease can be studied or treated in an abstract way, divorced from the culture in which it flourishes. I have been interested in the history of human illness— what illness or kind of illness seemed to dominate a given period of history. I imagine it's a difficult subject to research because of the constant changes in terminology—what would "an apoplectic fit" or "an attack of the ague" be called in modern medical terms? But instinct tells me that a given society, with given assumptions, given dominant drives, will harbor a given group of pathologies that seem to flourish in that particular culture. I don't know the history of the various types of cancer or of some of the other "modern" degenerative diseases (multiple sclerosis, muscular dystrophy, etc.), but it seems to me that these are diseases doing exceptionally well in this society at this time.

Certainly one of the dominant historical facts of the past hundred years—a prime determinant of American energies and an event with worldwide repercussions—is the closing of the frontier, the end of the limitless West. The precipitancy with which the white man proliferated across the landscape of this continent, the recognition of this precipitancy, will, even now today, take your breath away. The millions upon endless millions of bison roaming the prairie were reduced to a handful—largely in a period of only twenty years. And the door of the frontier slammed shut, just when the tide was in full flood.

One cannot resist the temptation to think of cancer as the playing out of those same energies—the drive to explore and dominate the landscape turned inward, exploring and dominating the host.

We Americans love to think of ourselves as a young country— and in many ways we surely are. It is only in recent years that the Sears Tower in Chicago has exceeded the Empire State Building in New York as the world's tallest building. How much longer can that sort of thing go on?

In cancerous cells, if recent researchers are correct, the aging process ceases. Imagine—cancer as the fountain of youth!

All this, at the very least, suggests a different philosophical approach. Destroy the landscape, and we destroy ourselves. So, instead of treating cancer as an evil, a pathology, to be eliminated, it becomes instead an energy, a source of hope, perhaps the ultimate vitality. The direction, then, is not toward eradication but toward diversion, harnessing—in the literal sense of the word, incorporation.

There are other areas, even more modern, in which some of these speculations break down. We read that a few teaspoonfuls of radioactive plutonium deposited in the water supply of a major city will produce malignancies by the millions. Facts like this are, to my imagination, simply unmanageable. We have to treat them as facts—we have no choice. But when the whole subject attains an inhuman, purely chemical level, such as this, my tendency is to return to the historical, cultural levels which may assume certain shapes in the imagination. This may be a cop-out—may very well be. But there is enough in these speculations that I have outlined to intrigue me. If I were a doctor, particularly a cancer researcher, I would want to think about them.

—N.D.

CHARLES OLSON

Charles Olson: A Gesture Towards Reconstitution

Several writers on whales—particularly modern writers, whose attitude is scientific and sympathetic, lacking the practical hostility of the earlier whalemen—speak of the shock on first coming in close contact with one of the great giants of the ocean. It is the onslaught of the sheer *size* of the creature, the very quality for which they had imaginatively prepared themselves and for which all preparation proves useless. The fact of finding oneself that close to such enormity simply intrudes, and all constructions planned for the experience melt and vanish.

It is in this sense that I remember swimming with Charles Olson at Edisto Beach, South Carolina. It was a warm day in late spring or early summer, the sun was bright, the air and ocean gentle. We swam out past the soft breakers, and, still standing on the shelf of sand or floating up and down with the waves, we let the ocean deal with us, while I needled him good-humoredly about Gertrude Stein, whose work he never liked.

Charles stood six-foot-eight or-nine and weighed close to three hundred. He was in every part—head, features, shoulders, arms, all ways—an enormous man. Bobbing slowly with the waves, in a world so absolutely benign, with only his head, and occasionally his hirsute shoulders or the backs of his great hands, emerging above the glistening water surface—dipping his mouth now and then to take in and squirt out a mouthful of ocean—he gave me, swimming and floating close to him, that overwhelming sense of submarine enormity. And it is perhaps because I am not a small man myself—six-two and two hundred pounds—tending in the same direction but stopped short of those geographies of physiology that he attained—that I found the experience so compelling.

When the world deals kindly with us, when Nature smiles in all her beneficence, we tend at times to think that this may not be permanent, and we may hinder our enjoyment of the occasion with such thoughts. The placid whale may nuzzle peaceably to your side—and with a flip of its flukes destroy you. So with Charles: within our pleasant literary banter there was an edge not altogether benign—and this was related to my sense of the ocean-hidden vastness of the man.

His attitude toward his own size was filled with contradictions and extremes. He was prey, particularly in his younger years, to levels of embarrassment stemming from a concept of himself as at least a social alien and at worst some sort of monster. (He mentioned once, in his maturity, the difficulty he had in making it with the young chicks: "When I was younger, I was too tall; now I'm too old.") Yet he never let these feelings overwhelm or dominate him for long, he never succumbed to self-pity. He would instead come charging forth, in voice, intelligence, and physical presence, and quite simply take over the world in which he found himself.

He had a habit, when we were sitting around talking, of rising from his chair, coming over to mine, pressing his thigh against the arm of my chair, forcing my eyes to rise to his, in that great head that occluded all other realities, and, his voice now deceptively gentle, allowing his bulk to carry the weight of his argument.

I have a cousin, Barton Chapin—a tall man himself, perhaps six-four—who was headmaster of a school in Buffalo at the time Charles was there teaching at the university, and I asked him once if they had ever met. He smiled, and recalled that he had been introduced to Charles at a party, when both were standing in a narrow doorway—and he had found dialogue there impossible.

On the same visit to Edisto Island, Charles spent the night with us in a little cottage we were borrowing, and all we could offer him for a bed was a narrow camp cot. The next morning, Charles, who normally slept until noon and often until twilight, was up and about early—incapable of dealing with that damned cot.

He came to visit us once in North Carolina, when our oldest daughter, Anne, was perhaps two or three, and he insisted on riding on the seesaw with her, laughing the fool all the time—and squatting to play in the sandbox with her.

In his relations with women, he seemed to go out of his way to dramatize his size. His two enduring connections were both with slight girls, shorter than average. The first, Connie, was perhaps four-foot-ten, and when they came for dinner in our first apartment—a tiny, low-ceilinged affair on West 18th Street—they sat side by side on the double bed that served as a studio couch during the day. Connie, head and shoulders against the wall, spread her figure out straight, and her feet didn't reach the edge of the bed; Charles, his head and shoulders beside hers, spread torso and rump across the coverlet, while his thighs rose to mountainous knees, and calves descended to feet planted flat on the floor, seemingly in the middle of the room.

In contemporary professional basketball and football, where teams employ creatures of the same bulk and grace as Charles, such figures have perhaps become more commonplace. Forty years ago, however—which is about when I first met Charles—these people didn't seem to exist. (It is as though the genetic reservoir had quickly produced physiques for which there was a pressing cultural demand.) Charles, being physically unique, at least in his own day, reinforced a sense one had of him as an original.

When I first met him, I was perhaps fourteen, and he would have been twenty. I was living at home with my mother and father in Cambridge. My older brother was away at school, and I was shortly to leave. Charles had sought us out because of his interest in Melville—my mother was Melville's literary executrix, and this was the period of the Melville revival—all the scholars were zeroing in on us. Charles's health, which was never secure—partly because he abused it—was particularly bad at that time: he was going through the business of losing his teeth, and he suffered massive, accompanying head colds. With my brother and me gone or leaving, a residue of maternal instinct in my mother must have been called forth by this great colorful invalid. What a child to nurse! Take him in and nurse him she did.

Out of this emerged another strong element in him, the opposite and complement to the role of social alien, quasi-monster, and absolute loner: *the need to belong.* So consumed was he at this time with Melville, so identified with him, that he determined to become one of us, to become a brother or cousin to me. I recall running down the list of my first cousins with him, reviewing who they were, where they were, what they were like, etc. My mother was his mother, and he had joined the bloodline. He had absolutely become a neo-Melville. The title of his book became *Call Me Ishmael.*

He wanted very much to meet my grandmother, Melville's youngest daughter, who was still living then. A sweet, gentle woman, she still so loathed her father that she refused to speak of him, to anyone. Mother knew full well that a meeting could never be managed—so one day she hid Charles in the bushes outside her mother's Boston apartment building, and, squatting as best he could behind the greenery, he caught a glimpse of this pathetic old lady as she emerged and made her way down the walk. That was enough, he was satisfied. He had identified with his grandmother.

This same drive—the need to belong—surfaced in other ways. Some years later, when he had made up his mind that the Melville blood-game wouldn't work, or he no longer wished it to, he discovered that the poet Yeats had great respect for the Hines family in Ireland. Charles's mother was a Hines, and this meant much to him, this genetic affirmation, coming as it did from Yeats.

Again, still later, when he was well into *The Maximus Poems,* and identifying with Gloucester and its fishing heritage, endeavoring to establish a brotherhood with those he considered his fellow fishermen, I visited him one day, at 28 Fort Square, and together we walked down to the fishing docks. It was a windy day and the boats were in harbor, the men on the docks mending nets. They indeed knew him, and talked with him for a while, civilly, about fish and weather—Charles, I felt, quietly staging all this for my benefit. But the fishermen were never warm, and after a while became quietly hostile: they stopped speaking English and spoke among themselves in Italian. Charles was slighted, and we moved off.

Counter to this, and much more powerful in his nature, was the role of dynamic outsider, radical independent—with time sense, money sense, practical sense—all the usual channels and weapons of interpersonal relations—absolutely fragmented.

Years ago, when he was still a young man, he secured a Guggenheim Fellowship, and all or a large part of the stipend came to him in a single check. He promptly went out and bought a horse for his mistress, and later commented, "They should have known better than to give it to me all at once."

Later, when he was living in Washington to be near Ezra Pound, I visited him, wiring ahead that I was coming. He failed to get my wire, so when I arrived at midday, I woke him up. Irritated and cordial at the same time, he tried to cook bacon and eggs for us, burning everything, laughing about it.

When he was at Black Mountain College, I found him one day, with Duncan and others, with matches and kerosene in a field of weeds, trying to burn the weeds off. They dumped kerosene, lit matches, ignited weeds, laughed, and nothing happened, nothing burned, all afternoon, an exercise in absolute futility and good humor.

While still at Black Mountain, he went to the West Coast for a short time, he, Betty and Charles Peter, taking the Pullman from Asheville. I offered to take care of his car for him while he was gone, running it occasionally to keep the battery up. We agreed to meet at the station. I arrived ahead of time and waited. The time arrived, the train pulled in, and I waited. The train pulled out, and I waited. Some ten or fifteen minutes later, in roars Charles—Chevrolet and Olson breathless. I think he was a little miffed with me for not having held the train, but I told him to his face that I didn't think he was reliable enough to warrant my intercession with the Southern Railway System. Slight irritation, but he got over it. Consulting with the station master, we decided we had a good chance of beating the train to Knoxville, across the Great Smokies. With Charles at the wheel, Betty and the babe at his side, and me in the back, we passed a pint of booze back and forth, and fishtailed around the S-curves at insane speed. In Knoxville, the train was waiting for them in the station. I saw them boarded, and drove back alone, arriving home near dawn.

After Black Mountain had closed, and he was back in Gloucester, my wife Nancy and I, and Nicholas Dean, the photographer, drove out one day to see him. We arrived about midday, having announced our plans in advance. There was a note on the door, please do not disturb, he was sleeping. More than a little irritated, we went out for beer and lunch, becoming angrier as the beers went down. By three o'clock, we were ready for no further nonsense, so we went back. The note was still on the door, and no answer to our knocks. We yelled, kicked, beat the door, virtually dismantled it. No response. Nancy wanted to throw stones at the windows. Later, I heard, indirectly, that he was awake, and had heard us, but didn't come out because he was afraid to face Nancy.

Clark Coolidge told me a story of Charles walking in the street one night in Asheville when some redneck, probably drunk, approached Charles and hit him. Charles, according to the story, seemed to go through a deliberate process: he stopped, thought to himself, let's see now, I've been hit; yes; let's see now, where did it come from? over there? oh; yes; and—he flattened the guy.

(But that was a process of the mind moving through and generating the processes of that great slow body. Where the mind moved alone, it moved instantly: "oxy-acetylene, we come in that close when we do come in.")

And Nick Dean tells a story of the great fisherman and mariner, Charles Olson, stepping into a canoe—and sinking it.

*　　*　　*

It was at Black Mountain College that Charles really came into his own. He arrived first on a commuting basis, maintaining his home in Washington, but it wasn't long before he moved in permanently—and when he did so, it quickly became apparent that he intended to take over. The college at that time was dominated by Josef Albers and the Bauhaus refugees, which gave it a distinct Germanic flavor, as well as a certain reputation and security, at least as much as an experimental college could hope to have. I don't know much of the details of this period, but Olson gradually moved in, the Germans moved out, and the great contemporary American period of the college came into being, attracting such figures as Creeley, Duncan, Dorn, and Williams in writing, Kline and Motherwell in painting, Cage and Tudor in music, Merce Cunningham in dance, to name but a few. And this was the most exciting, self-confident and productive period of Olson's life. As he moved into a position of power in the college, he took command of his own voice as a poet. *The Mayan Letters* and the beginnings of *The Maximus Poems* came from this time. He was like a gigantic spring, bound tight ("the ball still snarled"), primed to unwind—and as he unwound, the energy poured out. An evening with him was an endless night of eating, talking, drinking beer, talking, eating—all the appetites and energies at work.

It is hard to tell whether he himself knew that in making the college, in replacing the old guard with the avant-garde, he was also wrecking it as an ongoing economic entity. So strong was his confidence that, if he did know, it made no difference to him. He simply did what had to be done. It was one of those rare instances in the life of a poet of the external and internal man ripening together.

Later, when the college had closed, when it had died financially, he stayed on alone, to preside over the distribution of the physical remains, landlord of the detritus of his educational ideals. And of all those closely associated with the last bitter years, he seemed the only one immune to nostalgia. When the property was sold, to become a successful boys' camp, with that gloss of post-World War II affluence that he so hated in America—it didn't seem to bother him. He had done what had to be done.

He returned to Gloucester and plunged further into *Maximus.*

*   *   *

My own friendship with Charles was a winter-summer affair, blowing hot and cold. Our paths separated from time to time, but when they converged, it was not always smooth. He gave me a copy of his first published poems, a tiny pamphlet called *y & x* (Black Sun Press, 1950), which he inscribed, "For Paul and Nancy, early recognizers, now that the others are catching up." I became infuriated at the arrogance of this, felt that if I didn't protest, make some gesture, I would allow myself to be used endlessly. I wrote him an angry letter, and received an angry letter back in which he accused me of betraying him, of offering my friendship and trust, and withdrawing them. I felt at the time, and still feel, that I had made the right move: although this fight kept us apart for some years and established an edge of mutual suspicion that never disappeared from even our warmest subsequent friendship, I had maintained my own balance, kept myself from becoming fodder for his demands.

Charles could be ruthless in using people. He alienated Jonathan Williams at one time by referring to him as "one of the soldiers in my army." And when I had just returned from South America, he welcomed me to Gloucester, insisted on taking me out for dinner (though I doubted he could afford it), so that he could pump me on the trip, find out whether I had discovered anything he should know. Although both of us were in the best of humor, I again felt used.

There was a sort of megalomania that accompanied his size: he once told me that he might give up teaching altogether, perhaps give up writing, and go into "big business."

And he was proud, immensely proud, in other ways. When he was in grubby poverty, we would invite him for dinner, and he would always bring wine for us, or ice cream for the kids; and it was a battle gesture, not simple generosity. He would never allow himself to be placed under obligation to another; and when, inevitably, such a relation became necessary, he was extremely reserved about it, even sharp at concealing it. When he had no money at all, and someone was supporting him, we never knew who it was.

His public appearances, as lecturer and reader, were often memorable occasions, his presence, his sense of the theatrical, his fine voice all contributing. But he could at times be extraordinarily arrogant, and at other times—or perhaps both at once—suffer oddly from stage fright. I know of two occasions when he threw out a listener at a reading, refused to go on until someone he decided he didn't like had left. ("You! Out!") And there were other times when he drank heavily before a reading, to overcome the terror. (Except for his last years, he was not generally a drinking man.)

If the distances were right, he was capable of a genuine empathy, a sweeping feeling for his fellow man. I saw him once at Black Mountain when he had returned from visiting the local Veterans Administration Hospital. He had been in the ward where a long row of beds were occupied by ex-soldiers, all black, all amputees. The concept of these black men spending the rest of their lives lying in those beds, with their chopped arms and legs, nearly overwhelmed him. "Jesus!" he roared.

There was something about people in large numbers that he was unable to deal with. He never liked New York City, was uncomfortable there, couldn't take the mass of it, couldn't find the handle.

But on Edisto Island, he met an ancient black man, Edward Simmons, tall like himself, to whom he responded immediately. Edward spoke a thick Gullah, and Nancy, a South Carolina native, had to interpret for Charles. They got along beautifully. Edward had spent his entire life on Edisto, with only an occasional visit to Charleston, forty miles away. Once he was taken to Columbia, the inland capital of the state. When he returned to Edisto, he asked, "Is there anything the other side of Columbia?" The remark delighted Charles.

Although Charles responded to a large number of friends, the terms of any relationship had to be just right: too close, too distant, too numerous, it just didn't work. He and my father, Harry Metcalf, were immensely fond of one another, and when Harry died, Charles wrote me a letter of condolence. It was a long, convoluted, involved thing in which he felt called upon to lecture on the cosmic meanings of death. The plain gesture—*he's gone, we loved him, we shall miss him*—that sort of simplicity was denied him. And, most sadly, at the end of his letter, he asked me to pass on his sympathies to my mother—forgetting that she was already dead, that he had sent me a letter of condolence, earlier, at the time of her passing.

At times, though, he was able to cut through complexities and cant with a marvelous directness. Clark Coolidge tells me of a television talk show on which Charles appeared. Charles hated television, only agreed to appear because they told him that Bill Russell, the great basketball player (six-foot-nine), would be on with him—he was furious when Russell didn't show. The commentator began to question Charles about the "inner meaning," the "deep significance," the "symbolism" of *Moby-Dick,* and Charles said, "Listen, *Moby-Dick* is a book about a man got his leg tore off by a whale."

*   *   *

Throughout his life, Charles—sort of like W.C. Fields—hated pets—dogs and cats—and only barely tolerated children, on his own special terms. And he was not the easiest husband or lover. He quite cavalierly abused all the obligations and privileges of domesticity. There is a poem written at Black Mountain (I thought it was in the *Maximus* series, but I don't find it there now) containing the great, galvanizing line, "Loneliness is a god damn lie!" That line, for me, more than any other single gesture, drew those of us who were his contemporaries together, introducing to one another "the islands of men and girls," shattering the meaningless rigidities in which we had locked ourselves. Duncan says that it was Olson who turned it all around for us, in the fifties, thereby making possible the entire modern (or "postmodern") movement in American poetry. If a single turning point, a single fulcrum can be chosen, that line is it. And it is the tragedy of his life, to me, that in his last years he was the loneliest of lonely old men.

He always envied me that I had a ballast in my life, other activities lacking in his, to weigh off against writing. Twenty-four hours in every day, only so many of them he could sleep, and for the rest there was writing. And if the writing didn't come . . . ? "You have been more commodious to yourself than I have," he said to me.

Nancy and I went to visit him in Gloucester shortly before he died, having no idea what his condition was. He was living alone, the apartment a worse chaos than ever. We took him out to lunch at the Tavern, and he allowed us to pay the check, a gesture to which he would never have submitted earlier. He was pathetic. He puffed desperately on a clay pipe that wouldn't burn—his answer to the emphysema that forbade cigarettes. His conversation rambled, and I was surprised to hear reactionary attitudes, anti-youth positions. He brushed his long, yellowy-gray hair. He spilled his water, and the waitress babied him.

Nancy and I left, badly depressed.

*   *   *

We didn't attend the funeral. In fact, I didn't know anything about it until some time after, when Nick Dean called. "Have you heard about Olson?" No, what about him? "He's dead."

I understand a number of his friends gathered at the cemetery for the service . . . and then repaired to the Tavern . . . and sat down to become quietly and seriously drunk.

What else is one to do?

—1974

The Maximus Poems: Volume Three

Recently—September 14, 1975—I attended an open house held at Arrowhead, Melville's old home in the Berkshires, to celebrate the acquisition of the property by the Berkshire County Historical Society, and, in this genteel way, to put the arm on the members of the Society, and anybody else they could grab, to raise funds to restore the house to the condition it was in, exactly 125 years ago, to the date—September 14, 1850—when Melville purchased the property. At age fifty-seven, I was one of the younger people there. We watched the overdressed and elderly, the quiet rich of the Berkshires, doggedly hefting their frames out of their Chryslers to lend their presence and perhaps their pocketbooks to yet another historic moment; we toured the house, read the posters, each announcing a proposed restoration, with price attached; we chatted with the long skirted, lapel-labeled hostesses (in order to read a name, you had to stare at a breast) and found everything from total ignorance to serious scholarship in knowledge of what they were talking about; we listened to the speeches over the public-address system, under the rented jonquil tent; witnessed the presentation of the latest inflated artist's edition of *Moby-Dick;* we gabbled under the great white pines on the becalmed green lawn, and admired the flower beds, tailored by the Berkshire Garden Club; we drank the pale yellow punchless punch, and nibbled the little petite fours; etc., etc. . . . and then I came home and reread "Letter for Melville 1951," Charles

Olson's bitter, personal diatribe against the Melville Society, against all official organization of the celebration of Melville's work.

This occasion, at Arrowhead, was not self-serving in the sense that Olson saw the activities of the Melville Society (you meet and talk and publish on Melville, the department head takes note, and your salary improves); no one seemed to stand to gain, personally, from what occurred on this brisk and sunny September day. Rather it was, indeed, a historic moment, the great wheels of society turning and pausing for an instant at a new notch: these old crocks creaking out of their Chryslers, fixing their glazed eyes on the speakers—these people who had never read *Moby-Dick* and never would, wouldn't know spermaceti from Gelusil—come now to put their seal of approval on this acquisition (for a hundred thou), restoration, and preservation (another hundred and twenty-five thou) of the Great House where the Great Man wrote the Great Book.

Olson wondered about the meeting of the Melville Society in 1951—what would Melville think? But I wonder today—what would Olson think, about this occasion? And this leads at once to—which Olson? The angry young man of 1951 (he was barely forty then)—this strong, angry, bitter, somewhat paranoid but supremely confident young man who was single-handedly taking on the Melville Society in defense of the dead man they presumed to celebrate—and through them, ready to take on society at large? Or are we talking about the later, ingrown, Gloucester-obsessed older man—the man whose politics, whose political confidence, had by then turned to water—the man who wrote *The Maximus Poems: Volume Three*?

*　　*　　*

There is a type of American, several in the forefront of the arts, who believed throughout their lives that the Golden Age, in at least one place and time in the past, really did exist and who offered this as evidence of the Perfectibility of Man. These beliefs are often irrational and simplistic, and seem to coexist, in oddly good health, with an otherwise vast and cynical range of intelligence and erudition—

the two areas of the mind somehow balancing each other. Pound felt that if he could just sit down and talk with Roosevelt for half an hour, explain the world to him, the international Jewish conspiracy, etc., Roosevelt would quickly see the light, change his approach accordingly, and the world would thereafter move forward on its proper course . . . and Pound was profoundly disappointed and frustrated when he couldn't even get an interview with Roosevelt. Charles Ives, who believed in the Perfectibility of America, based on some concept of the country derived from his childhood, simply couldn't understand why somebody didn't _do_ something about Hitler . . . "why doesn't somebody talk to him?" Buckminster Fuller, whose descent from transcendentalist Margaret Fuller has left its marks on him, is a kind of scientific revivalist: the right use of the right technology will Save Us. And Charles Olson, the early Olson: the poem is an object in a field of force, is itself a force, with political potential.

This I take to be a Jeffersonian inheritance, and like so much else that Jefferson left us, it is deeply rooted in the American mind: the vigorous intelligence, often with vast accretions of knowledge, borne up, made buoyant, by a singular and anomalous naiveté. Jefferson believed in the Golden Age of Greece, and imported its forms, believed that forms could perfect modern American man. And Olson writes, near the beginning of *Maximus: Volume One:*

> one loves only form,
> and form only comes
> into existence when
> the thing is born.

But, particularly in *Volume One*, Olson fluctuated between two positions. The one:

> these things
> which don't carry their end any further than
> their reality in
> themselves

. . . things formally self-contained, endeavoring to be only themselves, without political extension; and, on the other hand, the possibility of the poem extending itself outward, as political weapon:

> as the news that the almond
> was in bloom Mallorca
> accompanied the news
> that the book was in print
> which I wish might stop
> the workings of my city
> where so much of it
> was bred

And:

> the demand
> will arouse
> some of these men and women

And:

> It is still
> morning.

It is this political faith, this faith in the possible political power of the poem, that gives *Volume One* its early buoyancy. And the passage, through *Volumes One, Two,* and *Three,* is a record, among other things, of the gradual loss of that faith.

This, the original faith, is Jeffersonian: the Grecian forms, the architecture that Jefferson planted in the Virginia hills, peopled with imported European professors and the bright youth of Virginia—that was to be a practical factory leading to the Perfection of American Man. (And then one reads of Edgar Allan Poe as a student at the new university: the rich kids, sons of Virginia planters, with their houseboys, their horses, their drinking and gambling, the cat houses and moneylenders in Charlottesville.)

*   *   *

In *Volume One,* Olson addresses his readers, not as "dear readers" but as "fellow citizens"—or, at one point, "Ladies & Gentlemen." This is as we might be addressed from the White House. But elsewhere, he reduces his political range, becomes more realistic about his possible reach, and speaks to us as "you islands of men and girls."

*   *   *

> On ne doit aux morts nothing
> else than
> la vérité

. . . and, as throughout the poem, throughout all three volumes, whatever changes he may go through, whatever fluctuations between poles, one is required never to doubt that Olson knows precisely what "la vérité" is.

*   *   *

There was a strong element, in the Olson of *Volume One,* of what we call today "investigative reporter." He felt that merely by exposing what he called "conantry" he could reform Harvard; and he seemed to want to give the impression that this was just a beginning, beyond Harvard there was the educational system, and beyond that the whole American nation; and he looked to you, the reader, to see if you seemed to believe that he had that power, and if you gave the impression that you did, if the feedback from reader to poet was positive, then he shared that belief, and extended its range—much as politicians are reassured, fortifying their belief in themselves, by "pressing the flesh."

His obsession with history seems at times a corrective matter, almost mechanical, a realignment (tow and camber, kingpin and ball joint) so that henceforth the social machine will run according to its ordained design. As Don Byrd says, holding thumb and forefinger close together, "He was *that close* to being Jonathan Edwards."

Yet it was his political faith, and the buoyancy resulting from it, infusing *Volume One*, that energized him, and, in turn, energized American poetry, in the "postmodern" period of the fifties. As Duncan says, it was Olson who turned it all around for us.

But toward the end of *Volume One,* the faith begins to fail:

> . . nothing now your credence
> start all . give over . . .

*   *   *

Volume Two opens with continental drift, the Atlantic rift: a seismic disturbance in Olson . . . which leads straight into the story of Merry and the bull:

> died as torso head & limbs
> in a Saturday night's darkness
> drunk trying
> to get the young bull down
> to see if Sunday morning again he might
> before the people show off
> once more
> his prowess—braggart man to die
> among Dogtown meadow rocks

Not that Olson was a braggart—or not that that is the point here—but that this is the first shift, the first major rift, in his front of confidence.

Symptomatic of this change is a turn to the land, which to Olson is feminine (and dirty), as opposed to the sea, which is masculine (and clean). There is the burial of Merry:

> Then only
> after the grubs
> had done him
> did the earth
> let her robe

> uncover and her part
> take him in

And:

> the Sea—turn yr Back on
> the Sea, go inland, to
> Dogtown: the Harbor
>
> the shore the City
> are now
> shitty, as the Nation
>
> is . . .

Masculine, seafaring Olson is no longer putting out for fish, but heading back to port, escaping disaster by mere luck (*Cashes*), and dreaming of the woman envenomed by the snake, the woman fucking the spirit of the mountain.

Not to belabor the psychological, but Olson himself says, in these poems,

> a mother is a hard thing to get away from

. . . and he said to me once, in conversation, something to the effect that concern or obsession with *rock* is psychological.

Note the venom with which he speaks, earlier, of the landscape at Yellowstone . . . and, in these poems:

> where moraine, and the more
> evident presence of rock-tumble
> gives the road, & center, its
> moor character—moonscape
> and hell)

*   *   *

Volume Two is the straddler, the linkage, the second act of a three-act drama.

He speaks of drinking, the sailors who will not put out to sea, even in fair weather, for drinking. It was somewhere around this point in his life that Olson's own drinking increased . . . he started indulging himself whereas hitherto he had been abstemious—*that close* to Jonathan Edwards.

*   *   *

In the poem *Maximus, at the Harbor,* he gets into the full conflict, sea and land, Okeanos and rock, male and female, man and woman:

> Okeanos rages, tears rocks back in his path.
> Encircling Okeanos tears upon the earth to get love loose,
>
> that women fall into the clefts
> of women, that men tear at their legs
> and rape until love sifts
> through all things and nothing is except love as stud
> upon the earth
>
> love to sit in the ring
> of Okeanos love to lie in the spit
> of a woman a man to sit in her legs

. . . and ending with:

> The great Ocean is angry. It wants the Perfect Child

Later, there is mocking (as in the nesting records of the Mocking Bird):

> The Young Ladies
> Independent Society
> of East Gloucester
> has arisen
> from the flames:

                    the Sodality
                    of the Female Rule
                    declared: We will Love
                    with Kisses

                    Each Other, and Serve Man
                    as Our Child

                              *   *   *

Again, in *Volume Two,* he is no longer putting out for fish, the
energy is in heading home for port:

        . . . but the roar of this guy going through
        the snow and bent to a north easter and not taking any
        round about way off the shoals to the north but going
        as he was up & down dale like a horseman out of some
        English novel makes it with me, and I want that sense
        here, of this fellow going home

Arrived at port, little by little he slips into the Earth—presaging
Volume Three. Not, as in the earlier poems, *placing* himself in
Gloucester, but immersing, slipping, identifying himself, his own
body, with the rocks, soil, gravel, contours, landscape, geography,
geology, topography, in ever-narrower, more precise detail.

            and open an opening
            big enough for himself

At the same time, the division—Father-Ocean/Mother-Earth—
becomes clearer, more exact:

                Mother Dogtown
            of whom the Goddess
            was the front

                Father Sea
            who comes to the skirt
                    of the City

And later, he runs the two together:

> gardens ran
> to the water's
> edge . . .

There is also a concern, through *Volume Two*, and reaching a climax in the next-to-last poem, with the River: the fresh water, flowing out of the Earth, invaded by the tides of Ocean, carrying the Flowers, on the outward tide, out to sea.

And, the final poem, a sort of decision, a decision we don't quite believe, a little thumbtack on the map of himself, his own tides:

> I set out now
> in a box upon the sea

*   *   *

Finally, there is *Volume Three*, of which this essay is presumably a review:

> A View, in the Mirror, of Myself,
> Age 52

This is a turning point, the pivot on which a revolving door revolves—or like the fishing boats he describes earlier, in the storm, anchors dragging, some slipping past the others, others crashing: Olson/Olson.

There begins, now, to be a drawing in, a concern with his own physical self: there is the poem titled "Maximus to himself June 1964":

> And my arm
> on my own body,
> my own hand
>
> mine

And:

> not even able to get off into the land except
> twisting
> like the hair
> from my own pubes

*   *   *

September 9, 1964: the poem about meeting Death. This was a little more than five years before his own death.

> a stranger, suddenly
> showing up, makes the very thing you were do-
> ing no longer the same.

*   *   *

We see, for the first time, a terrible, searing loneliness:

> police cars turn my corner, no one in the world
> close to me, alone in my home where a plantation
> had been

. . . and we are thrust back to a line from the very earliest stages of *Maximus,* a line written and later cut (he read it in a public reading at Black Mountain College, but it is not in the printed version):

"Loneliness is a god-damned lie!" We recall being addressed, in *Volume One,* as "fellow citizens," "Ladies & Gentlemen" and "you islands of men and girls," the sweep of the arm, gathering us in, turning it all around for us (as Duncan says), a political gesture; and one is reminded that politicians are *never* lonely.

More and more, the images in *Volume Three* are of completion:

> the earth
> is only round when water
> fills up ocean to the
> top

And:

> all that one cares for
> proven
>
> and come true

But *in*completion is his natural state, and will not be that easily buried (see *Mayan Letters,* his admiration for the Maya, "the ball still snarled"). Angrily, bitterly, the incomplete returns: "Has March now been added so I have to live a 2nd month/of fear & Hell each year?"

Earlier, the exigencies of incompletion exhilarated him—but it is now all too painful, and he escapes to another completion: the candid identification of himself with his father, thereby completing the cycle that began back in the 1940s: see *The Post Office,* and the quotation at the beginning of *Call Me Ishmael* ("Loke, fahter: your sone!").

>   My own
> was so loaded in his favor as in fact so patently
> against my mother that I have been like his stained shingle
> ever since Or once or forever It doesn't matter The love I
>   learned
> from my father has stood me in good stead
> —home stead—I maintained this "strand" to
> this very day. My father's And now my own

It can be said that all of *Maximus* is the exposition of a stance, a position in relation to the world, that was fully taken, and exists in its most compact form, in his earliest writings, back in the forties. (This is an attractive approach to many writers, for example, Joyce: was anything essential or substantial added, subsequent to *Dubliners* [even the title says it all]?)

This same poem, the one dealing with his father, ends in a crazy circular faint reprise on his earlier secular confidence (I won't attempt to copy the wild layout, on this page):

as Your son
goes forth to create Paradise
Upon this Earth
Secular Praise
of You and the
Creator
Forever
And an End to Hell

Later:

Scene: I said to my friend my
life is recently so hairy honkie-
hard & horny too to that ex
tent I am far far younger
now than though of course I am
not twenty any more, only
the divine alone interests me at
all and so much else is other-
wise I hump out hard &
crash in nerves and smashed
existence only

And:

in loneliness & in such pain I *can't*

And:

off-shore out the Harbor for the 1st
of all the nights of life I've lived upon,
around this Harbor I hear also
even in the fair & clear near round
& full moon August night the
Groaner *and* the Whistling Buoy in their
soft pelting of the land I love

Lonely, painful, personal—signals of the nakedly emerging *romantic* poet:

> Full moon [staring out window, 5:30 A.M. March 4th
> 1969] staring in window one-eyed white round clear
> giant eyed snow-mound staring down on snow-
> covered full blizzarded earth after the
> continuous 4 blizzards of February March   5 feet
> of snow all over Cape Ann (starving
> and my throat tight from madness of isolation &
> inactivity, rested hungry empty mind all
> gone away into the snow into the loneliness
> bitterness, resolvedlessness, even this big moon
> doesn't warm me up, heat me up, is *snow*
> itself [after this snow not a jot of food left
> in this silly benighted house   all night long sleep
> all day, when activity, & food, And persons]
> 5:30 A.M. hungry for everything

If we take as the definition of the classical writer the one who objectifies his material, pushes it outside the self, presents it in some inherited or given pattern . . . and the romantic is the one who infuses into his material as much of the self as he can manage, the forms dictated by every idiosyncratic ripple of individuality, his material virtually a sexual partner, into whom he must plunge all! all the body! all the self! . . . then, by these definitions, the progression of *Maximus* is from Charles Olson, the man who started writing about Gloucester when he was in North Carolina, to some extent objectifying it, and who told me, when he moved back to Gloucester, he was nervous about the move, uncertain he could get *at* Gloucester when he was that close to her—from such a man, the progression is to the *Maximus* of *Volume Three,* who is utterly identified with and infused into Gloucester . . . a man who becomes the Last of the Great Nineteenth-Century Romantics.

> little aluminum massed cat boats were glinting
> in recently settling sun behind my yellow sweater over my

non-Buddha non-healthy American-nerve Golden Triangle sensitive
back between and below shoulders

And:

> looking up through my back & to topknot
>   of Head to
> the eye of the apex of the bowl of the
> sky

. . . Seeing Gloucester—reality—through his body, his body become
eyes, and reality—Gloucester—determined by the position of his
body. This is under control, but it is not far removed from the kind
of out-of-control experience that Theodore Dreiser went through as
a young man—alone, lonely, broke, in New York, sitting alone in his
room or standing, isolate, on a street corner, he would have to effect
a circle, turn completely around, 360°, in order to bring himself into
line with something, to align himself—perhaps with himself.

* * *

Near the end, the penultimate poem is like death and rebirth, the
opening lines an act of self-burial:

> I live underneath
> the light of day
>
> I am a stone,
> or the ground beneath
>
> My life is buried,
> with all sorts of passages
> both on the sides and on the face turned down
> to the earth

As though having attended his own funeral, spoken his own brief eulogy, he finally gives up on this life, this people, this Gloucester, this America—gives up, and aims, vaguely, for the next:

> the initiation
> of another kind of nation

Finally, the last poem—the ultimate thumbtack on the chart of his life:

> my wife   my car   my color   and   myself

Olson/Olson: glimpsing himself in the mirror, he turns away, and climbs into the earth—or, to use a self-image from this volume, he is the crazy mole, spinning on the highway, and he takes an oar from the back of his car and lifts himself off the tarvia, into the marsh . . .

—1976

Ten Years Later

Nancy and I recently—4 and 5 August 1980—paid a visit to Gloucester. The ostensible purpose was to meet and spend some time with that neglected poet Vincent Ferrini—a man both abused and loved by Charles Olson, and a man who, despite the gratuitous abuse, is now devoted to Olson's memory.

In "Letter 5" of *The Maximus Poems,* Olson tells Ferrini "you are more like Gloucester now is than I who hark back to an older polis"; he brags that he (Olson) is "not named Maximus for no cause," and finally dismisses Ferrini as "you who come after." Ferrini was angered and hurt—but, although several of his friends wanted to make a public issue of it, he was able to quiet them.

To understand Olson's motives, it is best to put his attack into historic perspective. *The Maximus Poems* was started at Black

Mountain, and when the college folded, and Olson finished his duties presiding over the remains, he returned to Gloucester, settled in, and focused his energies on the poems. I don't know just when "Letter 5" was written—either before or after Olson returned to Gloucester—but in any case, Olson returns to Gloucester and finds Ferrini, Gloucester poet, already there . . . and The Big O, all six-foot-eight of him (he had been raised, remember, an only child) simply had to sweep the decks clean . . . there could be no competition.

Some time later, Olson gave a lecture at Berkeley. I don't have the text in front of me, and can't verify the wording, but Ferrini tells me that Olson said something to the effect that "Ferrini writes nothing but shit." Sitting on the beach the other day, at Brace's Cove, Vincent tells me, "Well, I felt like I'd just been knocked clean out of the arena." The double blow—left-right combination—first in "Letter 5" and then in the Berkeley lecture, was almost too much for him. But however he may have smoldered, he developed a curious defense, which became a subtle but not unkindly counterattack: he began writing a long series of poems in Italian-American dialect. By retreating to his ethnic sources and regrouping with those specific energies, he had created for himself an arena where Olson could not get at him!

Olson was Swedish-Irish. The great majority of Gloucester fishermen are Italian. I remember the time Olson took me down to the docks one day, to jaw with his "buddies" the fishermen. The men paid him barely polite attention—and then ignored him, began to speak among themselves, in Italian. Olson was miffed, and we departed.

This Ferrini, he was not only a Gloucester poet, he was, like the fishermen themselves, Italian. (The race that produced Dante!) Was that cause for resentment?

At the beginning of this essay, I referred to Ferrini as "that neglected poet." The judgments that critics wish to make about Ferrini's poems, their qualities and virtues, are one matter. And of course almost all poets are neglected—it comes with the trade. But the neglect I'm concerned with here is that afforded him by so many serious Olson scholars. I don't see how it is possible to come to an understanding of Olson without dealing, centrally, with his amo/odi relation with Ferrini.

Vincent has his own version, his own definitions, of their respective roles. In a letter to me, he writes: "Olson spoke to the intellectuals and the academic world, I speak to the non-poetry reader, the man in the street"; and elsewhere he writes: "the scholars scavenging Olson's big bang/the provincial mute catching up on my slang." Of course, nothing can be that simple, that clean-cut. In fact, the relation between "natural man" or image-seeker in both men is complex and fascinating, central to the study of *both* men, and well beyond the scope of this essay. But one point seems clear: lacking Olson's range or flamboyance (choose your term), Ferrini, almost (but not quite) without effort, was and is the man that Olson tried to be and wanted to be and to some extent was able to be—that is, the native, the man whose worldview originated in, whose eyes looked out to the world from, the city of Gloucester. (It should be mentioned, I suppose, that neither man *is* a native of Gloucester, Ferrini coming from Lynn, Olson from Worcester.)

Ferrini believed, and believes, in the Power of the Poem:

> do you think this moment
> after reading this
> you will be the same again

It is my contention that the Olson of the early *Maximus* poems shared this belief, and drew from it major energies; and that the poems thereafter are, among many other things, a record of the gradual loss of that belief, a gradual draining of those energies. But that, too, is beyond the scope of this essay.

*　　*　　*

While in Gloucester, we got in touch with Linda Parker, who occupies Olson's old apartment, 28 Fort Square. She had company, and lots of food—fresh Gloucester flounder—and invited us all for dinner. Ferrini was nervous about going; he had tried only once before, since Olson's death, to visit that apartment, and had been unable to stay . . . the spirit of that man who had so abused him, and whom he so deeply loved and loves, overwhelmed him. But this time, after ten years, he was able to stay, felt comfortable.

Linda runs a seaweed business, and the stuff was all over the place, outside and in. Generally, the apartment looked even more cluttered and raffish than when Olson was there. But we crowded around a big table, the flounder was delicious, the salad rich, we had brought homemade bread, there was ground sesame-seed-and-seaweed for the fresh local corn, and the wine was from everywhere.

Vincent talked comfortably and easily, as we all did—of Olson, poetry and life. If The Big O was present that evening, the mood of his ocean was benign.

—1980

WHERE DO YOU PUT THE HORSE?

> *"Sometimes I have the feeling that Metcalf is asking too much of the reader, that we must almost BE him to appreciate his work fully. In fact he is asking no less than this of the reader: change the structure of your mind."*
>
> —Douglas Macdonald, proprietor, Two Hands Bookstore, Chicago.

As the subject of this remark, I guess I am both flattered and disturbed.

As a boy, growing up in Cambridge, Massachusetts, I used to eat something called an "Educator" cracker. And I think that's a fine and appropriate comment on that one-industry town where education is everything and where the educators, descendants of transcendentalists who were themselves descendants of Puritans, went about their daily business with a vigor aimed at no less than changing the structure of the student's mind.

Beyond school, I was exposed to—and learned to resist bitterly—other reformulators of my consciousness—not the least of whom was that modern version of New England hellfire and damnation, Charles Olson.

So, to find myself thrown into this group—standing in the pulpit, pointing an accusing finger—"You can't understand THE TRUTH until you restructure your mind"—it's a role in which I'm not comfortable.

I *am* at ease, though, to find myself following a path more or less of my own making, often isolated from those with whom it would be easier for me to join, people who nevertheless seem to follow certain directions and respond to certain assumptions that I cannot share.

These directions and assumptions are complex, not always uniform, but there are certain common denominators.

* * *

Not long ago, that clever journalist, Tom Wolfe, wrote a magazine article called "The 'Me' Decade" in which he pointed out that the period since World War II has been one of unprecedented affluence in this country, with money pouring into all class levels, one of the results being a national obsession with self-improvement, the alchemical dream being "changing one's personality—remaking, remodeling, elevating, and polishing one's very *self* . . . and observing, studying, and doting on it (Me!)." He cites Bergman's *Scenes from a Marriage* as a typical Me-Decade film: over three hours of two people trading off: "I'll let *you* talk about *you* if you'll let *me* talk about *me*." A sort of adult version of "I'll show you mine if you'll show me yours." And he quotes Alexis de Tocqueville: "Not only does democracy make each man forget his ancestors, it hides his descendants from him, and divides him from his contemporaries; it continually turns him back into himself, and threatens, at last, to enclose him entirely in the solitude of his own heart."

So we have all classes of Americans, particularly that vastly and only recently enlarged middle class (filled with sons and daughters of the downtrodden proletariat of the thirties), with newfound leisure and affluence—indulging, absorbing themselves, in ME: Synanon, Esselen, Arica, est, analysis, lemon sessions, scientology, encounter sessions, Jesus-freaking, consciousness-raising, clearing, rolfing, women's liberation, gay liberation, primal scream theory, Noetics, ESP, TM, pot and acid, Moonies, swapping & swinging, orgasm, orgone Zen, Tao and mantras . . . and poetry.

* * *

The world is aflood with poetry. Guy Davenport has remarked that literature used to be a river flowing between banks, now it's a river flowing through an ocean. Vast numbers of Americans, striving to define the self by immersion in the self, emerge as poets. And as obsessively interesting as the self can be, these poets nonetheless feel the need to join one another—not a true herd, but a kind of shared narcissism. Each group or school begins to develop and share certain cultural referents: the books read, the pictures on the wall, the jazz or classics on the stereo. And they begin to write poems about poetry, about being a poet, about writing poems . . . and the poems become filled, not with life observed, experienced, and celebrated, nor with the peculiar idiosyncratic nature of the author, but with the group-shared cultural referents: Coltrane, Kline, or Creeley, whatever is current.

The poet ceases to speak in a personal voice, to speak out of himself or herself, but rather of what he or she has *learned*: they are poems of education, rather than of the authentic self.

And the sad part is that the original motive—to define oneself following absorption in oneself—is absolutely defeated: the poets quite simply become anonymous, all that they share rendering them impersonal.

The poets gather and hold "open readings": "I'll listen to yours and applaud, so that you'll listen to mine and applaud"—a social contract. They get grants to support themselves. And they are very "supportive" of one another.

The river flows into the ocean . . .

*   *   *

Some years ago, when I was young and impressionable, a knowledgeable academic said to me, "There are two interesting things in the world—integration and disintegration—and they are equally interesting." My response was the nineteen-thirties equivalent of "Wow!"—I felt that I had learned everything worth knowing, if I could just hold onto this formula.

More and more, I have come to realize how wrong it is. Integration and disintegration are *not* equally interesting. Pathology is *not* as interesting as health, the journey to chaos is *not* as interesting as the journey to order. The poet may—in fact *must*—plunge into disintegration, pathology, chaos, maintaining as best he can his own freeboard, his balance—but it is the return to the surface, the return to sanity, where the experience may be recorded, that confirms our interest. Ishmael *survived* the sinking of the Pequod.

Most people's personal souls, my own included, are a rat's nest, and I find them just plain dull. My own approaches to history are very similar, another kind of dive into the soul: "I would think of history—and the varieties of language that ride with it—as a vast resource, into which one plunges with energy, comparable to sexual energy, demanding and focusing all one's vitalities. Following this, there is the second phase, which I learned absolutely from the poet Charles Olson: History is important only insofar as it impinges on the present. First, the plunge, the descent into hell, the near-drowning, if you wish; then the return to the surface. Because, if you drown, who cares? And if you don't plunge, who cares?" Two of my books—*Patagoni* and *I-57*—follow this pattern explicitly: the plunge into the past, and the return—the final chapter in both cases being a journal, a recording of the present.

It is precisely at this point that I part company with so many of my contemporaries. To them, the plunge—into one's personal soul, or whatever—is all there is, there is not even a thought of emergence, of return. And that's the tip-off, that the poet is in fact playing a kind of game: he's not *really* going to hell, he's not *really* going nuts—because if he were, the instinct to sanity, inherent and deep in all of us, would be disturbed and come into evidence.

But because it's a game and rules can be formulated and recognized, it gains support from the arts councils and foundations, all the officialdom of the arts.

Poetry, as a game, is much less interesting than baseball because it pretends to be concerned with such things as Truth and Beauty and the Soul, whereas baseball is explicitly a game, never pretends to be anything else, and therefore has direct and uncluttered appeal to our emotions.

*   *   *

Much of this so-called personal poetry is not really personal at all, in that it reveals nothing of the authentic self, or reveals qualities and materials most common and repetitious amongst us. And it is curious that this kind of poetry is apt to be decorated with—and numbed by—shared cultural referents. The urge toward the personal becomes, in fact, the very opposite of itself: a drive to anonymity.

It is difficult to write good baseball fiction because baseball is itself a fiction, and you're trying to build a fiction on a fiction. By the same token, and for the same reasons, it is difficult to build a poem on cultural referents.

*   *   *

I don't believe, as Douglas Macdonald suggests, that I am asking the reader to "change the structure of your mind." I do believe that the most interesting journey is the one from chaos toward order, that it is best enjoyed in good health, and that the whole trip will be most commodious for all concerned if, initially, the horse is placed in advance of the cart.

Is this so radical?

—1979

THE MAKING OF A PLAY

In February, 1979, I was introduced to John Dillon and Sara O' Conner, artistic director and managing director, respectively, of the Milwaukee Repertory Theater. This was arranged by the indefatigable Karl Gartung, manager of that remarkable Milwaukee bookstore, Woodland Pattern.

John and Sara had been reading some of my books, and we listened to a tape of a reading I had given. They asked me if I would be interested in putting together a play made up of materials from various of my books, and would I then come to Milwaukee to direct it. [See *An American Chronicle*, pp. 221]

I had a year to think about this while plans were made, funds were raised, etc. Although I had done some work in theater, both as actor and playwright, thirty-five years ago, I had broken with theater— under the influence more of poets and novelists—with strong feelings about the impurity of theater as a medium, feelings that sustained the separation during those thirty-five years.

It was curious, therefore, to have professional theater people— John and Sara—looking into my work, finding something I felt I had abjured. And this led me to examine again my thoughts about theater, to discover what theater is, for me; to determine if I still find it an impure medium . . . or is there such a thing as "pure" theater?

I was flattered, challenged, and a little nervous, I guess, in consideration of the great liberty John and Sara had given me—to write as I please; and the responsibility—to serve as both playwright and director, working with experienced professional actors. It was clear that the enterprise was developed largely for the benefit of the actors, as an exercise for them, an engagement with language and mime outside their usual range.

I was told there would be four actors; the play should be written with this number in mind. Initially, I didn't know whether they would be male, female, or a mix; in fact, the play was written and finished with the consideration that I might have men playing women, or vice versa, or blacks playing whites, etc., and that this would be simply another challenge to the actor or actress, another "illusion" to be dealt with.

Getting down to the work of writing, I went through all my books and unpublished manuscripts, looking for episodes, chapters, vignettes that suggested *movement*, where I found myself visualizing live bodies behind or amidst the language. This did not necessarily involve dialogue; in fact, as it turned out, there was very little dialogue, so that when it did occur, it came, I felt, with a certain freshness. Instead, there was a good deal of action, or mime, described either by the participants or by narrators.

I came up with a surprising number of possible scenes, some of them highly complex. My original version, I suddenly realized, would run some three-and-a-half hours—I had to whittle it down to an hour and a half. I finally got it into two acts and sixteen scenes, and it began to take a certain obvious shape and form: it became apparent that I was putting together a kind of American history and that the scenes should be placed in chronological order, running from the Cherokee myths (that I had taken from *Will West*) through Columbus (from *Genoa*), to the Civil War (from *Waters of Potowmack*). I called it *An American Chronicle*.

From the beginning, the idea was *simplicity*. Well after I had planned and written the play, I read Jerzy Grotowski ("Towards a Poor Theater") and felt my notions confirmed . . . that the centripetal force of theater drives toward the actor, that the actor is voice and body; that theater, therefore, in its simplest terms, is language and mime.

The language exists already in the text. And the play should be a joy and satisfaction to read, by itself, *before* it is embodied on the stage . . . so that the act of giving the words to actors, adding flesh, limbs, and movement to language, is an enrichment of forces already present.

Grotowski pleads that it is absurd for theater to compete with film and television in the realm of costume, setting, props, lights, special effects, transitions, etc. Just as representational painting became somewhat absurd with the development of the camera, so representational theater became somewhat of an anachronism.

The set for *An American Chronicle* was to be simply a platform. Later this was elaborated to two platforms, and masked entrances upstage. Costumes for the four actors were uniform: blue jeans, T-shirts, and sneakers. Lighting was of the simplest, and the actors could be seen moving between scenes and seated offstage. Props consisted of a tambourine, for one scene. Sound effects: a harmonica (one scene), and an actor beating his hands on a wooden cube to simulate gunfire (one scene). Scripts were carried in hand for some of the scenes, others were memorized; in some cases, the scripts were integrated into the substance of the play. (One audience member told me that the play should never be memorized, that the scripts were a positive *addition*.)

Because of this simplicity, transitions from scene to scene were executed rapidly, and contrasts from scene to scene—in pace, tone, substance—were enjoyed in a way that a cumbersome production never would have allowed.

As it turned out, I had four male actors, all white, ranging in age from early twenties to late thirties. As I look back now, I would say that one of the four was absolutely brilliant; two were above average; and one was competent, but with a large and volatile ego.

The most difficult part of directing came on the first day: I had to meet the actors, none of whom I had seen before; try to give them some sense of what the play was about, what I was attempting; and cast the play at once, all sixteen scenes, before rehearsals could begin.

I became aware of a peculiar double dynamic at work in my relation to the actors. On one level, I was their superior: the playwright, the director, the "literary" man, a good deal older than they—someone in whom John and Sara obviously believed, or I wouldn't have been there. On another level, that of experience in theater, I was at best a neophyte, and possibly an ignoramus. This became touchy at times, particularly in my dealings with the scene-stealing propensities of the man with the volatile ego.

All the actors, however, without exception, were cooperative, trying to deal sincerely with these factors.

The casting, of course, was crucial, and here I was either shrewd or lucky: as I came to know the actors, their limits and abilities, during later rehearsals, I don't think I would have changed a single casting decision that I had made on the first day. For example, I had a scene taken from Walt Whitman, his account of the defeated Union soldiers straggling into Washington after the first Battle of Manassas: the man I cast as Whitman told me, *after* I had cast him, that he had done a one-man Whitman show . . . his knowledge of Whitman far exceeded mine, and he brought this to bear on the role in several useful ways.

In another case, the man I cast as John Wilkes Booth, mouthing materials taken from his diary, had great difficulty with the role; I asked him to ham it up, emote all over the place, break all the rules of good acting, let it all hang out, etc.—and he was oddly stymied. This was the closest I came to changing a casting, in midrehearsal. I let him struggle, however, and quite on his own he came up with a marvelous device: to break the monologue into sections, play each of it as a different Shakesperian villain—Iago, Richard III, etc.

The actors were professionals, Equity members, with years of experience. But none of them had been trained in mime. And none of them, I think, had done anything quite like this before. The play at times called for silent mime, it called for speakers describing an action mimed, it called for actors miming and speaking at once, it called for conventional dialogue, it called for language with little or no mime. After rehearsals were over and we were in production, the actors became candid with me about the difficulties. One spoke of the difficulty in communication, the fact that they and I didn't share a common language. Another spoke of a particular scene, "John Marr," a long quote from Melville with very little stage action: how he hated that scene at the begining, couldn't understand or mouth the language, how he came around to it, learned to love the language, it became one of his favorite scenes.

Three of the actors bought several of the books from which the play was drawn.

Response of the actors and audience demonstrated a point of which I think I was aware from the start: *An American Chronicle* steers a narrow course between literature and theater, drawing on resources of both. One of the actors said that, in the process of rehearsal, "we simplified." I think he meant by this the process of translating or transposing language into bodily action, and it is interesting to me that a theater person would think of that as "simplifying."

My effort in all the books, beginning with *Will West,* has been to collapse time, to create a plane on which events of all periods may occur at once, to create tensions that one finds in the static arts, that I found so forceful, for example, in the color associations of Josef Albers—the chemistry of a red against a green, etc. Can these tensions be created in theater? To read a book requires *time,* although a reader is somewhat in control of that time, being able to go backward, forward, etc. Watching a play or hearing a symphony, the audience is locked into the time sequence. There is no "going back," save in memory.

An American Chronicle, as the title suggests, is a chronology, a sequence. Before writing the script, I read Aeschylus, listened to Bach, Ives, Coltrane, and Mingus. At some point, I realized that Ives and the jazz composers were not appropriate, or could not be factored into this effort. But *An American Chronicle* is a first: for myself as playwright, for myself as director, and for the actors, in this kind of theater. It is interesting to me that the three performances of the play represented a progression, each successively better than the one before, as the actors became more comfortable with the material.

I'm not at all sure that the complexities of Ives and Mingus, a complexity in which events occur on a single plane and all the lines are tense or taut—I'm not at all sure that this isn't possible in theater. And this idea represents a challenge.

—N.D.

TOTEM PAUL: A SELF-REVIEW

The other day, my three-and-a-half-year-old granddaughter Rachel saw a totem pole, and she wanted to know all about it, who carved it, why there was a bird at the top, etc. So the next day I went to the children's room at the local library and said to the lady in charge, "totem poles."

She came forth with one of those marvelous books that one occasionally finds, written for children. Direct, factual, straightforward—don't try to bullshit a kid!—the book laid out in good, clean prose, and in just a few pages, everything one would want to know as an introduction to totem poles: what they are, what they mean, who made them, where and when, how they were made, what is being done now to save them, etc.

Rachel and I looked at the pictures, and then she quickly lost interest. But not grandpapa. I brought the book home and read it carefully.

*   *   *

A totem pole was in no sense a religious icon or object; the Indian did not think of it as representing his spiritual life. Commissioned by a wealthy chief and carved by a team of expert craftsmen, it was an historical record, from animal to man, of the clan or tribe to which the chief belonged. Neither patron nor craftsman was aiming for spiritual or aesthetic qualities; the intent, rather, was for historical accuracy. And it is for this very reason—because they were not trying consciously to be beautiful—that so many of the totem poles are, in fact, so extraordinarily beautiful. It is the virtue of indirection.

Studying a complex totem pole, one can see how the various figures, and the tales they represent, bear upon one another: the claws of the raven are on the back of the beaver, etc. I realized that I was dealing here with an unusual hybrid form: generally, works of art fall into one of two categories, those that may be taken in at

once, like a painting or a sculpture, and those that require time for
their reception, such as a symphony, a play, or a book. A totem pole
combines both conditions: one can see it at a glance, or one can read
it like a book, the chapters merging, top to bottom, or bottom to
top. And to describe this mix, I have come up with the term, "The
Narrative Hieroglyph."

*　　*　　*

Genoa is the last book I wrote which may be described as a novel. Guy
Davenport calls it an architectonic novel. Since then, with the fiction
dropped out, I think all of my books, individually and collectively,
may be called "narrative hieroglyphs." True, unlike a totem pole, a
book may not be taken in at a glance; it requires time to read. But a
totem pole, as I have said, may be read like a book. And the effect of
one of my books—which I have commissioned myself to carve, to
record the "histories" of our "tribes"—the effect is one of the various
elements or "figures," in a line sequence, each perched upon the back
of its predecessor. In the past I have used terms such as "mosaic" or
"collage"; but the totem pole, with its tribal, historic sequence and
organic juxtapositions, is a much more powerful analog.

*　　*　　*

One final point. I know of a poet today who writes his poems on
expensive acid-free paper designed to last forever. He is consciously
and directly courting posterity.

But posterity, like beauty, is unpredictable and responds best to
indirection. The Indian chief who commissioned a totem pole
intended it to last only his lifetime . . . let his heirs and successors
make their own. In fact, due to exposure to weather, many of the
finest poles have fallen, rotted, and disappeared. It is the archival
white man, with his hunger for aesthetics, who is now preserving
them, bringing them indoors, oiling and staining them.

The Indians who made them were concerned only with the
making of the object in the moment, the object finished and raised.
Let the future take care of itself. It is perhaps the intensity of

the moment carved into the figures that gives the poles the very posterity of which the chief and his artisans were heedless.

* * *

Am I courting posterity with my books? Well, not consciously. How could I care, or what good will it do me, what people think of the books after I'm gone? I would like to see them read *now*. They are printed on what paper the publisher chooses, to last as long as it may . . . the books to be reprinted as anyone may or may not wish, as time goes on.

Let the future take care of itself.

—N.D.

OLYMPIAN IMPRESSIONS

There are areas on the surface of the earth where the landscape or, often, the conjunction of landscape and climate are so dramatic, not to say melodramatic, as to be the primary and unrelenting daily challenge to one's attentions. The north shore of the Olympic Peninsula, where I am now visiting, strikes me as such a place.

The sky is seldom altogether clear; more often there is cloud cover; or, more often still, a shifting—and quickly shifting—succession of clouds, of sunlight dimmed through shallow clouds, of narrow shafts of sunlight patching the water surface. As Nancy says, it looks like pewter.

Our house overlooks Admiralty Inlet, at the junction of the Strait of Juan de Fuca—opening, as we know, to the ocean, far to the west—and Puget Sound—with Seattle, Tacoma, and Bremerton to the east. When the sun *does* shine, we have clear views of pine bluffs, beach, and water; of Indian, Marrowstone, and Whidbey Islands; in the distance, Mount Rainier, in the center of the view; to the left, the Northern Cascades, with Mt. Baker permanently snowcapped; and to the right, the jagged Olympics.

This is what we see through the sliding glass doors in the dining area or through the window over the sink in the kitchen. It is what commands our attention many, many times each day—from our first arising in the morning to the last light at nightfall.

We are living on the outskirts of Port Townsend, a relict Victorian village that boomed and busted along about 1890 and that still retains much architectural charm, although being nibbled, now, by strip development at the edges. Because of this charm, because, by West Coast standards, it is "old," Port Townsend is now expensive and chic. Boutiques, antiques, bed-and-breakfast mansions, etc.; well-heeled Wisconsin retirees; Californians weary of their hot tubs, now looking for something "real"; trust-fund hippies, off the slopes at Aspen; day-trippers from Seattle; young survivors, scratching a living at the edges, etc.

Along with all this, of course, Port Townsend has become "artsy"; there are painting, poetry, crafts. And what little I have seen of this so far presents an odd appearance: if the artists were attracted presumably by landscape and climate, they are producing work that is strangely disconnected from just those factors; it could be anywhere—Provincetown, Soho, the Berkshires—or Port Townsend.

There is one exception that I have discovered so far, a man named C., who lives, appropriately enough and by choice, not in Port Townsend but in ugly, roughneck, redneck Port Angeles, a nearby lumber and fishing town. C. has been meeting the challenge head-on exploring and painting the shoreline, foothills, and mountains, the cloud and landshapes, with wonderful persistence, for years. I have seen examples of his work in dated sequence, and one can follow the growing intensity, the meticulousness, the forces channeled.

I am also aware that C. has been married and divorced twice, and that no human figures, or even human artifacts, appear in his recent paintings. The specifics of what the landscape offers him command his constant, almost ferocious attention: a concentration of energy that works well in the paintings but that might not be easy to accommodate in a human relationship.

Is this what the landscape does to one?

*　　*　　*

Shortly after arriving, we drove from Port Townsend to Port Angeles along Routes 20 and 101, the latter the highway that makes the circuit of the Peninsula. Initially a pretty road, somewhat hilly, through evergreen forests, with occasional glimpses of water, it takes us first to Discovery Bay, known to the locals as Disco Bay—the village itself a grungy little roadside excrescence. It is a curiosity of the times that the two most famous representatives of Olympic cuisine—Dungeness crab and the native oyster—are not to be found in the markets of Port Townsend. For these one drives twelve miles, to a run-down general store in Disco Bay. And the crabs are all precooked, the oysters shucked and jarred.

Next, driving westward, there is Gardiner, whose general store contains what has got to be the dirtiest, most dilapidated branch of the United States Postal Service to be found on the face of this our fair land. I have no confidence that the letter I mailed there ever went beyond the bottom of the dusty slot where I dropped it.

Beyond Gardiner is Blyn, and on to Sequim—pronounced *Skwim*. From Blyn to Sequim. Whereas Disco Bay and Gardiner were simply old and grungy, Sequim is modern and affluent, and the strip development, both in and out of town, assaults both sides of the highway like a flash flood, a slap in the face.

From Sequim to Port Angeles the highway is pockmarked with little disasters. And Port Angeles, the "big city" of the peninsula, with fish and lumber money, is the vulgarity of Sequim compounded exponentially.

Here we pick up C. He tells us that he likes Port Angeles, that all those cancers along the highway help to preserve the landscape; they keep the white trash, and many of the tourists, huddled to the asphalt. In five or ten minutes off 101, one can be in time immemorial.

With C. as guide, we drive into the Olympics. First the foothills, on the very edge of Port Angeles: rolling, open farmland, with a backdrop of jagged mountains. For the first time here—and perhaps for the first time in my life—I have a genuine feel for the word "homestead." Despite the occasional jeep or chain saw, it is frontier, pure nineteenth century.

We drive further into the mountains, to some old, man-made lakes that antedate the establishment of the national park. The dams have been condemned by the Corps of Engineers, but nobody much cares; should they go, only the Indian reservation below would be wiped out.

On to Crescent Lake, and here we park the car and hike into what is my sense of the rain forest—although I'm told the true rain forest is further west, where the rainfall is 150 inches annually. Nevertheless, here we have enormous firs and hemlock, moss all over everything; and the nursing trees, trees that fall and serve as sustenance for new sprouts, which then grow and become enormous.

We are following a mountain stream—the water a curious gray, or (again) pewter color—and come, at the head of our hike, to a powerful waterfall: volumes of water forced into a long, narrow drop. Everything here is cool, wet, gray, potent, and channeled.

Lunch this day is taken at a roadside café, where we have "widow-makers" with "timber logs." These turn out to be hamburgers on sourdough toast, and french fries with the skins on.

Driving is a challenge, with the huge lumber trucks menacing us at every curve.

Quite a day.

* * *

Indian Island, directly in the view from our cottage, is taken over largely by the u.s. Navy. Mile after mile of immaculate chain-link fence, with signs, "Government Property. KEEP OUT." I'm told that every incoming vessel carrying live ammo is required to stop here and unload before entering Puget Sound. And I am told of a local girl, just out of high school, who was hired by the navy—at minimum wage—to count the bombs. She finally couldn't stand it, quit her job, went to work at the local health food store.

* * *

Port Townsend is ringed by three abandoned army bases, now state parks, all with massive, rotting gun emplacements. These were constructed at enormous expense during the Spanish-American War to defend the entrance to the sound against an utterly non-existent enemy fleet. Today they are beautiful.

* * *

When one arrives in a new community, a roadside café, preferably an older one—as William Least Heat Moon has pointed out—is a likely place to get a feel for the area; or, at least, a look at the faces that inhabit it. Another likely spot is the public library; the types—the retirees, the cranks, the eccentrics, the family historians—who spend their days reading the papers, snoozing, gossiping, perhaps mulling over some real or invented research project. Again, the faces.

I drove out again one day, stopping in a coffee shop in Sequim, observing the country types, the farmers, the ranchers, and then went on to Port Angeles, where I spent the day in research at the library. It struck me that, among the men at least, I was seeing the same face, or a varying version of it, over and over again. And it was a face, or a look at least, that I had seen before: on C., and on another friend T., who was raised in nearby Bremerton.

Years ago I went to an exhibition of Rembrandt paintings, portrait after portrait of the aged, the faces heavily lined, incised like a relief map, each line seeming to mark an episode or an epoch in the subject's life, so that the face became an autobiography, and one felt that imminent death would be a natural conclusion, the completion of a life fully lived and recorded.

These peninsula faces, however—and I'm speaking now of the older ones—are altogether different. However old they are, there seems to be an underlying freshness, a bloom of youth, across which age, as an instant event rather than process, has been suddenly slapped, like a flash flood. So that the face is not a map, not an autobiography, because the young man, who has barely learned how to live, let alone record his life, is still in there, peering out through clear-blue, somewhat watery eyes, with a look that is plainly abashed over what has happened to him. Again and again I have seen this same face, this same look.

A friend who has lived in coastal areas of England, as well as here, points out the similarities in climate, and says that the high degree of moisture in the air, the frequent rains, may be responsible for the fresh complexions to be found in both areas. I wonder. This may well be part of it; yet I believe that I've been observing a genuine peninsula type, perhaps Northwest type, because it goes beyond mere complexion, it is often a shape of face, or, more importantly, a look in the eye, that denotes a shared character. It isn't even furtive, because it hasn't had that much time to think about itself. It is a quiet shock of surprise: what has happened to me?

*　　*　　*

l return now to the four general areas discovered thus far: 1) artsy, self-conscious Port Townsend; 2) some lovely, backwater, homesteading farmland; 3) the unspeakable trash of Route 101, Sequim and Port Angeles; and 4) the pure wilderness, the Olympics.

I'm told that 80% of the peninsula is in national park or forest. A look at the map would seem to confirm this. The wilderness will be preserved.

Port Townsend will probably thrive, becoming less and less what it pretends to be the more it succeeds. But it remains an isolated pocket.

The homesteaders, the less affluent retirees or survivors who are seeking a quiet life, will probably retain pockets of attractive farm-land—land that for one reason or another nobody else wants.

Most of what happens on the peninsula, though, is tied up with communities such as Sequim and Port Angeles, and stripped along 101. I can't help feeling that the unspeakable chrome and plastic vulgarity, the planned obsolescence of these communities, slapped across the face of the land—leaving the land looking somewhat abashed—is more than just a metaphor for what I take to be the characteristic Olympic face: the little boy peering out, too surprised to be hurt, from behind the hard fact of age, an age that has only just this moment been slapped upon him.

—1983

THE BUSINESS OF POETRY

"The United States is the world's first nation to go directly from adolescence to senility, without the intervention of maturity." That is a truism—or witticism—or both—that has been kicking around in my head for many years. I don't know whether I invented it or stole it. No matter. It is probably not original.

I think it has something to do, much to do, with the question at hand—the business of poetry; with the aborted growth of so many poets, the subtle diversion from original aspirations.

*　　*　　*

Any young American who charts a course wherein the financial rewards are not clearly in sight necessarily leads a strange and uncomfortable life. While adhering to the principles that dictated the choice, one is constantly vulnerable to two nagging seductions: first, money, and all that it can bring; and secondly, fame.

In free-enterprise capitalism, with greed sanctified, the lure of money is always with us. But fame, I think, as an expectation, is peculiar to only two professions in America: sports and the arts. (Perhaps also politics, where it is impossible to succeed without being known.) The gifted athlete or the rock star can expect fame and expect it fast. To a lesser extent, so can the poet. At least, he has the example of those whose names are known in literate circles, whose books are read and taught across the land, and who, in consequence, command the better teaching jobs and reading fees. As I have pointed out, except for politics and sports, this expectation of fame is peculiar to the arts. How many lawyers, doctors, electricians, plumbers, and architects enter their professions or trades *expecting* to become famous?

There is a special affinity, I think, between the poet and the rock musician—particularly when the poet goes on the reading circuit, becomes a performing artist. There was tacit recognition of this when Allen Ginsberg and Bob Dylan went on tour together. They share a nominal common currency in language, although this is minimal in most rock music. And they also share in music, to the extent that all language is musical. But more to the point, the poet has before him, constantly, the example of the rock musician who becomes rich and famous at a very early age.

Beginning, I suppose, with Hollywood, but affected more by the great dislocations caused by World Wars I and II, and now the computer revolution, time sense in America has become grossly skewed. Most young writers I know live in terror of those great watersheds, the birthdays marking the decades in their lives: ages twenty, thirty, and forty. Forty, I think, is the crucial one: beyond this, it is no longer useful to be "promising"; by now, there must be solid accomplishment and consequent recognition, or it all goes down the drain.

This is a novel phenomenon, novel to the present generation. I have great difficulty explaining to young students how it could be that Herman Melville wrote *Moby-Dick* when he was thirty-two, that it was badly received, that he lived and wrote for more than forty years longer, that he died in obscurity, and that he remained obscure for more than thirty years after his death.

(The one person whose recognition Melville most actively sought was Hawthorne, and Hawthorne evidently responded enthusiastically to *Moby-Dick*. In thanks, Melville wrote to him as follows: "People think that if a man has undergone any hardship, he should have a reward; but for my part, if I have done the hardest possible day's work, and then come to sit down in a corner & eat my supper comfortably—why, then I don't think I deserve any reward for my hard day's work—for am I not now at peace? Is not my supper good? My peace and my supper are my reward, my dear Hawthorne. So your joy-giving and exultation-breeding letter is not my reward for my ditcher's work with that book, but is the good goddess's bonus over and above what was stipulated for— for not one man in five cycles, who is wise, will expect appreciative recognition from his fellows, or any one of them. Appreciation! Recognition! Is love appreciated? Why, ever since Adam, who has got to the meaning of this great allegory—the world? Then we pygmies must be content to have our paper allegories but ill comprehended.")

The kind of patience required of Melville—postmortem patience, no less!—is simply baffling to most young writers today. I have had students, age seventeen, come to me and ask how they go about having their poems copyrighted. Paranoid before they start! If they are serious, they push forward, past age twenty, past thirty, approaching forty—and here the terrors set in. Generally speaking, the subtle shifts towards careerism become evident: how can I get published here? who is sleeping with whom? if I praise her, will she praise me? whom should I stroke to get invited to teach at the writers' conference? etc.

And all this occurs just at the entrance upon what are, in the normal course of things, the mature middle years, when human capabilities are at their richest and ripest.

Hence, the truism: Americans pass, sadly enough, often enough, from adolescence to senility, without mature intervention.

*　　*　　*

One could legislate the MFA writing courses, the NEA grants, etc., out of existence, returning to some sort of Darwinian state, where only the toughest and truest (and independently wealthy) survive. But it's not going to happen. The students, the poets, the teachers all demand these services. No bureaucracy once established ever dismantles itself. I think it was Guy Davenport who said that literature used to be a river running between banks, now it's a river running through an ocean. The winnowing process that took so long in Melville's case is now infinitely more crowded and complex; but it will still happen.

Meanwhile, a number of poets, both good and bad, some with academic degrees, some without, are enabled to teach these courses. The jobs offer a wage, and, depending on one's energies and temperament, this may or may not be better than driving a taxi or tending bar. And although the students may not be greatly helped, they're probably not badly harmed.

And no doubt each generation of this literary river, coursing through the great ocean of scribblers, will yield up roughly the same number of genuine poets as before: the few who somehow or other buck the prevailing current and make their way to some extended growth and ripening.

—1983

THE CREATIVE PROCESS

Choice of the daunting title for this essay is deliberate. In opening a magazine, we all tend to skim titles and authors' names to determine which pieces we want to read, and I am fully aware that this title will cause many a reader to skip on by or at least begin reading with an unconscious negative bias.

There is good reason for this. Experience teaches us that whenever an editor invites a so called "creative" person to diagnose and expatiate on the so-called "creative" process within that holy instrument that is his or her own "creative" self, said editor is opening the floodgates to a seemingly endless freshet of mystical nonsense.

The fact is, few of us who write or paint or compose or otherwise "create" know what the hell it is we're doing. In general, if we're any good at what we do, we're moving too fast, too much in thrall to our obsession, our muse, our daemon, to be intelligently aware of process.

But that ignorance doesn't seem to stop us. Given permission by a well-meaning editor, we're off to the races. And it piles up. And piles up. And piles up.

Very well. Don't say that you haven't been warned. *Caveat lector!*

*   *   *

I have always been fascinated by the term *the quick and the dead,* as though there were no allowance for anything in between. One cannot be slow or lethargic or lazy. One is quick. Or one is dead.

The confusion, of course, derives from earlier meanings of the word *quick.* It meant, originally, to be alive. An entity that is quickened is given life. *Quick* is associated with *quiver, quaver,* and *quake* —all very early signs of vitality.

Another synonym for quick is *sprightly,* and this leads us into the manifold layers of meanings deriving from the Latin *spirare,* to breathe.

Latin offers two words meaning to breathe—*halare* and *spirare*—but *halare* seems to describe merely the mechanical process, whereas *spirare* brings us to the noun *spiritus,* whose meanings unfold from breathing and breath to include air, life, soul, pride, and courage. In English we may be spiritual, spirited, sprightly, and in good spirits; we may indulge in ardent spirits, and may be spirited way to the spirit world.

There is little we can do without breath, without spirit. We aspire, conspire, and perspire. All that transpires requires respiration. In sadness we suspire, and eventually we expire. But—and here we come around at length to the topic of our discussion—we may, at one or more points in our lives, if we are creative souls—we may become *inspired!*

*   *   *

Inspiration.

The intake of breath.

The way that something exceptionally beautiful—or exceptionally frightening—causes one, *involuntarily,* "to catch one's breath."

Is this what true poetic inspiration is?

*   *   *

I find myself now standing on the tip end of the diving board, my knees quivering, quavering, and quaking, as I'm about to take the plunge into a great bath of mystical nonsense.

I step back, try to feel solid ground under me.

I remind myself that I've always been suspicious of people who claim William Blake as a cultural ancestor. The watery, distant look in the eyes, the tendency to talk about "the infinite," "the light," "paradise," etc., to indicate that they have already taken the plunge from which I have just stepped back.

Is there such a thing as too much inspiration? Too much breath?

To compound my metaphors: it is not a good idea to catch one's breath when one is under water.

* * *

If not mystical inspiration—then what are we talking about?

A couple of quotations might be useful here. Edgar Allan Poe: "There is no greater mistake than the supposition that a true originality is a mere matter of impulse or inspiration. To originate is carefully, patiently, and understandingly to combine."

Herman Melville: "And here it may be randomly suggested . . . whether some things men think they do not know, are not for all that thoroughly comprehended by them; and yet, so to speak, though contained in themselves, are kept a secret from themselves."

The Poe remark is perhaps oversimplified, but is valuable, at least as a corrective.

Melville's thought is more complex, involving areas of experience, of conscious/unconscious knowledge and data, that we know or do not know or do not think we know that is factored in some physiological way into our being, and that may be a larger element than we are aware of than that which flies under the airy banner of "inspiration."

Julian Jaynes, in *The Origin of Consciousness in the Breakdown of the Bicameral Mind,* claims that early, preconscious man lived his life largely by habit, and whenever he found himself in a situation requiring a decision, the right lobe of the brain gave orders to the left, and the left promptly executed them. These were auditory hallucinations: preconscious man heard voices, and he projected them into an elaborate structure that he called "the gods." As the cities grew larger, life became more complex and sophisticated, and modern consciousness came into being, the voices of the gods became weaker and more confused; no longer did they speak forth, clear and true, in any place and at any time . . . their appearances became ritualized and isolated, and, most particularly, they could be expected to perform in only a few unique and geographically dramatic places.

This period of overlap—between the primitive and the sophisticated, preconscious and conscious—began some three thousand years ago, and, according to Jaynes, it is still going on. As the gods retreated, became increasingly temperamental, it was the oracles

and the poets who became increasingly important: the former, as
the channel through whom the gods occasionally spoke, and the
latter, the poets, as the ones especially sensitive to the gods' places,
and as the gatherers, presenters, and at times performers of a
people's history, the restructuring of the preconscious era, that time
of infallible authorization, for which modern man, capable and
confused, has never lost his nostalgia.

Following left-lobe-right-lobe theory, the gods speak to us from
the right lobe, the intuitive lobe. In the case of Joan of Arc, the
voices of her saints spoke to her, literally, in her garden. Such voices,
in Melville's words, are "things men think they do not know"
but "are not for all that thoroughly comprehended by them; and
yet, so to speak, though contained in themselves, are kept a secret
from themselves."

We are inspired, take in a breath; and when we die, we expire, and
are spirited off to the spirit world.

But here again I approach the diving board, knees quivering . . .
and again I step back. Back to crazy Edgar Poe. Because it is not
just inspiration, not the involuntary intake of breath—it is knowl-
edge, the fruit of hard experience, things we do and do not know,
brought to the surface.

Brought up carefully, patiently . . . but at times, also, *quickly!*

*   *   *

David Kadlec, in an unpublished essay, describes the theory of
bricolage, as developed by the French anthropologist, Claude Lévi-
Strauss: "*Bricolage* is distinguished from the work of the craftsman
insofar as the materials used are those salvaged from the wreckage
of previous constructions rather than materials designed specifically
for the task at hand. Lévi-Strauss views mythical thought, which
draws from an extensive but limited repertoire, as a kind of intell-
ectual *bricolage.* New myths can be wrought exclusively from the
fragments of old ones."

Fragments of old myths, old voices, are caught up as they float to
the surface. Original meanings may be lost or incomprehensible
or conceived only in the abstract. But carefully and patiently put

together in new relationships and in a current context, they are charged with new force.

In our multiethnic, multicultural, severely disjointed world, *bricolage* may be our most natural mode.

*   *   *

It is sometimes forgotten that a work of art is conceived and brought to life by a process of *in*direction. We are all familiar with the metaphor of courting the muse. Courting—or, more bluntly, seducing—the muse involves all manner of guile and ruse. I remember reading a poem some years back in which the poet speaks directly, bitterly, to the muse: "You squint when you read my poems!" This may relieve the poet's feelings, but it won't impress the muse. I don't think she likes to be addressed directly. And it is plainly obvious that she doesn't want to be raped. Going back to etymology, *to seduce* means *to lead aside.* This implies that the muse has another purpose from which the successful poet is able to divert her, distract her. There are indications that, when circumstances are just right, the muse enjoys playing this game, this dance of courtship and seduction—both for the pleasures of the process and for its ultimate intention and culmination. But, given the cultural explosion in this country today, the proliferation of little mags, etc., she would appear to have more suitors than Penelope. And I suspect she is particularly resistant to those with the boldest and least subtle blandishments.

Bearing all this in mind, I am amazed at the number of poets and other artists in America today who are throwing themselves upon the muse in full frontal attack. Each has made a "commitment to Art," or a "commitment to a Life in Art." All other human, social, ethical bridges have been burned; the poet is out there naked and alone before the muse . . . and he or she seems to behave as though the muse were exclusively attentive.

It is my feeling that this direct approach is often self-defeating. These are the artists who seem the least self-critical, the least aware of both the virtues and vices of their own work. Encapsulated in their fundamental commitment, they have denied themselves all manner of leverage. Often they wind up simply playing a role, fulfilling an image: "I, the artist" or "I, the poet."

Most parents are surprised, be it positively or negatively, by the choices their children make for lifetime partners. For those of us who follow the arts, the muse similarly surprises and amazes us. Be it to the corporate executive, the family doctor, the alcoholic housemaid, or the impoverished field hand, her granting of favors seldom ceases to astonish. And she seems to take an almost perverse pleasure in passing by those who have made the most spectacular courtship displays.

*   *   *

Charles Olson once wrote, "Art is the only morality." I think this a questionable premise, on the face of it. But, more importantly, I wonder how his vision may have been damaged, how his awareness of himself and his work, particularly his later work, may have been skewed by such an absolute commitment.

On the other side of this coin, I am reminded of a book called *Landmarks of Old Prince William* by one Fairfax Harrison. Dealing with colonial Virginia, it is a work of dense scholarship written in a wonderfully open and rich prose. I was amazed, subsequently, to find out that, besides this kind of endeavor, Harrison was also president of the Southern Railway. America has produced numerous other avocational scholars like Harrison: small-town lawyers, businessmen, whatever, who kept alive aspects of their local culture. Many of them, like Harrison, wrote a remarkable prose; and I wonder how much of this ease with language stems from the fact that they were not singly committed to it; they were beneficiaries of the manifold layers of activity in their lives.

Then, of course, there were Stevens and Williams and Ives.

*   *   *

It is dangerous to draw absolute conclusions from the above. I could easily paint myself into a corner as isolating as that which threatens the "all-for-art" people. True creating is, at best, an obsessive, compulsive process; one accommodates it as best one can.

It is particularly dangerous to attempt conclusions that presume to apply to all historical periods. We are, so much more than we realize, the product of the history that has produced us, that has produced the culture in which we live.

It does seem to me, though, that here, today—United States, 1984—the role of "The Great Artist"—the lonely one, alone with the muse—is a romantic, nineteenth-century notion that has long outlived its value.

Perhaps the only historical constant, since man has first courted the muse, is the muse herself: a wily and wonderful and still utterly unpredictable creature.

—1984

BUSTER

I received a letter recently from someone who was commenting on a book we had both read, a recent biography of Buston Keaton by Tom Dardis. He complained that the book didn't really reveal the nature of the man, that Keaton remained for him still a beautiful puzzle.

I find this remark puzzling. For me, Keaton's nature emerges almost painfully clear: the physical abuse he took as a child, in the family vaudeville act, that immediately became a part of the way he was to survive; the suppression of emotions, the refusal ever to speak to anyone of his inmost feelings, feelings that found release only in the energetic enthusiasm for his work, in a succession of sexual conquests, and, perhaps most of all, in blasts of alcohol. But perhaps more revealing and most exciting in the book was the definition of what I would call his physicality. Uneducated, unburdened with any sort of literary language, his expression as writer, director, and actor came entirely through his body. The extraordinary intelligence therein, the ideas that generated from it, were never separate from the sinew and muscle that put them into action.

Charles Olson said somewhere that he could not have a soul without a body. There is a dichotomy suggested here, that I find most intriguing, which may be demonstrated in many areas of the arts in America: the dichotomy between what we might call the intellectuals and the corporeals.

The intellectuals, generally, are borrowing and importing from Europe; the corporeals are developing something native to this country.

Keaton and Chaplin come first to mind. Both immensely skilled with their bodies, Chaplin—the European—is almost more a dancer, whereas Keaton is an athlete. Ballet vis-à-vis baseball. Chaplin's body is the embodiment of his ideas, it is pure and delicate; Keaton's body has the force of just that, a body—it is never less important than, or in service to, the ideas that are woven into it. In Keaton, thought and action are one.

Once could argue—and I am tempted to argue—that this physicality, or corporeality, is peculiarly American, and those artists who demonstrate it and embody it are the deepest and most important people in their fields, for the simple reason that our history as a country, the physical nature of it, the discovery, exploration, settlement, building, etc., are so close to us, as opposed to the European experience, where even the modernization is imbued with inherited traditions.

Other pairs immediately suggest themselves in this dichotomy. Melville and Eliot, or Whitman and James. Williams and Pound—although Pound is a special case, his materials, so much of them, being imported, but his flavor, his speech rhythms, being physical and American. (Pound once told Williams that he, Williams, had never been west of the March Chunk switchback, but he, Pound, had known the pee-rar-ee.) We have Charles Ives, who poured new American cultural baggage into his work, and Schönberg—such an intellectual system! Harry Partch and John Cage: Partch couldn't stand Cage's music for the very reasons I'm talking about, and it is from Partch that I have borrowed the term *corporeality*. And, god knows, the best of American black jazz is marked by the hard, sometimes buffeting, physical impact of the notes.

There is a revealing vignette reported by Tom Dardis in the Keaton book. Chaplin hired Keaton to play a cameo role in *Limelight*. He offered Keaton a non-negotiable fee, below what Keaton deserved. Keaton didn't care, gladly accepted. Keaton performed brilliantly, endeared himself to the entire film crew. And Chaplin eventually cut a good portion of Keaton's scene, the implication being that he was a little annoyed with Keaton's success.

The tortured physical language in Hart Crane, the hard Maine rocks in a painting by Marsden Hartley, the incredible physical feats performed by Buster Keaton, never using a double . . . these are forces that come strong out of our own culture, with an impact on the whole corporeal being.

—1981

WHITMAN AND MELVILLE

Those two great giants, Whitman and Melville, bestriding the nineteenth century, provide striking parallels when considered together. And perhaps even more striking contrasts.

The coincidences in their lives are astonishing. Both were New Yorkers, Melville of the city and Whitman just outside, on Long Island. They were born the same year, 1819. Melville's heritage was aristocratic, and Whitman came from commoners; nevertheless, both men were of combined English-Dutch heritage—a mixture that seemed to produce more conflicts than one might expect. The English were a restless, adventurous people, settling and moving on, whereas the Dutch, at least in this country, were stable, rooted in the communities they established. I hope to point out that these varying degrees of restlessness—evidence, perhaps, of their mixed heritage—are keys to both men, providing both parallels and contrasts.

Another comparison involves their homosexual or bisexual drives. This is a well-known matter in Whitman's case—less clear cut, more open to speculation, in Melville. Nevertheless, Melville *did* write: "Nature, in no shallow surge / Against thee either sex may urge."

Another curious similarity that I don't think has been heavily investigated is the inability or unwillingness of either man to deal in any direct, human way with individual human beings. So many of the characters in Melville's novels are prototypes or archetypes— representatives of human or philosophic positions that he wished to establish. The English critic Ronald Mason has written: "Having limitless sympathy with man, he had dangerously imperfect sympathy with men and their activities; his preoccupations were with the elements, and the terrors and joys, the passions and speculations which close contact with those elements provoke." Similarly, Whitman wrote grandly of the "brotherhood" of man, but less well of individual, idiosyncratic human beings. (A sharp distinction should be pointed out here in passing: Melville's characters were the product of his ideas—he was a philosopher; with Whitman, on the other hand, as John Jay Chapman has pointed out, "the revolt he represents is not an intellectual revolt. Ideas are not at the bottom of it. It is a revolt from drudgery. It is the revolt of laziness." This is not to demean Whitman, by comparison; laziness, in his hands, seems almost a positive energy.)

Nineteenth-century scholars have speculated at some length as to whether the two men ever met. Apparently, they did not—although we know they were aware of each other, late in the lives of both. It is hard to imagine what they would have made of each other at this stage . . . and it is not a surprise that neither left anything in writing about the other's work. There was, however, a critic, E. C. Stedman, who was personally acquainted with both men. He and his son Arthur visited them both, in Camden and New York. In a letter to Melville, the father mentions in passing, "as you said so much of Whitman . . ." That's all we know.

Finally, in the catalogue of similarities, it can be said that the two men contrived to die within a year of each other: 1891 and '92.

*　*　*

Many of the distinctions between the two are obvious, while others are not at all clear. The discussion may be centered on the differences between the gentleman and the commoner, but the issue is confused by the changes that Melville went through during his life. Early, seafaring Melville was a Whitmanic rebel, identifying with the common sailors . . . the Pacific became his "Open Road." Whitman may have been the great celebrator of vagabondage, but Melville actually traveled—throughout the Pacific, to Europe, the Near East, the Midwest—infinitely more than Whitman. And one of Melville's Pittsfield friends reported that his neighbors thought him something of a "beachcomber." Thus, as D. H. Lawrence pointed out, Whitman and the early Melville had much in common: "The true democracy, where soul meets soul, in the open road. Democracy. American democracy where all journey down the open road. And where a soul is known at once in its going. Not by its clothes or appearance. Whitman did away with that. Not by its family name. Not even by its reputation. Whitman and Melville both discounted that."

But as Melville grew older, made a "white" marriage, bought property, became a father—and failed as a novelist—the gentleman, the aristocrat in him came more and more to the forefront. Whatever was going on inside him, much of his exterior behavior became conservative.

Curiously enough, Henry David Thoreau may claim, or have thrust upon him, at least a portion of the paternity of both Melville and Whitman. Whether from inner nature or force of circumstances, Melville gradually converted to the very sort of cautious Yankee that Thoreau was and remained all his life. Manifestly, a juxtaposition of Walden Pond with the Pacific Ocean is absurd. Or is it? We are all amazed, sometimes appalled, by the outrageous behavior of our children. Whitman's lineage, meanwhile, back to Thoreau, is well described by Wright Morris:

> The word *saunterer*, ill suited to Thoreau, slips onto the relaxed figure of Whitman like a glove.
>
> It is left to Whitman, the democrat en masse, to spell out what Thoreau glossed over, to yawp out over the roofs what a respectable Yankee would keep to himself.
>
> It is Whitman who carries to its conclusion Thoreau's admirable beginning. It is Whitman who *lives* the prevailing tendency.
>
> With his usual accuracy, Thoreau described his romance with Walden as an experiment—it is the safe Yankee testing the ice to see if it will bear the load. Whitman does not test or experiment. At the risk of exclusion, that is, he does not discriminate. All roads lie open, all friends are good friends, and all journeys perpetual. As Thoreau is the archetypal honest man, the square peg in the world's round holes, Whitman is the archetype that lurks even deeper—the professional tramp. The man whose business is no business, whose roof is the sky, whose house is the road, and whose law is the law of comrades.

Thoreau might risk the *experiment* of friendship, but he would flee like the plague the *movement* of brothership.

Having given sanction, if not birth to such a child, Thoreau would have been horrified to see it in operation.

* * *

Whitman at one point sheds his clothes and takes a sun bath: "So hanging clothes on rail near by, keeping old broad brim straw on head and easy shoes on feet, haven't I had a good time the last two hours!"

One could never imagine Melville—even in his beachcomber phase—writing such lines! In fact, Melville at no point in his life would have written something that he would call "Song of Myself." He knew full well that writing is an act of self-revelation; nevertheless, even if one is an exhibitionist, there are proprieties to be observed. His most famous first-person narrator, the Ishmael *Moby-Dick,* is as elusive a character as one could imagine.

* * *

The gentleman-vis-à-vis-commoner issue has earlier roots in American history, much earlier than Melville and Whitman. Consider, first, the dispossessed, displaced soldier farmers, paid off in worthless scrip after the Revolution, striking out in what became known as Shay's Rebellion. Earlier than this, there were troubles in Massachusetts with uprooted citizens following King Philip's War (1675). And, still earlier, there is Roger Williams and his difficulties with the authorities in Massachusetts Bay; and this is important because he *walked,* repeat *walked* from Massachusetts to Rhode Island—and this is the special, dignifying, characteristic activity of the rebel, the liberal, the beatnik, the hippie, the naturalist, conservationist, and Indian lover: he *walks.* (Still earlier, there were Cabeza de Vaca and David Ingram.)

Perhaps Whitman never got beyond his Brooklyn ferries, but in *Leaves of Grass* he *strides*—or, as Wright Morris has it, he *saunters.*

Strider or saunterer, he was the unconscious publicist, front man for a tradition already established: the tradition of John Chapman, Johnny Appleseed—more than Thoreau, perhaps, Whitman's authentic parent and original.

Son of a Massachusetts carpenter and farmer, Chapman emigrated west, wandered about Ohio for three decades, an "apple missionary," moving with the shifting frontier. His clothes were ragged and ill-fitting, his hair long and beard scraggly, he wore his mush pan on his head for a hat, and his feet were knobby, horny, and frequently bare. The Indians discovered that he had healing powers, and they often sought him out. They also thought him crazy, and therefore regarded his life as sacred.

If Johnny Appleseed is Whitman's antecedent in this tradition, Vachel Lindsay is one of his clearest successors. Lindsay was much taken with Johnny, wrote about him frequently, and emulated him: he went on walking tours in the country, begging food and lodging, offering poems in exchange instead of apple seeds. Avoiding cities, he walked through villages and farms, from Illinois to Colorado, speaking of something he called "the Church of the Open Sky": "Thanks to the Good St. Francis who marks out my path for me, I start to-morrow morning to trot unharnessed once again." Others in this tradition would include the two Bartrams— and George Catlin.

Finally, closer to our own time, we come to the Beat Generation, the Kerouacs and Ginsbergs, and *their* descendants, the hippies: the scores of backpackers, hikers, and hitchhikers of the sixties.

Opposed to all these are those whom we may call the conservatives or the gentlemen or the insiders—they stayed *inside*, wrote from what they carried within them, rather than risking the weather *outside*. Theirs was the sense of history and the cultural tradition, generally European—immaculate survivals of the Atlantic crossing. As already indicated, Melville is hard to pin down, depending on what stage of his life one deals with, but he certainly wound up an insider. Following in this tradition are Pound (a line of descent from Melville to Pound would please Pound not at all, but it can be found), and Pound's satellite, Eliot. Olson and Creeley probably belong here; they are perhaps bohemian but nonetheless conservative . . . the bohemian and the beatnik are different creatures, the former a transatlantic tradition, the latter Chapman-Whitman resurfacing.

American culture began as the transplanting of foreign seed in virgin soil. To the conservative, the emphasis is on the seed and its growth; to the beat, it is the soil itself that matters; the loss and nourishing of the altogether-altered seed becomes secondary, so that the soil, the land, ultimately outweighs the crop in value. Thus, it is through the liberal-beatnik that Nature comes in: our passion for land and conservation. The conservatives are concerned with man and culture, and find Nature, per se, uninteresting. Pound is not exactly a liberal-beatnik; nor is Olson what one would call a Nature poet.

The liberal-beatnik lets in *all*; there can be no exclusions. On the other hand, Eliot fled Missouri, and finally even New England wasn't cultured enough for him . . . Pound slammed the door on the Jew . . . as Olson on extra-New-England America . . . and Melville on all twentieth-century life (see *Clarel*).

But as surely as the door is slammed, some nut, daft in the head, skips out the window, pocket full of seed, and starts *walking* . . . the tradition surfaces anew.

*   *   *

One of the fascinating aspects of this Melville-Whitman dichotomy, conceived as a valid double tradition, is the fact that hardly any of the major figures fits neatly into either slot. Crossfertilizations abound. I have spoken of a line of descent from Melville to Pound, but there was also a good deal of Whitman in Pound. Olson and Ginsberg were good friends, had great respect for each other. And many a bearded backpacker is shrewd and knowledgeable behind that cloud of grass. It is often difficult to untangle the threads. But the capacity of a tradition to leave its own limits, to interweave itself intimately with its own opposite, is testimony, it seems to me, to its enduring validity.

—1982

THE SCENE

Being a gathering and a ripping apart, brimming with bile and bias, spleen and prejudice, and offering, at the very end, a glimmer of hope.

Perhaps the most striking aspect of Robert Hughes's recent book *The Shock of the New* is the assurance with which he treats the entire world of modern art—painting, sculpture, and architecture—as a completed cycle, a fait accompli. One can imagine the dilemma of the contemporary painter faced with such a proposal: a world in which the economic values are inflated—art as investment—and its deeper values, the forces that drive him to palette and canvas, are adrift in shifting quicksand: one world finished, a new world not yet born.

The obvious question arises: does this proposal apply also to the world of poetry? Does the fragmentation of the art world—op, pop, surreal, hard-edge, postmodern, whatever—have its parallel in the fragmentation of the various schools of poetry? In a letter to me some time ago, a friend spoke of the "avant-garde primitivists," "the backpacking whale freaks," "the theosophists," "the I-must-be-hip-at-any-cost ideal personality clones of New York," "the new L=A=N=G=U=A=G=E types," etc.

It would appear that the world of poetry is indeed filled with quicksand . . . and the poet thrashes about, searching for something substantial that will support his weight.

*　　*　　*

> I shall at last see my complete face
> Reflected not in the water but in the worn stone floor of my bridge
> I shall keep to myself.
> I shall not repeat others' comments about me.

This poem by John Ashbery represents at least one sad aspect of the contemporary poet's dilemma: Ashbery has chosen a kind of hermetic narcissism as a retreat from the noisy fragmentation of the modern world.

I would suggest that the majority of poets writing and publishing today have, at some early, elemental point, suffered a failure of courage. I would suggest that:

1. They are writing to defend themselves against reality rather than to engage it;

2. Many of them have forsaken the traditional artist's role of making and are satisfying themselves with simply naming; they have, in short, substituted nouns for verbs; and

3. Gertrude Stein, with the collaboration of the reductive and arrogant French, is the Great Earth Mother of this present American condition.

*   *   *

Your poet is often a frightened soul. And this fear seems to express itself as, first, self-indulgence, and second, a terrifying dedication to poetry. These poets have, in fact, placed the cart perfectly in advance of the horse: poetry trying to pull life.

This can be a very seductive stance: the poet, with his towering belief in poetry, would seem to have the True Cross. But, along with it—and this is evident in both his life and his poetry, damaging both equally—there is an ethical failure: we are dangerously close to the-end-justifies-the-means.

This is not necessarily Machiavellian, but the underlying premises are at least questionable: poetry is good, life is bad. The modern world is evil (oddly Calvinist, isn't it?); poetry is the only refuge. These assumptions are so easily made—it's almost like the click of a turnstile, you put a quarter in the slot and instantly you're on the other side. And a second world is created, a second view of the world you just left, which your poetry is supposed to celebrate and which will now be so difficult to recapture in that state of original innocence (you can never get that quarter back!). So now, irrevocably on the subway side of the platform, you do the only thing you can: churn out that daily poem, or daily six poems, or daily sixty, as your only defense against the loss of Eden. (Yes, Eden . . . that evil, corrupt world that you willingly paid a quarter to escape . . . what is it when you can no longer go back to it?)

Such writing is a perfect adjunct to, perhaps product of, a drug culture. It is compulsive, obsessive—and addictive. The daily poem or poems as a demanded daily fix.

It is also the product of a culture hag-ridden by analysis and "therapy": the poet certifying his couch spoutings by funneling them through a typewriter and getting them printed.

Such poetry is not without public support—from patrons, foundations, arts councils, the National Endowment. (For over a year now this writer has served as literature panelist for the NEA . . . this is as good a place as any to confess my sins.) Insofar as both private and public giving to the arts are acts of cultural conscience, the donors are apt to seek out, or at least play along with, the trivial because the trivial will rock no *real* boats. To the typical rich, an overage adolescent sticking out his tongue at him is an image with which he is comfortable; it is *containable.* The rich—and arts boards—tend to recognize *style*—that is to say, no particular content or substance.

Compulsive poets, too, are perfect products of a consumer culture. They fit in, better than they can imagine, to that world they thought themselves to have rejected.

*   *   *

At some point in *The Shock of the New,* Robert Hughes speaks of the Surrealists, of how they abandoned the traditional artist's role of making things and resorted to simply *naming.* And Hannah Arendt has made the following remark (quoted by Jonathan Williams): "To quote is to name, and naming rather than speaking, the words rather than the sentence, brings truth to light."

Somewhere recently I have read comments about the cult of the writer in America, how the public is often more interested in the writer's personality than in the work produced. Following from this is the proposal that good writing is that which *radically differs* from the known or apparent personality of the writer—writing that, just because of this difference, "surprises" us. Conversely, bad writing is that which endlessly restates, without change or growth down through the years, the known and demonstrated personality of the writer. Such bad writing is called *self-expression:* the poet is *saying,* and often naming—but not *making.*

*   *   *

Clark Coolidge, Bernadette Mayer and the L=A=N=G=U=A=G=E poets, have, in recent years, experienced some divergence, but I would suggest that they still have much in common. The L=A=N=G=U=A=G=E poets, as one friend of mine described them, claim that "the poem should have no other reference than to other neighboring phrases, words, & measures upon the very same page—a totally enclosed, hermetically sealed, self-sustaining world. . . . They stuck their tongue out at content, and closed the outside world, or even their own inside worlds, off from the center of their poems." As I shall propose later, there is a powerful connection here with Gertrude Stein, but more immediately, I think, the influences come from the abstract expressionist painters and from black jazz: the notion that the pigments on the surface of the canvas, the notes and tones that strike our ears, contain *all* that matters, the full range and substance of the work; that content or subject matter, in any traditional, referred sense, must be rigorously excluded.

In no way do I wish to include in this critical approach the painters and jazz composers themselves. It is an odd phenomenon that what works so magnificently for them, both in practice and rationale, becomes something altogether different when the medium, the pigment if you wish, is language. Tones of music and pure colors are able to penetrate our senses and consciousness altogether free of the burdens of history and meaning inherent in words. And the effort to expel from words precisely those burdens, all in the name of "freedom," comes across as an oddly Calvinist, Puritan gesture. It could happen only in a country that has tried to clamp upon itself the Eighteenth Amendment!

And this sort of piety produces, or will produce, not only its own demise but its own opposite. A recent book of Coolidge's—he is smart enough to stay ahead of his followers—is entitled *Own Face.* Out of the flat, anonymous plane of names and words, the ego is purified. The piety produces a sweet nostalgia for ego!

And in little of this, as I see it, is anyone doing what Melville referred to as "the ditcher's work" of making a book.

*   *   *

At a recent appearance in New York, I read a piece of prose—a section of a larger work—made up entirely of firsthand, subjective accounts written by schizophrenics. Toward the end, one of these unfortunates thinks of himself as Shakespeare reincarnate:

> Write, damnit—write something—write anything—write faster, faster!

> I write in columns on the wall, three feet wide, on huge sheets of wrapping paper, pasted together, running down the corridor, twelve feet an hour!

A poet in the audience, someone with long associations with New York, came up to me afterwards and said with a chuckle, "We'll make a New York poet out of you yet." It was a bit of banter, and I took it as such. But some time later I thought: these people, these schizophrenics, with whose words I was constructing my piece, were—yes—crazy.

*   *   *

After World War II there was a young GI who hung around Paris, attached himself to Gertrude Stein's salon, listened to The Great One holding forth. He noticed that if anyone had the temerity to interrupt her or even to present an idea at variance with her own, she would stop talking, stare at the offender, then start up again as though nothing had happened, but in a slightly louder voice.

He decided to test her. The two were out walking one day, Gertrude uttering her customary pronouncements. He interrupted. She stopped in her tracks, stared at him, then proceeded, her voice a little stronger. He interrupted again. Same process. Again. And again. Until finally Gertrude, standing on the street in Paris, was literally bellowing at him.

This self-confidence to the point of arrogance was her trademark. And I suggest that it was not inconsistent with at least a part of the French national character. A comparison here between France and England is illuminating. Despite their bullying in Ireland, the English seem to know, to have accepted the fact that Britannia no longer rules the waves, that the sun *does* set on the British Empire. Something in the French psyche, however, that refuses to dislodge itself is arrested in the days of lingua franca, when Paris and France were the hub of the civilized and cultural universe. (American tourists with whom I have talked report without exception that the French are the rudest of all European peoples.)

Arrogant—and reductive. It was Francis Ponge who wrote a book called *The Voice of Things*. Things—and names. It is the French, I suspect, who are at the heart of this move to dismantle the paragraph, the sentence, to reduce language to individual words. Lacking energy or inclination to *make* something and assured within themselves that they remain at the heart of things, they have created and exported a culture shrunken and fragmented that shrinks and fragments whole segments of the American scene.

*　*　*

I would suggest that Europe is the land of nouns, America the land of verbs. The nearest concession to a verb a true European will make is at best intransitive, grudging. As in Samuel Beckett: "I can't go on. I go on." And Beckett, when asked why he wrote in French, replied, "Because French is the most beautiful language in which to say absolutely nothing." And Meridel LeSueur, that grand octogenarian lady of the midwestern American Left—whose name but nothing else may be French—has recently said, "I'm doing away with the noun now. The noun is a capitalist invention."

* * *

"And it is no common coincidence if we can see our words shine in the dark, held like epitaphs frozen in their eternal order." These are the words of Edmond Jabès, celebrating The Word. And what a fine introduction this would make to that mortuary that we call concrete poetry, where the words, the very letters, are frozen epitaphs, absolutely and forever drained of life and energy!

Roland Barthes: "This subject is never anything but a 'living contradiction'—a split subject, who simultaneously enjoys through the text the consistency of his selfhood and its collapse—its fall." Ah, that ego again, dancing on the flat plane of words!

Finally: "To go towards death, to make a death for himself as one would make a life . . ." To Edmond Jabès, life and death might as well be equivalents.

* * *

Is it more than coincidence that so much of the "new" American poetry seems to flourish in the Bay Area, where the quality of the light is so Mediterranean, so like that light which drew so many of the French painters, late-nineteenth-early-twentieth century, south to the Côte d'Azur?

* * *

So what is the answer? For us? Here? Now?

One endeavors to shake off these "foreign devils," to rediscover and build upon those powerful native voices who have preceded us for two centuries. But to go back to the original question: Is the cycle of modernism for writers truly complete, as Robert Hughes suggests it is for artists? And if so, freeing ourselves of the reductive, what sort of ground remains?

In a recent letter, Don Byrd writes as follows: "What would you say to the notion that ART AS SUCH IS BY NOW A SENTIMENTAL HANGOVER OF THE TIME THAT THERE WAS A KULCHA, and that now the techniques of ART are useful as means of research, directing research, and presenting research, to make the necessary information available for public use? The thought is that the poem now is not usefully an object to contemplate, but as discovering the information and putting it into a context for use."

I wouldn't go quite that far. I think there is still energy to be infused in the poem, in the poem to be made, perhaps in a quite traditional way, building on Olson, Pound, and Williams, drawing on Whitman and Melville, back through Shakespeare, all the way to Homer.

In other essays I have hammered on the idea of the physical, the physiological, the corporeal—the notion that the poem is not the product of the poet's intellect, of his "culture," of his sweet little heart or his tender little soul—but of his whole historical-cultural- genetic-inherited-physical presence, existence, and being.

Recently I was delighted to read an interview with Robert Creeley (published in a magazine called *O.ARS*). Creeley is recounting a trip he made through southern Mexico, where he stopped to visit a self-styled anthropologist named Franz Bloom:

> He said, "How would you like to meet a Mayan?" I said "Terrific!" He said, "Actually the man is a Lacandon Indian. He's the first person ever to come out of his particular situation *ever*. The first human being of that particular cluster ever to go beyond its stated boundaries and to move out of its area of habitation into this world."

The Indian comes into the room.

> What was extraordinary about this man was that all the senses were absolutely alert all over the body in the same way you'd experience the situation of a so-called wild animal as opposed to a domestic animal. I mean the sensory system was absolutely alert, not worried, but he was entirely *there*. I've never met a human being who was so completely where he was, not that he knew where he was or was determined to stay there, but was absolutely

alive in the moment of each instant. I mean there was no abstraction in him. It was fantastic. I thought, "You *can* do it." I mean you can arrive at a consciousness that's present as opposed to one that's thinking about what happened last week or what is going to happen tomorrow as an imposition on the present instance. Extraordinarily fresh. He was healthy and, as one might expect, his whole sensory nervous system was absolutely incredible.

In a somewhat like sense, as a younger man during the war and coming into contact with Gurkas, their central nervous system was fantastic. They again had not as purely, let's say, as this Indian but they had two aspects of that same centering of physical being without consciousness of being otherwise. So that when they were given things like sodium pentathol as an anaesthetic—the average Caucasian the average European or American will tend to go out certainly by ten in the count down. Most people are anaesthetized by the time they get to eight or nine. These men have been known to count to 100. I mean they have a central nervous system that just won't quit . . . I've seen . . . operations performed on these men when in all respects they should have been long gone with shock.

And again and again as I'm reading these various texts of poetry, say from Whitman's time to the, not to the present actually but to the '40s and '50s, the crisis seems to be endlessly the awful success of the process of objectivity and abstraction so that the mind seems to have almost no consciousness of the body it lives in even when it's preoccupied with that . . .

So there it is: the wild animal, with no abstraction, the centering of physical being, the sensory system absolutely alert . . . vis-à-vis the awful success of the process of objectivity, the mind with almost no consciousness of the body it lives in.

The noun may or may not be a capitalist invention, but it is an abstraction. In the verb, however, mind and body are integral, active, unself-conscious. And Creeley experiences that wonderful moment of illumination: "You *can* do it."

With this sort of possibility in prospect, what are we waiting for?

—1983

STAMPERS AND HAWKERS

On August 1 this past summer—Herman Melville's birthday—the U.S. Postal Service held ceremonies in New Bedford in connection with the first-day issue of a new Melville stamp, part of the literary arts series. As one of Melville's surviving descendants—I am a great-grandson—I was invited to attend, representing the family.

My wife and I drove down the day before. It was a typical sweltering summer day. We checked into the Whaler Inn, kindness of the New Bedford Post Office, and made tracks as fast as we could for Horseneck Beach and a swim in one of the two great oceans on which Melville had voyaged.

The next day blossomed even hotter: a soggy, blistering day, and even at the harbor there was not a breath of wind. We made our way to the Whaling Museum, where, an hour before the stamps were to go on sale, the collectors were already lining up. We were escorted to the director's office where we drank coffee and hobnobbed with some of the visiting dignitaries. These included the assistant post-master general from Washington; the postmaster of New Bedford; the mayor of New Bedford; a rear admiral from the Coast Guard; the president of the Melville Society; a chaplain; the port director of customs; assorted other local postmasters; etc. Among such I was a sort of minister without portfolio, with nothing but my bloodline to offer—and feeling a little bit silly about it.

At the appointed hour, we were lined up military fashion and marched through what had now become a seething mob of stamp collectors, to the auditorium, where we took our chairs on the platform. Gracing the ceremonies were the First Marine Band and Ceremonial Guard, in full button-down regalia—on this steamy, steamy hot day! Following opening remarks, we had the presentation of colors, the National Anthem, and the invocation. We were patriotic and blessed, and ready to sail into a sea of speeches—which indeed followed. (During one of these, Dr. Milton Stern, president of the Melville Society, scribbled a note on an envelope and slipped it to me: "What do you think Melville would have made of all this?" I wrote back, putting it in quotes: "I don't believe it!")

To vary the program, we had a group of musical selections: a rousing performance of "Stars and Stripes Forever," and some semi-classical pieces, with that peculiar tone that occurs when a good military band tries to be "aesthetic."

With the conclusion of the final speech, and the presentation of albums, we filed out of the auditorium, and I thought, that's that.

But that was not that. That was just the beginning. There occurred now a phenomenon that left me shaken, and that still somewhat mystifies me. There were more than four hundred in the auditorium, most of them stamp collectors, and, picking me out from among the other dignitaries, a swarm of them descended on me, seemingly all at once, all shoving programs and ballpoints under my nose, demanding my autograph. I'm as vain as the next man, and anyone who asks for my autograph generally has my attention. But this turned into a mob scene, I scribbled and scribbled and scribbled, the sweat of my brow fogging my glasses, and I began to think to myself: Who are these people? What do they think they're getting? I'm three generations removed from The Great Man, and yet they seem to think they're getting a piece of Him, as though I were Herman himself signing their programs. One insistent woman demanded that I sign *six*—"for the grandchildren." After nearly an hour of this, when my fingers were cramping and my legs felt rubbery, the last of these strange souls finally departed.

We were collected once more and made our way over sunbaked sidewalks to the harborside. Here we boarded the u.s. Coast Guard cutter *Unimak* and sat down at tables on the afterdeck. Without benefit of canopy or awning, we lunched on elegant broiled haddock under the broiling, broiling sun—and listened to more speeches. My wife thought she was going to faint.

When it was finally over, the crew stood at attention and piped us ashore.

We drove back to the Whaler Inn, slithered out of our sopping clothes and into bathing suits, and headed once more for Horseneck and a cleansing, cooling plunge into the waves. Swimming underwater and on the surface, bobbing with the waves, bodysurfing, I thought again of that swarm of locusts that had descended on me. I thought of Dr. Stern's question: "What do you think Melville would have made of all this?" I recalled that *Moby-Dick* had been published in 1851, when Melville was thirty-two; that it was panned by the critics and sold poorly; that Melville lived and wrote for another forty years after this, and died in almost complete obscurity; and that still another thirty years passed before interest in *Moby-Dick* began to develop. I thought: suppose it had been Melville himself, and not I, who had signed all those programs? What, indeed, would he have made of it?

Finishing our swim, we went back to the Whaler Inn for a dinner of motel fish and an evening watching the Red Sox lose another one on television.

There are some things in this world that are just too mad to contemplate.

*   *   *

I have no idea whose birthday falls on September 16. But that day, here in the Berkshires, blossomed sparkling clear. Following a day and night of humidity and rain, a weather front passed through, and the morning air was fresh and crisp, with a northwest breeze. I had become interested in the migration pattern of hawks and discovered to my surprise that we were only a forty-five-minute drive from two of the better spots in the northeast from which to observe these flights.

We had gone first to Mt. Tom—or, more properly, Goat Peak, adjacent to Tom. Here there is a steel tower rising above the treetops, and the platform at the top offers a panoramic view: the Connecticut River valley, with the oxbow; Mt. Monadnock; the tall buildings of the University of Massachusetts; Westover, Northampton, Easthampton, Holyoke, Springfield, and Hartford. It had been a beautiful sunny day, but the hawk flights were disappointing: only a few birds, and these at a distance. The greatest excitement came from an eagle—whether immature bald or golden could not be determined. (My fellow observers, all strangers to me, were obviously experts, with years of study and watching behind them.)

This day—September 16—we decided to go to another spot, also nearby. It is simply a hilltop, located in—ah, no, dear readers:

I think I shall keep this to myself. It is one of the most spectacularly beautiful and apparently little-known spots here in the Berkshires, and if I locate it and publicize it, you and your family and friends will discover it and flock to it, and it will cease to be what it is now: the top of the world, in a near-perfect state of nature.

It is just a bare hilltop, and not particularly high, an easy climb from the road. It is spectacular, though, because the land around it is all slightly lower, and one looks for miles and miles and miles in any direction before discovering a higher configuration, so that the sky is an enormous blue bowl, and one stands on the hilltop at the center of what seems a near-perfect circle. Well-known mountains were visible, some at a great distance, but I shall not name them, dear readers, for there lurks among you someone with a cartographic mind who would use this information to help pinpoint our hilltop.

There were two hawk-watchers present when we arrived, and perhaps eight or ten others showed up as the morning wore on. They were all carrying picnic lunches, folding chairs, and the inevitable binoculars; they were there for the day, to make an official count for their local chapter of the Audubon Society.

On the platform at Mt. Tom, and here on this hilltop, I became aware at once of a rare kind of camaraderie. It was rare in that it mixed openness and friendliness with respect for one's privacy. In both places, we were outsiders: amateurs among experts. I quickly discovered that if I wanted to be alone with my thoughts, or with the birds, or with nature, they would leave me alone; but if I wanted to ask questions or share perceptions, they were more than helpful, going out of their way to indoctrinate us into the wonderful world of hawks, without being patronizing or condescending.

At Mt. Tom I had been wearing my Red Sox cap, and this brought me into conversation with some of the men, mostly older, all of whom were dedicated baseball fans, as well as bird-watchers. I thought of John Kieran, the late sportswriter for the *New York Times,* who was also a serious bird-watcher and naturalist. I have meditated some on this affinity, between bird-watching and baseball.

Here on the hilltop, we had come only for the morning, had not brought lunch. Our new friends opened their picnic boxes, offered to share with us. We politely declined.

At both places, I observed and tried to speculate on the backgrounds of these people. They seemed to come from different walks of life, some giving evidence of the "advantages," others clearly from the working class. They were brought together by their single compelling interest.

I felt, too, that their response to the world of birds was an aesthetic experience; but, in most cases, it was the single aesthetic in their lives. These were not gallerygoers, poetry readers, music lovers, but their artistic passion was every bit as powerful. One of my favorites among them was a young man in ragged jeans, a work shirt, a baseball cap on backwards, and his hair in a pony tail. He described what is called a "kettle" of hawks rising in a thermal wind, reaching the top, and then, one by one, peeling off: "That's neat," he said. "Neat." That single monosyllable said it all.

When we first arrived, the sky was clear, with only a few clouds on the horizon. Although the sun was warm, it was breezy and cool enough for a down jacket. Initially, the hawks were few and distant. We stood or sat among the low-bush blueberries, conversed casually, and scanned the horizon. The first excitement was a flight of twelve broadwings, directly overhead. By now some wispy cumulus clouds had spread over us, and we lay on our backs looking directly up at the seemingly chaotic, swiftly moving patterns of flight, in and out among the blue of the sky, and the white and soft gray of the clouds. The birds were near enough to be seen with the naked eye, but to be seen much better of course through the glasses. The whole flight lasted only a few moments, and they were gone.

Later there was a much larger kettle, again directly overhead. As before, we lay on our backs, the glasses lifted and lowered, lifted and lowered. This flight lasted for several minutes, and the official count came to 214. If you think that's a lot, dear readers, consider: on September 13, 1983, at Mt. Wachusett, during the space of one hour—12 noon to 1 P.M.—the official count of broadwinged hawks came to 16,216! No such prodigious numbers at our hilltop. Still, the few minutes that it took those 214 to pass were strangely exciting.

At Mt. Tom we had been disappointed because the birds were few, and distant. Here, the birds were more plentiful, but similarly distant; and it occurred to me that that's part of the aesthetic, the excitement: those magnificent creatures, swirling, soaring, rising, diving—keeping their distance. Closer, they would lose their wildness, which was their signal virtue.

* * *

A little after midday we took our leave. On the way home my wife pointed out to me how strange was the contrast between these two events of our summer: New Bedford and the hawk-watch.

Strange, indeed.

First, the weather, that framework in which all events occur, and which is seldom far from the attention of a New Englander: there was the cloying, steamy humidity of New Bedford . . . and the brisk, dry, early-fall warmth-and-chill on the hilltop.

I thought of Herman Melville, the man whom we were presumably celebrating in New Bedford, the man whose restless, roaming spirit carried him to the South Seas . . . as the instinct of the broad-wings overhead led them in their southward migration.

I thought of the people: the stampers and the hawkers. The stampers, cornering me, crowding me, clutching their programs and ballpoints in their sweaty palms, seemed a people possessed, as though fighting an unseen enemy, seeking security in their collections and autographs. The hawkers, on the other hand, were without an ax to grind.

There was the almost military formality of the ceremonies in New Bedford, vis-à-vis the relaxed informality, both at Mt. Tom and the hilltop.

For the stampers, there seemed some demonic significance in possessing a family member's autograph. I wondered: suppose I were to tell the hawkers who my great grandfather was? I imagine they would be polite about it, but I doubt that they would really care. I would neither rise nor fall in their estimation. And the hawks themselves wouldn't give a tinker's damn!

These thoughts give me great pleasure.

—1984

LOUIS THE TORCH

To the unknown poet,
whose name and poem I have long since forgotten,
but one of whose images
has burned itself into my memory:

There's an arsonist lives in my belly

Obviously there is no tolerance for sham or lies in either science or philosophy. But within the category of each there is the same congruence as the infinitely more sensitive relationships of great art—in which only does the time element enter, in that the same truth in art must be restated continually in each age in the materials of that age to be true: whereas the crudity and grossness of both philosophy and science is that they attempt to do away with time in an absurd absolute which—by the very lack of time makes them—to say the least inhuman.

—William Carlos Williams

ONE

There's an arsonist lives in my belly:

Louis the Torch!

All the warmth, heat, ardor, spreading through the Sun's
Weaving, comes from Louis's fires.

But, for a fee . . .

> (What is your fee, Louis? and who pays you, in whose
> service do you ignite? What is your incentive, who sends
> you in to incend, slips to you those coins now burning a
> hole in your pocket?
>
> (Your fee, Louis: *feo, fief, fie, feu, fiu* from the Anglo
> Saxon, *feoh,* cattle . . .
>
> (Are you paid in cattle, Louis?
>
> (Should I feed you a Big Mac?
>
> (Or a Golden Louis, a Louis d' Or?
>
> > (to pay is to pacify *(pax)*. . .

For a fee, you will waste any structure, any frame . . .

. . . and it is in me, Louis, that you are living:

My structure! *My* frame!

It is *fire,* Louis, I know it, that's your game: *fyr, pyr,* fire and pure, pure fire, from the Sanskrit, *pu* . . .

(But you give me pyrosis: heartburn!

Where are you, Louis? No longer in my belly (that bag, that swelling, that waxing waist, that boil and bubble at my middle . . .

Wandering, Louis, a gypsy in my body? I'll smoke you out!

Louis Spina, that's your name—Louis the Thorn, with your little candle kindling my spine, to burn my back bone to spinach!

Smith me, forge me, if you will, I'm malleable . . . but I'll see you behind bars, within my rib cage, trapped behind the spine branches . . .

And, like any jailbird, you'll incendiate your cell, enflame my lungs, 'til my tubes are roiled, my breath smokes, my brain in fumes, *fumos, thymos, theos* . . . enthuse!

Louis, you are ardent and enthused!

But the Torch, where did you get that Torch? *Torche, torge, thorche, tourche, tortche, towrge*—a bit of twisted tow dipped in pitch. Ah, the twisted mind of the arsonist!

Where are you, Louis? Posturing in my torso, flaunting your flambeau, flamboyant, flagrant . . .

And in the next moment I'll break out in itches, a rash of little inflammations!

But don't get proud, big Louis, I'm gonna fight you, every little inch: I'll study, pyrosophy, pyromancy, and pyrotheology, become downright pyrolatrous; I'll master the laws of pyronomy, my tools will be pyromachal, pyrergical and pyrobolical. You will be pyrometamorphosed!

You're working me into a fever, Louis, where are you? what are you doing? my torso—tortured! The torque, the torsion, distorted, contorted, the wringing and griping of my bowels!

You're in my joints and my throat, the articles of bone, the knuckles of speech, I cannot articulate—my *artus* will be arthritic!

I am scorched and flayed, charred to a turn, you're a lousy firebrat, a burn bastard!

Okay, I'll fool you. Listen to this, Louis:

> The head bone's connected to the ankle bone,
> The wrist bone's connected to the knee bone,
> The neck bone's connected to the hip bone . . .

Where are you, Louis? Lost?

Oh, God, my kidneys and gall bladder, you're cooking up stones: bezoar, calculus, calx!

Dear sweet God, let me fight your fire with flowers!

Give me the Torch-Wort, the Great Mullein, give me the Torch-Lilly, Flameflower . . .

. . . the feverfew will drive away fever . . .

You say an arsonist is an artist, Louis, a fine artist, practitioner of the fine *ars* . . . my arse! You're nothing but a petty extortionist!

. . . and you're in my arse-ropes, my arse-gut . . . I'll make gas, chaos . . .

. . . and you'll ignite my blooming farts!

TWO

When the rising sun first shoots over the horizon, catch a beam in your mouth and bite it off.

A man of great power may bring down the sunheat and fire without leaving the earth.

Go westward to the setting sun, and just as the orb sinks beneath the horizon, chip off a piece, bear the fragment back.

Only the crows possess fire . . . it is stolen from them by the fire-tailed finch.

The swallow-tailed flycatcher brings fire down from heaven.

It is the hawk discovers fire: flying to a great height, with a mighty swish of his wings he causes a whirlwind, spreading flames among the grasses and forests below.

A man pursues a gigantic beast, kills it with a club. Pulling out the male organ, which is of great length, he cuts it open, and finds within it a very red fire, which he takes out and uses to cook the meat of the beast.

An old blind grandmother draws fire from the nails of her fingers, the nails of her toes.

An old woman spits fire from her mouth, cooks with it, and licks the flames back in.

A woman discovers fire, guards it jealously from men. She hides it from them, gathering the glowing ashes and thrusting them into her vulva.

Seated on the floor, legs spread wide, the woman gives her belly a great shake, a ball of fire rolls out of her genital canal.

A man hugs his wife. They become locked together, unable to break the embrace. A supernatural being appears and shakes the pair, turns them this way and that, in order to part them. As he does so, smoke and flame burst from the friction of the two bodies.

Zeus will not give the power of unwearying fire, for the gods keep hidden from men the means of life. In the anger of his heart Zeus hides it. But Prometheus steals fire for men, in a hollow fennel stalk . . . Zeus, who delights in thunder, does not see it.

Fire is stolen, Louis, always . . . it is never a given.

Louis, where did you steal your fire?

THREE

The whole world, Louis, was once a globe of flame, a fireball
spinning in space. The flames quieted, earth and ocean came
into being, and fire entered the roots of trees, ascended into
trunk and branches, where it is stored to this day . . . from which it
may be released by rubbing or drilling, wood upon wood, wood
within wood. A lambent flame within, rubbed or drilled, the
flame springs forth.

Wild olive is male, oak female. The woods are husband and wife,
their rubbing is union, begetting off-spring in the shape of fire.
Let the priest twirl the pointed olive, let the priestess hold fast on
the ground the invaginated oak, blowing into flame the rising
sparks . . .

> (let none but persons of pure life, Louis, blow up the
> fire with their mouths, never a vile man who has
> polluted his lips . . .

Or place a nubile boy and girl, perfectly naked, in a darkened
room, let them rub together two rollers of lime wood, that the
friction may blow up sparks.

Impregnation by fire is impregnation by wood of the tree from
which the fire is kindled.

Louis, light the torches in the grove, in celebration of Diana! as
she herself bears a glowing torch, upraised . . . !

> (like the iron lady, torch-bearer, in whose shadow
> your forbears passed, to arrive at Ellis Island . . .

Where is your torch, Louis, your sacred fire? Do you have virgins
to guard it?

> (According to that doctor from Vienna, women
> were always set to guard the fires, 'cause it was
> more difficult for 'em to extinguish 'em, by
> peeing . . .

Remember, Louis, the vestals, though virgin to you, are regularly
conjugal with the firegod, the phallic flame shooting from the
sacred hearth . . .

But it is the Sun! and fire but a piece of Him, the little bit of
magnet here on earth to capture and re-capture, to hold
Him . . . ! On cloudy days, re-kindle the fires . . . When the Sun is
eclipsed, shoot fire-tipped arrows into the air, to bring Him
back . . . at the winter solstice, when he is at His threatening
lowest, burn a mighty logfire on every hearth, to raise Him once
more above the horizon . . . !

In the Spring, the vernal renewal, the winter fires, in which the
vital principle has grown weak, the old fires on every hearth, must
be extinguished . . . ignite a new fire, a Spring fire!

A bonfire brings good marriage, crops, weather, and health . . .

Drive your swine and cattle through the smoke and flames, singe
their hides, to halt the ravages of plague . . .

The *need-fire,* the *will-fire,* the *new-fire,* first and original fire,
from which all other embers may emanate . . . that the cattle may
be healed, the fields yield, infants engendered, the Sun rekindled
at the solstice . . .

A leap through flames cures the sterile . . . a mother-to-be passes
through the fire to ease her delivery . . . the nursing mother holds
her breasts in smoke over flame, to strengthen the nurseling . . .
and holds the child in the bonfire to protect from fevers.

Build fires of fennel, thyme, and rue, of chervil, camomile, geranium, and penny royal, and in the smoke of these flaming herbs you are purified . . .

> (and while you're at it, Louis, burn an
> effigy of that heretic, Martin Luther . . .

Build a sacrificial fire, in the open air, on the highest hilltop . . . offering the grandest view of Nature, and being nearest to the Sun, it will be close to the seat of warmth and order.

> (or like the Greeks, Louis, jump through the flames
> to get rid of your fleas . . .

Build bonfires at Twelfth Night to ward off sorcerers and wizards, the witches who steal the cows' milk . . . to drive out all maleficent spirits . . .

The dragons are flying overhead, Louis, copulating wildly in the midsummer heat, their spilled seed falling, poisoning wells and rivers . . . ! Build bonfires, bone fires, fires of bones and filth, drive them off with noxious smoke!

Set the faggots afire, drive off the fairies!

Louis, are you there? Pay attention, now, and listen:

The hearth, with the embers of the fire, is a place for fantasies and festivities, for roasts and reveries . . . it strengthens the eyes to stare steadily into a fire, without blinking.

FOUR

First on the scene, the first question: what is the point of origin? Where did the fire begin. And was combustion accidental, or is this a touch-off? (Did you touch me off, Louis . . . ?)

Or perhaps two or more fires started at once, in the same structure—a sure tip to arson . . . (When everything hurts at once, Louis, I know it's your fires . . .)

Look for the lowest point of burning, look to the point where heavy items—sofas, refrigerators—have shifted, as the structure weakens, the point of longest burning . . .

Look for the honeycomb of charcoal, the cone of scorching, with the arcing lines that mark the rising heat waves. On floors and doors, frames and panels, look for the *alligation* (ah, yes, Louis, I know your terms!): where burning knobbles the surface—like the hide of an *alligator* . . . the fiercer the fire, the deeper and closer these crimp marks . . .

What is the set, the plant, the device for touch-off?

A few jerry cans of gas? (Pretty crude, Louis . . .)

Perhaps a candle, set in a box of crumpled papers . . . slow-burning, to give you a chance to escape, establish an alibi (but there it is, Louis, we'll find it, beneath the scorched cone: the little pool of wax . . .

If the smoke is heavy and white, with the stink of garlic, we'll
look for phosphorus . . . chlorine smoke is irritating, biting the
nose and throat, forcing tears . . . flames deeply red mean petro-
leum, tongues of flame leaping from the run-off water . . .

Maybe you got clever, Louis, a device of phosphorus and water in
an ice bag: you put a pinhole in the rubber, the water seeps out
slowly, and when it drains below the level of the phosphorus, the
chemical ignites, on contact with air . . .

> (and maybe you're not so clever, either
> like the time you spread too much gas,
> lit the match, and damn near got killed:
> we found you in the emergency room, the resi-
> dent picking the threads of shirt
> and jeans out of your scorched flesh . . .

The set, the plant, device to ignite . . . and the trailer; what is your
trailer, Louis? Crumpled papers? oil-soaked rags?—to trail the
blaze from point of origin, spread it through the structure . . .

Set, plant, trailer—and exclusive opportunity: these are what we
need, to haul you into court . . .

"Any person who willfully and maliciously sets fire to or burns or
causes to be burned, or who aids, counsels or procures the burn-
ing of any dwelling house, whether occupied, unoccupied or
vacant, or any kitchen, shop, barn, stable or other outhouse that is
parcel thereof, or belonging to or adjoining thereto, whether the
property of himself or another, shall be guilty of Arson in the first
degree, and upon conviction thereof, be sentenced to the peniten-
tiary for not less than two nor more than twenty years."

Two to twenty, Louis . . . would you do it? . . . would you risk it?
. . . sell me to the insurance company?

And would you risk Murder One, Louis . . . if I become your
roast?

FIVE

Tell me about yourself, Louis, your folks, your family . . . Where do you come from? What were you like as a kid?

(Did you suffer anoxia, pre-, intra- or postnatally?

(Did you observe your mama and papa in intercourse, find their mutual thrust threatening?

(Were you a bedwetter and shiteater, did you attack your siblings, pull hair, have tantrums, vomit, and steal money?

(Did you set fire to your little brother's crib, and cut off his finger with a razor?

(And, later, adolescent, was there a ringing, buzzing in your head?

(Would you walk and walk and walk, finally enter a house, search for women's clothes, fondle undergarments, to scatter and ignite?

(Did you thrill to the sound of a passing siren?

SIX

Pyro!

Ah-ha! So that's your story: you're not a Torch, not an Arsonist, you're a Pyro! Not for loot, not the lust for money, but for the Fire itself, the sheer love of it!

monomanie incendiare!

A tough kid, lousy home life, no job, no sex, you get into the bottle . . .

Restless, tense, an urge to move, to have a finger into something . . . maybe headaches, palpitations, ringing in the ears . . . a merging into unreality . . . and the fire is set:

the world is in confusion! people run, scream, the sirens ring, trucks roar . . . !

Then, only then, with a sigh of relief, are you released . . .

Only then, do you feel *natural* . . . no longer furtive, you go home, omnipotently passive, and drop into peaceful sleep . . .

It was you, Louis, back on the farm, you got mad at your neighbor and waited twenty years before you burned his barn.

You went to a ball game, and afterwards, gathered all the score cards, made a lovely fire, and watched, as the stands burned down . . .

. . . steal a piece of firewood, drill a hole in it, put in a lighted candle with an opened shotgun shell, put this bomb on your neighbor's porch . . .

. . . burn churches, schools, barns, and homes, throw logs across the roads to block the firetrucks . . .

. . . set forest fires, tell the marshalls that you only wanted to improve the stand of blueberries!

And me, Louis . . . what do you have against me? Something you don't like? Voice? Posture? The way I walk? Race, religion, or point of national origin?

Will you roast me, Louis, because you think I'm a nigger or a kike—or, God help me, a protestant?

Are you a gypsy, Louis, a vagrant, a wanderer? Were you a hobo, in the Great Depression, leaving the city in the East where you were born, living in the jungles, the boxcars and railyards, enflaming the midwest, across the Rockies, to California, kindling your way, finally, to the Pacific Northwest?

Or is it sex?

Ah, that's it! You twisted, horny hotflame!

Have to kindle a fire, a *big* fire, gaze at all the hot tints, the flaming hues at the base of the blaze, to get it on, get it off!

Have a few drinks, and it's like a boy and girl petting, you get hot and bothered, just have to go ahead and ignite . . . the colors, the noise, the crackling, walls and timbers falling, there's a tingling, an itching, and all the flames in your trunk, your crotch, quiver, ascend, burn . . .

You dance nude around the flaming building, or the singing grasses in the open fields . . . !

The trucks arrive, the fireman, superhero, drags out his mighty hosenozzle, carries it to the height of the building in his cherry picker, pours into the hot flames an endless torrent of potent quench . . . or enters the building, cunnilingual with the flames . . .

What's that? You can only get it off in front of a fire? And they arrested you once, for setting 56 fires? In one day?

Quit bragging! You're a lousy faggot! A firebug, and you practice buggery! You and your buddy, hoboes in the jungles, setting fires all across the Great Plains, through the passes and over the Divide, to the Great Ocean . . . and after every fire back to the boxcar, the little pillow of rags in the corner, and you go down, go down . . .

Or maybe you've gone further, Louis, had that little operation:

Louise! Louise the Torchette! Louise the Firegirl!

You make a little fire at home, you want the insurance to redecorate, or buy you some new dresses . . . a little blaze, maybe it's in a closet or a bureau drawer, you feed it with toothpicks and perfume . . . then you get excited, you stare at the hot little flames, you get all dressed up, some fantastic rig . . . or strip bare, run into the streets and dance, waiting for the flaming red trucks . . .

Or you burn down your lover's house . . . you were carrying the torch for this guy, and he jilted you . . . so you put the torch to him . . . touched him off.

What's that, Louis? "A Song of Joy," you say? Sure, some joy . . .

What? Walt? Walt *who? Whitman? Walt Whitman?* "A Song of Joy," by Walt Whitman? Why, you lousy third-generation immigrant, you're going to quote the Good Gray Poet, the true American . . . to *me?*

"I hear the alarm at dead of night,
I hear the bells—shouts
I pass the crowd—I run.
The sight of flames maddens me with pleasure."

Oh, dear God . . . !

SEVEN

eau de vie, eau de feu . . .

"It is a water which burns the tongue and flames up at the
slightest spark."

"It is the communion of life and of fire."

". . . brandy burns before our entranced eyes . . ."

From the pit of the stomach it radiates heat to the heart, and
throughout entire trunk and structure . . .

. . . opens the brain, incorporated with language, pours fresh words
to the fiery tongue . . .

. . . and disappears with what it consumes . . .

As an old pyro, Louis,
you're a common drunk.

EIGHT

Salamander, Louis, the Spirit of Fire:

> There was the European lady—Eye-talian, like you:
> "Several times a night while she slept, a flickering
> bluish glow emanated from her breasts."

>> (and you, Louis: you're bilious, nervous, red-
>> haired, and alcoholic . . . when you cut yourself,
>> does the wound glow?

> And the Firewalkers, treading barefoot through
> charcoal pits, their feet, their soles, unscorched:
> achieving a state of unreality, the consciousness
> withdrawn, displaced, bestowed upon
> another—there is always a leader—and replaced by
> the body's aura, a sheath of protection, a shift in
> molecular vibration, so that you walk through the
> firepit, in absolute submission, the body warm from
> the ruddy coals, the feet cool and untouched . . .

> And the Poltergeists. Tell me, Louis, back to your
> youth, your early teens, sexual electricity of the
> muscle cells just awakening—could you create fires
> out of nothing, without means of ignition? Would
> a room combust, in your presence? Were you an
> agent, a Lucifer, a match?

> Were you trying to lobotomize yourself, to cut off
> the damaging portions of consciousness, so that,

broken loose, these fragments of your own soul dispersed in violent ignition?

Remember, Louis?

NINE

Well, Louis . . . it's all a dream, isn't it?

You and I have been together a while . . . getting on, getting it
on . . .

Where are you now? Wandering again, a vagrant? My belly, my
knees, that little rash, that little itch on my ankles? I never know
where you're going to break out . . .

Fire is the bastard son of two pieces of wood, Louis. Once brought
to life, it consumes its parents, the parents feed the fire, are
themselves its food. The spark ignited, released to the open air,
becomes the tongues of flame that eat the mother and father,
leaving only ash. The parents *become* the child.

All is consumed, Louis, the earth's exhalations feed the comets,
the comets feed the stars, the stars feed the Sun, the Sun will one
day feed and consume itself: all is flamboyant aliment.

What do you think of that, pal?

You're falling apart, you old pyro, I can tell . . . cataracts, bad
teeth, the hearing fails, arteries harden . . . testes dessicate,
atrophy . . .

What's that? You say you can still get it on? Rises like the Phoenix
from her own ashes? Well, Louis, you know how it is,
you get older, you know what I mean, the prostate enlarges . . . you

can still make it with the lady, you can still do it . . . but there's that slight burning sensation.

I guess the Chinese were right, ole buddy: the vital principle in old fire grows weary . . . let it extinguish, die from its own flame . . .

You live in my belly, Louis, have made fires from my toes to my skull, have tried by so many hot sets to incinerate . . . but you're getting old, now, falling apart . . . and the flame consumes the hand that lights it . . .

You have been chosen, Louis, look at it this way: it is the highest honor, an apotheosis raising you to the rank of a god, to be selected for the sacrifice. Bound hand and foot, you will be thrown alive into a great furnace, then raked from the coals, and from your scorched, blistered, and still writhing body, your palpitating heart will be removed . . .

Immolation—remember this, Louis—immolation consumes only that which is mortal, leaving your divine and immortal spirit . . . to return renewed and strengthened in your next life!

You're old, Louis, and you're a drunk . . . one of these days, in your gin-soaked dotage, you will incinerate yourself . . . you'll be out in the woods somewhere, with your booze . . . blue flames will dance from your gut, trip over your torso, only your hands, feet the top of your skull will remain, your trunk cindered . . . as you have tried to cinder mine.

Or maybe you'll die, as they say, from natural causes, but it'll be days, weeks, before they find you . . . and tiny blue flames—phosphoretted hydrogen—will burn from the pores, the minute pits, of your rotting skin . . .

Remember, Louis, death by flame is warm and sociable, a toasty expiration.

So long, Louis. I'll miss you . . . so long.

Bibliography

Aeschylus. *Prometheus Bound.* Trans. David Grene. Chicago and London, 1974.

Arlow, Jacob A. "Notes on Oral Symbolism." *The Psychoanalytic Quarterly.* (January 1955).

Bachelard, Gaston. *The Psychoanalysis of Fire.* Trans. Alan C.M. Ross. London, 1964.

Barracato, John, with Peter Michelmore. *Arson!* New York, 1976.

Battle, Brendon P., and Weston, Paul B. *Arson: A Handbook of Detection and Investigation.* New York, 1960.

Clough, A.H., ed. *Plutarch's Lives.* Boston, 1875.

Encyclopedia Brittanica. 11th edition. Cambridge, 1910.

Etsell, Karen Lee. *The Mechanism of Defense in Children Who Set Fires.* Northampton, 1968.

Faecke, Peter. *The Fire Bugs.* London, 1965.

Fedor, Nador. "Fire and Begetting." *American Journal of Psychotherapy.* (April 1948).

Frazer, Sir James. *The Golden Bough.* London, 1913. 10 VOLS.

__________. *Myths of the Origin of Fire.* New York, 1930.

Freud, Sigmund. "The Acquisition of Power over Fire." *The Collected Papers.* Ed. James Strachey. London, 1950. Vol. 5.

Gaddis, Vincent H. *Mysterious Fires and Lights.* New York, 1967.

Hesiod. *The Homeric Hymns and Homerica.* Trans. Hugh G. Evelyn-White. London, 1926.

Kaufman, I., et al. "Re-evaluation of the Psychodynamics of Firesetting." *American Journal of Orthopsychiatry.* (January 1961).

Macht, L.B., and Mack, J.E. "The Firesetter Syndrome." *Psychiatry.* (August 1968).

Murray, James A.H. *A New English Dictionary on Historical Principles.* Oxford, 1888.

Nurcombe, Barry. "Children Who Set Fires." *Medical Journal of Australia.* (April 18, 1964).

First Conference on Arson and Fire Investigation. *Proceedings.* Rutgers University. New Brunswick, 1964.

Rothstein, Ralph. "Explorations of Ego Structures of Firesetting Children." *Archives of General Psychiatry.* (September 1963).

Schachtel, Ernst G. "Some Notes on Firesetters and Their Rorschach Tests." *Journal of Criminal Psychopathology.* (October 1943).

Scott, Donald F. *The Psychology of Fire.* New York, 1974.

Skeat, Walter W. *An Etymological Dictionary of the English Language.* London, 1963.

Smith, William. *A Smaller Classical Dictionary.* London and New York, 1910.

Tennent, T.G., et al. "Female Arsonists." *British Journal of Psychiatry,* 119, 497, 1971.

Vandersall, T.A. and Wiener, J.M. "Children Who Set Fires." *Archives of General Psychiatry* 22, 63, 1970.

Yarnell, Helen, and Nolan, Lewis. "Pathological Firesetting." *Nervous and Mental Disease Monograph,* 82. New York, 1951.

Yarnell, Helen. "Firesetting in Children." *American Journal of Orthopsychiatry.* (April 1940).

GOLDEN DELICIOUS

I would like to thank the staffs of the following libraries and library systems where research for this book was pursued:

The Berkshire Athenaeum, the Lenox (Mass.) Public Library, The Forbes Library (Northampton, Mass.), Williams College Library, Smith College Library, Mt. Holyoke College Library, the Massachusetts Inter-Library Loan System, The New York State Library (Albany), The Beinecke Research Library at Yale University, The New York Public Library, the Library of the University of California at San Diego, the Suzzalo Library at the University of Washington, and the public libraries of Port Townsend and Port Angeles, Washington.

For special research assistance, I am indebted to Don Byrd, Paul Herder, William Matthews, and Ilana Smith.

I am also grateful to The Centrum Foundation, Port Townsend, Washington, for providing a winter residency that made possible my research in that part of the country.

*What I mean is, I would never
choose a subject for what it means to
me. I choose a subject and then what
I feel about it, what it means, begins
to unfold.*
—Diane Arbus

tranced anachronism
—Donald Wesling

ONE

It hath been deservedly esteemed one of the great and wonderful
works of God in this last age, that the Lord stirred up the spirits of
so many thousands of his servants . . . to transport themselves . . .
into a desert land in America . . . in the way of *seeking first the
kingdom of God . . .*

> Upon due consideration of the state of the Plantation now
> in hand for New England, wherein we, whose names are
> hereunto subscribed, have engaged ourselves, and having
> weighed the greatness of the work in regard of the conse-
> quence, God's glory and the Church's good; as also in
> regard of the difficulties and discouragements which in all
> probabilities must be forecast upon the prosecution of this
> business; considering withal that this whole adventure
> grows upon the joint confidence we have in each other's
> fidelity and resolution herein, so as no man of us would
> have adventured it without assurance of the rest; now for
> the better encouragement of ourselves and others that shall
> join with us in this action, and to the end that every man
> may without scruple dispose of his estate and affairs as may
> best fit his preparation for this voyage; it is fully and faith-
> fully AGREED amongst us, and every one of us doth hereby
> freely and sincerely promise and bind himself in the word of
> a Christian, and in the presence of God, who is the searcher
> of all hearts, that we will so really endeavor the prosecution
> of this work as by God's assistance, we will be ready in our
> persons, and with such of our several families as are to go
> with us, and such provision as we are able conveniently to
> furnish ourselves withal, to embark for the said Plantation

by the first of March next, at such port or ports of this land
as shall be agreed upon by the Company to the end to pass
the Seas, (under God's protection,) to inhabit and continue
in New England . . .

> . . . whereas God of old did call and summon our
> fathers by predictions, dreams, visions, and certain
> illuminations, to go from their countries, places, and
> habitations, to reside and dwell here or there, and to
> wander up and down from city to city, and land to
> land, according to his will and pleasure; now there is
> no such calling to be expected for any matter whatso-
> ever, neither must any so much as imagine that there
> will now be any such thing. God did once so train up
> his people, but now he doth not . . .

> . . . now the ordinary examples and precepts of the
> Scriptures, reasonably and rightly understood and
> applied, must be the voice and word, that must call
> us, press us, and direct us in every action.

> . . . we are all, in all places, strangers and pilgrims,
> travellers and sojourners, most properly, having
> no dwelling but in this earthly tabernacle; our
> dwelling is but a wandering and our abiding but
> as a fleeting, and in a word our home is nowhere
> but in the heavens . . .

*　　*　　*

That such, and so many Gentlemen of Ancient and Worshipful
Families should Combine in so desperate and dangerous a Design,
attended with such insuperable Difficulties, in the plucking up of
their Stakes, leaving so pleasant and profitable a place as their Native
Soil, parting with their Patrimonies, Inheritances, plentiful Estates,
to come into this Desert, & unknown Land, and smoaky Cottages,
to the Society of wild Indians; what less than a Divine Ardour could

inflame a People thus circumstanced to a work so contrary to Flesh
and Blood.

. . . soe vast an ocean . . . thousands of leagues . . . both turbulent
and dangerous . . .

. . . for a man to remove himself out of a thronged place into a wild
wilderness . . .

. . . a remote, rocky, bushy, barren, wild-woody soil . . .

But O how horrid and dismal do these newfound regions appear!
On the shore and rivers, nothing but sights of wretched, naked,
and barbarous nations, adorers of devils—the earth covered with
hideous thickets that require infinite toils to subdue—a rigorous
winter for a third part of the year—not a house to live in—not a
Christian to see—none but heathen of a strange and hard lan-
guage to speak with—not a friend within three thousand miles to
help in any emergency . . .

> Being thus arrived in a good harbour and brought safe to
> land, they fel upon their knees & blessed ye God of heaven,
> who had brought them over ye vast & furious ocean, and
> delivered them all ye periles & miseries thereof, againe
> to set their feete on ye firme and stable earth, their proper
> element.

> But hear I cannot but stay and make a pause, and
> stand half amased at this poore peoples presente con-
> dition; and so I thinke will the reader too, when he
> well considers ye same. Being thus passed ye vast
> ocean, and a sea of troubles before in their prepara-
> tion . . . they had now no friends to welcome them,
> nor inns to entertaine or refresh their weatherbeaten
> bodies, no houses or much less townes to repaire too,
> to seeke for succoure.

> And for ye season it was winter, and they that
> know ye winters of yt cuntrie know them to be
> sharp and violent, & subjecte to cruell & fierce
> stormes, dangerous to travill to known places,
> much more to serch an unknown coast.
> Besids, what could they see but a hideous &
> desolate wilderness, full of wild beasts and
> willd men? and what multituds ther might be
> of them they knew not.

> > For sumer being done, all things stand
> > upon them with a wetherbeaten face;
> > and ye whole countrie, full of woods &
> > thickets, represented a wild & savage
> > heiw. If they looked behind them, ther
> > was ye mighty ocean which they had
> > passed, and was now as a maine barr &
> > goulfe to separate them from all ye civill
> > parts of ye world.

The hardships, difficulties, and sufferings which you have exposed
yourselves unto that you might dwell in the house of the Lord and
leave your little ones under the shadow of the wings of the God of
Israel, have not been few nor small.

. . . and this merely on the account of *pure and undefiled Religion,*
not knowing how they should have their daily bread, but trusting
in God for *that,* in the way of *speaking first the kingdom of God, and
the righteousness thereof . . .*

*   *   *

*I will make the Wilderness a Pool of water, and in the dry lands I will
plant a Cedar.*

How wonderfully is the going of Christ into *America!*

. . . what glorious things might here be spoken unto the praise of free grace and to justify the Lord's expectations upon this ground!

God sifted a whole nation that he might send choice grain over into this wilderness.

. . . wherewith His Divine Providence hath irradiated an Indian Wilderness!

*   *   *

. . . whereas the good hand of God now brought them to a country wonderfully prepared for their entertainment by a sweeping *mortality* that has lately been among the natives.

> The Indians in these parts had newly, even about a year or two before, been visited with such a prodigious pestilence, as carried away not a *tenth,* but *nine* parts of *ten* (yea, 'tis said, *nineteen* of *twenty)* among them: so that the woods were almost cleared of those pernicious creatures, to make room for a *better growth.*

Laftly, if the Lord himfelfe have roared from Sion . . . fo from his Churches in *New England,* by a great and terrible Earthquake . . .

> . . . taking rife from the Weft it made its progreffe to the Eaftward, caufing the Earth to rife up and downe like the waves of the Sea; having the fame effect on the Sea alfo, caufing the Ships that lay in the Harbor to quake, the which, at that very time was faid to be a figne from the Lord to his Churches, that he was purpofed to fhake the Kingdomes of *Europes* Earth . . . to fhew he will ordaine Armies both by Sea and Land to make Babilon defolate . . .

Awake, Awake, put on thy strength, O New-English *Zion, and put on thy Beautiful Garments,* O American *Jerusalem!*

*   *   *

Consider that there are no persons in all the world unto whom
God speaketh by His Providence as he doth to us.

Mention, if you can, a People in the world so priviledged as we are.

Have you not observed that there have been more . . . awfull
tremendous dispensations of divine Providence in New-England
than in any place else . . . ?

Jerusalem was, *New England* is, they were, you are God's own,
God's covenant People . . .

There never was a Generation that did so perfectly shake off the
dust of Babylon . . . nor a place so like unto New Jerusalem as
New England.

N-Englands true & main interest . . . is a fixed unalterable thing.

*Without doubt, the Lord Jesus hath a peculiar respect unto this place,
and for this people.*

If my weakness was able to show you what the Cause of God and
his People in *New-England* is, according to its *divine Originall* and
Native beautie, it would dazzle the eyes of Angels, daunt the hearts
of devils, ravish and chain fast the Affections of all the Saints.

If we look abroad over the face of the whole earth, where shall we
see a place or people brought to such perfection?

> (. . . such of us are in exiled condition . . . shall know
> what God is doing, and about to do in the world,
> though others know nothing of these matters).

God himself hath been a Wall of fire to us . . . *He hath fenced us . . .
about as his peculiar garden of pleasure . . .*

. . . if we cast up the Accompt, the Summe of all our mercies, and lay all things together, this our Common-wealth seems to exhibit a *little model of the Kingdome of Christ upon Earth* . . .

. . . the *New English* Churches are a preface to the New Heavens.

The matchless favors of God unto New England are now to be set before you . . . Beholding so much of New England from every quarter, under such characters here come together, I shall take this opportunity to bespeak your hearty praises to the Almighty God for so dealing with New England as not with any nation. Indeed New England is not heaven; that we are sure of! But for my part, I do not ask to remove out of New England except for a removal into heaven.

. . . there never was any people on earth so parallel in their general history to that of the ancient Israelites as this of New England.

I knew that if God had a people any where, it was here . . .

O, God of Hosts, thou hast brought a vine out of *England;* thou hast cast out the heathen and planted it; thou preparedst room before it, and didst cause it to take deep root, and it filled the land; the hills were covered with the shadow of it, and the boughs thereof were like the goodly cedars . . .

*   *   *

I have been before God, and have given myself, all that I am, and have, to God; so that I am not, in any respect, my own.

. . . no right to this tongue, these hands, these feet, these eyes, these ears, this smell. I gave them to God, and I have been this morning to him, and told him that I gave myself wholly to him.

> (to *Hate* our *selves* and *ours*,
> the very name of Own,

the Vomit in its Cheeks,
the whole body of Sin . . .)

You are using my lips to speak—you!—
your words, shaping my lips,
passing under the roof of my mouth, inwards

and my mouth, and my own words, and my thoughts

are phantoms, shadowing the altogether
other, shaping words—yours!—

and I haven't the scent, the smelling
is your smelling, your inhalation in my nose!

my palm roots the beckoning of your fingers

you are in me! in me! you step in my pace,
your eyes in my hollows turn inwards,
stare into my head . . .

> . . . 'tis COTTON MATHER that has written all these
> things; *Me, me, adsum qui scripsis; in me convertite*
> *ferrum* . . . It was I, I myself who wrote this! Hurl
> your spears at *me!*

*   *   *

Then judge all you (whom the *Lord Chriſt* hath given a diſcerning
ſpirit) whether theſe poore New England People, be not the fore-
runners of Chriſts Army, and the marvelous Providences which
you ſhall now heare, be not the very Finger of God, and whether
the Lord hath not ſent these people to Preach in this Wilderneſſe,
and to proclaime to all Nations, the neere approach of the moſt
wonderfull workes that ever the Soones of men ſaw.

The whole earth is the lords Garden & he hath given it to the soones of men . . .

. . . the great Mountains standing before you . . . shall become a Plain . . .

The Mighty Works of Christ in Western Lands!

TWO

My dear Cousin I am a going to Write to you about our trubels
geting to Callifornia

> (elm or Osage for hubs,
> (oak or hickory for spokes,
> (ash or beech for felloes,
> (ash for framework
> (hickory for tongues . . .

Steamboats are coming into St. Joseph, three and four a day,
each with three hundred or four hundred passengers California
bound. The lower deck is filled as closely as they can stow them
with horses and mules, and the upper decks with wagons and
men. Some are playing cards, some fiddling, some drinking,
others dying, all at the same time and on the same boat.   if any
man has got 2 middling stubbed Horses from 8 to 12 years
old & a middling light waggon strong tires bolts every Fellow
that has his own provisions at Home & 50 dollars in money can
start to California   The crowd at the ferry is a dense mass—
fighting for precedence to cross. 2 teamsters kill'd each other on
one of these occasions, with pistols, at the head of their wagons.
2 crazy scows very insufficient for the occasion, as soon as a
wagon enters the boat, the next moves close down, while compa-
nies are falling in the rear, and this goes on from earliest dawn
till midnight day after day.   The rush now seems tremendous,
each determined to head his neighbor.   they now find things
different to what they expected, and everything is wrong and
they are wrong and crazy, too.   This was enough to make all
the world laugh. the moist boistrous day I have ever seen, the

wind is raving.   The multitude that is going is wonderful.
It seems as if the world is going to market.   DEAR WIFE: Kiss
the baby. Border line, all well. Kiss the baby, Independence, Mis-
souri. Kiss the baby. Had a good time. Last letter. Cross the river.
Tell the baby California. Dear wife all well. Tell Johnnie papa
plenty of money California. Kiss the baby. Robert   This day
we leave this post. Only He who knows all things . . . His will,
not mine, be done.

For Christ's sake let's go to California!

We commenced packing our mules early in the morning, but
owing to their wild and unbroken state, and being unacquainted
with packing, we were not prepared to start until five o'clock in
the evening . . . This appeared like a very tedious way to get to
California   If ever there were other vicious mules in this world,
they must have been amiability itself compared with ours. They
rolled, they kicked, they plunged, they screamed, they bit, as
though we had been submitting them to the torments of the
damned. Taking six men to each mule, we finally lashed the packs
on them so tight as almost to cut them in two. The moment their
heads were loosed, away they went into the river, over the hills,
and across the country as hard as they could lay legs to the ground.
Oh! it was a pretty sight! The flour and biscuit-stuff swimming
about in the river, the hams in a ditch full of mud, the new set of
pots and pans bumping and rattling on the ground until there was
not a morsel of shape left in one of them. And the pack saddles,
which have delayed us a week to get made, broken and smashed
to splinters.

> There is no dependence To be Placed in the guides you Buy
> or at least none That I have seen These That has made
> Them has either never seen the Plains or They must have
> been Drunk or asleep

> Brief Practical Advice to the Emigrant or Traveller: The
> journey is not entirely a pleasure trip.

everything that a man's wife or a boy's mother could think of was piled in the wagons—sheet-iron stoves, feather beds, pillows, pillowslips, blankets, quilts and comforters, pots and kettles, dishes, cups, saucers, knives, and forks.   Take no loose cattle excepting a cow for milk. Drive everything before your wagon, and learn the cow to keep the road in front of the oxen; when she becomes troublesome kill her for meat.

Two miles of Independence the parrieres comense.   Now we are out of civilization & the influences of civilized society entirely, & cut loose from the rest of the world to take care of ourselves for a while. I confess to a feeling of lonliness ... Henceforth we must work across these vast wild wastes alone and go in our own strength ... So be it.   Our camp this evening presents a most cheerful appearance. The prairie, miles around us, is enlivened with groups of cattle, numbering six or seven hundred, feeding upon the fresh green grass. The numerous white tents and wagon-covers before which the camp-fires are blazing brightly, represent a rustic village; and men, women, and children are talking, playing, and singing around them with all the glee of light and careless hearts.   There will be a continuous train of wagons reaching from here to the Rocky Mountains. You can see the white tents gleaming in every grove—wagons, oxen, mules, horses, men, children and dogs lining the road from morning till night. The Exodus of the Israelites was nothing to it.   there cannot be less than 2000 wagons ahead of us on the road.   It was alarming to see the long strings of wagons that were on the road. I counted just passing before us as we came into the St. Jo road 90 ox teams in one string. And as far as the Eye could reach forward and back the road was just lined with them. It would appear from the sight befor us that the Nation was disgorging its self and sending off its whole inhabitance.   When we reached the prairie we found that all the emigrants who had crossed the river during the five previous days had gone into camp waiting for the rain to cease. ... It was a grand sight to look over the prairie as far as the eye could discern and see the new white-covered wagons and tents clustered here and there and the great number of horses and cattle, scattered

in every direction, trying to get a bite of the short spring grass that
had just started to grow. It was estimated at the time that at least
10,000 emigrants were camped within a distance of ten miles of
this point   As the shadows of evening gather, while I sit in the
tent door and watch the declining sun above the horizon, bathed
in a sea of its own effulgence, it seems to beckon us onward, be-
yond the vast prairies, beyond the rugged mountains, to what we
are prone to imagine its resting place, the yet far off mighty West!
Gold must be had & I for one am willing to brave most anything
in its acquisition.

The plains were an ocean, to be crossed in prairie schooners. Birds,
even seagulls, flew overhead. The wind whipped the land into
waves of grassy hillocks, or left it in a vast flat calm. Shoals of
bison, antelope, or tiny prairie dogs swams among the grasses. The
schooners were watertight, rising high at prow and stern, and they
set sail from the town of Westport at the ocean's shore, in Mis-
souri. moundy hills of fine, light rabbit sand, the Coast o' Nebrasky
Flocks of seagulls overflew the valley   And now commenced a
perfect gale which continued to blow all day with such fury as it
does nowhere except on these land oceans.   the broad expanse
of blue plains on the north side of the river, and below, looks like
the ocean, bounded by the dim blue mountains.   The beautiful
undulations of the plains are like waves of the ocean.   The
almost constant high wind which sweeps over the prairies like over
the ocean   like an ocean changed to a praraie in the midst of a
storm.   Betimes the prairies appears like the oceans rolling
waves, green & the rises or undulations of every conceivable
variety of shapes. When out of sight of wooded ravines it is easy to
imagine oneself out of sight of land.   Appearances often remind
one of being at sea.   One might as well attempt to describe the
sea to a person who had never seen it, as to paint in language the
calm grandeur, and boundless extent, of the rolling prairie.   like
the huge lazy swell of the Atlantic in a calm.   like the sea, with
the same boundless sweep to the eye.   smooth, ocean-like
verge of the prairie   broken into separate and rugged peaks and
elevations, like some gigantic ocean breaker dashing its immense

volume into a hundred different waves.   Like the long peaceful swell of an Old Ocean at rest.   The sundown seas were before us

We find we have twice as much of everything as we can carry . . . Hardly a company has left here but that had too heavy a load & every train before travelling 50 miles throw away quantities of provisions & articles not absolutely necessary.   Ham, flour, pilot bread, Beans, sheet iron stoves extra axletrees & wheels, medicines Tools of all kinds   lead crucibles, gold washers   The road and plain is strewn with them, hats, coats, boots, old iron, powder, balls, lead, boxes, trunks, valises, salt, bacon flour   barrels of bread, six dozen steel shovels   a complete outfit for a sawmill brooms and brushes, ox shoes and horse shoes, lasts and leather, jumping jacks and jewsharps, rings and bracelets, pocket mirrors and pocketbooks, calico vests and *boiled shirts*   a boat   anvils, feather beds, rocking chairs, overboard goes everything.   Rifles are thrown by the dozen into the river and worthless white beans almost cover the ground.   a diving bell   some wooden buckets, and all our pickles   towels, gowns and hairpins There is more clothing on the ground . . . than would fill the largest store in Boston.   and green bonnets enough to build a foot bridge across a creek.   meet and flower   good geese feathers in heaps   old clothes boots provisions, particularly beans   King Bolts, Crow Bars, Picket pins   spools, soap, scythes   a great walnut bedstead   The bacon was piled like cordwood, and some of the men poured turpentine on the provisions and set fire to them, so the Indians couldn't eat them. sugar on which turpentine has been poured, flour in which salt and dirt had been thrown, and wagons broken to pieces, or partially burned, clothes torn to pieces   A few hundred yards from my camp I saw an object, which reaching, proved to be a very handsome and new Gothic bookcase! It was soon dismembered to boil our coffee.   Costly trunks torn to pieces.   2 large kegs of gun-powder, which we put in a wolf-hole, on a hill, close by, and blew up.   A Dutchman here, was discarding some tools, which he could carry no further: and was busy breaking saws, &c. over a stump. "Day cosht me plenty of money, in St. Louis, and nopoty

shall have the goot of dem, by Got!" a general destruction and
devastation appeard to take Place   I have never seen before in
no place, such destruction of property
     Saw a fine sheet iron stove sitting beside the road, took it along
cooked in it that night, & then left it   Found an old stove and
baked some bread.   great piles of bacon and flour, piled higher
than my head, a notice on every pile "This is clean: help yourself"
     an old man would pick up all the old iron lying along the road
even to old iron tires which he would bind up with his immense
strength and throw in the wagon telling his companions that it
would come in good play later on. And his companions, later on,
when the old man was not observing, would throw them out again.
     a fair-sized library   books of every sort and size from Fanny
Hill to the Bible.   law books, novels   Several Law Libraries
     Lying by the way-side, are a great variety of books. . . . From
this extended library I frequently draw a volume, read and return
it.   an escritoire of rare workmanship   Huge piles Bacon are
fired & affords a fine light

Wild flowers are scattered over the prairie beautifully.   Prara
pinks were in abundance and the odor arising from them delightful
to ones allfactorys.   We have found the wild tulip, the primrose,
the lupine, the teardrop, the larkspur, and creeping hollyhock
The grass and the wildflowers growing so luxuriantly about us, our
horses feeding in their midst   Cacti, tulips, and the primrose
The wild rose, which is now in full bloom, perfumes the atmosphere
along our route   Wild roses on both sides in great abundance
     we now found grass brisket deep and wild flowers to the waist; a
perfect sea of flowers   Trees are a perfect luxury to our Prairie
sick eyes.   No one can imagine how delightful the sight of a
tree is after such long stretches of desert . . . to lay down in their
Shade . . . & hear the wind rustling their leaves & whistling
among their branches.   the breeze was fragrant with the scent
of southern-wood   Beautiful warblers of the prairie, they are
rather less than the robin, in black with red breasts.   The
singing of the meadowlarks, clover fields shimmering with hum-
mingbirds.   Springs of cold, pure water gushing from the cliffy

banks of the small branches and ravines   The moon and the countless starry host of the firmament exhibited their lustrous splendor in a perfection of brilliancy unknown to the night-watchers in the humid regions of the Atlantic   hills green to their tops, and the vallies rich with vegetation, wild wheat, clover and oats, whilst the clear, pure, invigorating atmosphere renders it the paradise of the mountaineer in summer. It is well worth a trip to California for the slothful, ease-loving denizen of lower countries, to see the country, and recover their manhood.   As the rays of the setting sun kissed the hills the scenery was grand.   The golden beams of a brilliant sun lighting an Italian sky kissed the distant peaks & threw a charm over this fairy-like scenery. What a scene from here! The Snow Butte, and his blue neighbors, deep vales, silver-thread like streams, near mountains, dense forests, bright deep valleys, &c. Pshaw!—enraptur'd with a landscape!—how ridiculous!   a succession of high, round, grassy ridges with running water in the hollows, and distant points of timber nearly always in sight. We made seventeen miles, and passed numerous fresh graves.

hear we go winchind our way threw the black
hills this is ruf country   If I had not seen
wagon tracks marked upon the rocks I should not
have known where the road was, nor could I have
imagined that any wagon & team could possibly
pass over in safety.   A man was endeavorous
to urge 2 weak oxen up the hill, but they would
not attempt the laborious ascent, in spite of
kicks, banging and stoning.   all day giting up
hill.

> Some verry steep descents where men hitch a tree behind
> waggons to hold back.
> Oh, snub by a fir, or snub by a spruce.
> Get a rope and turn the bull-teams loose!
> Snub by a cedar, snub by a pine,
> And lower your wagon down the steep inn-cline!

in many places we had to chain all the wheels, and assemble all our force to hold the wagons back.   The bank was so steep & the pitch into the water so abrupt that the men would have to hold onto the hind part of the wagon to keep the bed from pitching over the fore wheels.   My wagon seemed as though it stood on end.   It is so steep in places that it does seem that the wagon must fall over on the cattle   the road hangs a little past the perpendicular
over some places narrow enough to roll through with the hubs on the top of the rock other places again one wheel going over a Rock 3 or 4 ft high & the other grinding in a crivis below some places turn to the left one step the next step turn to the right one time cracking she goes another time grind & another time hop & another time bounce she goes it is awful to see it   larboard ox was on the starboard side—the starboard ox on the larboard side—the mare foul in the rigging and all going to hell together.   Cabins were built at such points out of wagon wrecks.

crawsing the Caw River the bote sunck with one family, tho all ways save.   We got sloughed once today, and had to carry our loads on our backs.   After a bad Knight, we went 5 miles for brec forst.   After we cross the creek and got on top of the hill look back the road is so crooked some of the teemes looks as tho they was going back   We overset one Waggon with a family some of which were slightly hurt and one lady fell and the Wheels run over her legs hurt her badly and had a marriage at night Parson Stewart officiating.

I have dreams my mind when I am asleep is like an uncaged Bird it is as ungeovenerable as the wild roe that runs over these mighty plains   As we rose from the bottom of the Blue, upon the high and rolling prairie, a vast diameter of country spread itself before us in all directions   One that has never seen these plains can form no idea of their vastness   turn which way you will nothing to be seen but the green grass stretching away   The eye aches

with looking for Timber & Water.   I can't see what God
Almighty made so much land for!   Our ignorance of the route
was complete. We knew that California lay west, and that was the
extent of our knowledge.   No wonder the resolution of these
hundreds of prostrate men and women all but faints in contempla-
tion of the uncounted desert miles yet to be covered, and knowing, if
they had never realized it before, that it is now too late to turn back.

Saw a man riding an ox; queer sights on this road.   Air'd &
sunn'd the clothes, clean'd out the wagon which was full of dust,
read the remaining 3 acts of Hamlet   it is quite asite to see the
prairies covered with Buffalow we had agreat time acilling one
Sunday was our day for cooking beans and eating pickles. We
never ate pickles except on Sunday.   Two women and a man
were baptized in a mud-hole today   "Come to the wedding.
Come kiss the bride, everybody."   There was fiddling and
dancing in the camp tonight.   Billy Collins . . . brought out his
old "fiddle." . . . Billy's music was of the "Rend a rock and split a
cabbage" variety.
    In the evening we had a *cotillon party*. Our *spacious room* was
illuminated by lighting two or three dozens of sperm candles, and
arranging them in the form of a circle.   To wander among these
vast ledges of rocks, to crall in the great caves, caverns, and holes,
which nature has formed in these rocks fills the mind of man, with
a wild romantic Grandeur, which raises him above his natural
sphere, and leads him, to aspire, to reach the angles

What goes the hardest with me is the total loss of the company of
young ladies.   I hear not the glad notes of the church bell, and
see not the neatly dressed brunette tripping her way   No habita-
tion in sight or within miles of us, and no telling how distant are
women.   To-day I saw a sight worth the while, which was a live
woman on the plains.   Such was the amativeness of some of the
train boys that they were glad to hug even a lousy squaw.   The
hardships, the toil, and privations endured while crossing the
plains in those early days were no drawback to love-making
Love is hotter here than anywhare that I have seen when they love

here they love with all thare mite & some times a little harder.
Jacob made love to old Blazard's daughter, and gets the woman-
kind to wash our shirts.

A tornado was whirling across the prairie
             We had rain in the valley accompanied with light-
             ning, also hail and snow on the mountains. A snow
             storm in the middle of June is not very comfortable.
It was dark by this time & the wind blew a perfect herricane,
whirled the tents topsie tervy and the fire Came in flames &
Sparks filling the whole heavens.
             This being out in the night guarding a herd of wild
             cattle the rains pouring down in torrents is no fun.
             Even if you are in serch of gold.
wind shakes wagon so much I cannot write.
             After the tornadow has passed clouds of Grass-
             hoppers fell from the sky which had been drawn up
             from the surface of the Whirlwind.

Wolves howled, musquitos pretty plenty.   They were as thick as
they could fly decentley.   forty bushels to the acre   the
muschetoes and knats were very annoying to the Horses.   The
musquitoes here are more ferociously savage and blood-thirsty
than those in a civilized country.   they bite as if they had never
seen a human being before.   They took right hold without giv-
ing any warning at all.   The mosquitoes here have been lied
about. None are as large as turkeys; the biggest one I ever saw was
no bigger than a crow.

             (Buffalow Bones, & dung laying as thick as it can lay
             (noon it is a valley of dry bones for it look as thou-
             sands of buffalows killed in the big platt it is a
             Delightful country it appears as though there were
             millions of buffalows killed on this place.

and this narrow road continues about a mile and a half, when we
get a view of the first water which flows into the Pacific Ocean.
This is called Pacific Spring   After we cross the dividing ridge

the watter went the other way.   Reaches Pacific Springs . . . and
drank the waters of the Atlantic and Pacific Oceans mingled in
one cup.   How near together the solitary mountain sources of
these little streams, and yet with half the world between them,
how widely severed their ultimate destinations!   We crossed
South Pass in about a week / And all spit in Pacific Creek. / Oh,
roll on, spit!

We hear on all sides the lowing of cattle, the neighing of horses,
the braying of mules, and barking of dogs, mingled with the clack
of human voices. To this is added the sound of the viol, bugle,
tamborine and clarionette. To fill up the chorus, rifles and pistols
are almost constantly cracking, responsive to the rumbling, grind-
ing music of carriage-wheels still passing along.   Such horrid
noises caused by the braying of the asses, lowing of oxen, scream-
ing of women and children with the fiendish cursing and swearing
shouted in all languages by furious madmen was enough to
becraze the greatest stoic in all Christendom.   sume may think
the children of Iserel in the Wilderness were a clammersome set
but they were nothing more than what folks now are.

It is hard to turn away a starving man 1500 miles one way, and 300
the other, from any source of supply, but we are obliged to do it.
    We constantly met groups of men, inquiring for lost cattle . . .
Among the unfortunate ones, one company, having an hundred
head, lost seventy; another, out of eighteen, lost nine; and we
passed two wagons with families, who had only three oxen tied to
the wheels. It was a kind of *terra firma* shipwreck, with the lamen-
table fact, that the numerous craft sailing by were unable to afford
the sufferers any relief.   Found a man dead by the roadside
today. Two stakes were driven into the ground, and over them was
drawn a piece of wagon sheet, under which the man lay. By his
side was a cup of water and a piece of hard bread. Near by lay a
card, with the following on it: "Please give this man a cup of water
and bread if he needs it. He was not able to travel, and wanted to
be left." The truth is, the inhuman wretches had left him there to
perish, while they rushed madly on the gold fields.

No earlier Cause called together in the New World such a strange
medley of men, so curious a mass as this Golden Army.   The
trip is a sort of magic mirror, and exposes every man's qualities
of heart, vicious or amiable.   It is strange that so many of all
kinds and classes of People should sell out comfortable homes
in Missouri and Elsewhere pack up and start across such an
emmence Barren waste to settle in some new place of which they
have at most so uncertain information. But such is the character of
my countrymen.   I'm going to the mines so I can be indepen-
dent of the darned fools that feel themselves above me back home
because I'm a poor cuss—damn their stinking hides!

Upon this journey the bad passions of men are apt to show
themselves . . . Appoint no captain—make no by-laws. Be quiet;
attend to your own business; make no promises . . . Try and go in
company with quiet, peaceable men   But what is there that
human nature, in the shape of a parcel of California boys,
cannot accomplish.
  There are yet some sunny spots in human nature. To enjoy such a
trip along with such a crowd of emigration, a man must be able to
endure heat like a Salamander, mud and water like a muskrat, dust
like a toad, and labor like a jackass.   old men young men one
legged men and some that don't happen to be men   upon experi-
ence, I am convinced there is no severer trial of a man's temper
than such a journey as the one we have undertaken. . . . it requires
a constant and vigorous effort of the mind to delude oneself into
the idea that one is performing a romantic and heroic act. I
discovered that the emigrant's true character was here developed;
all moral restraint thrown off, they become reckless in regard to
truth and honesty, and totally selfish.   so much discontent,
wrangling, and quarreling in almost every train.   Our train is in
a state of rebellion . . . The whole train is on the war-path.
Everything is wrong. The feed is poor. Wood is scarce. Wind is
blowing a gale from the north cold as a Christmas morning
Store sweep Clerks and Gentlemen are littel fitting for a trip of
this kind.   A company from Ohio dissolved—cause, too many
Doctors & Lawyers.

The mind, that which distinguished man from the beast, will be depraved. A vast number are underage, some mere boys, cursing and swearing, carrying knives and pistols; men, and that savage men, in their own estimation.   Men get cross sometimes on this trip and having all restraint thrown off they act rash.   Men often mad & here one can learn human nature in all its aspects. Yes, if a man has a mean streak about him half an inch long, I'll be bound if it won't come out on the plains.   men were decidedly more irascible on the plains than they had been at home   The spirit of selfishness has been here beautifully developed   Some, whom at home were thought gentelmen, are now totally unprincipled.   What were "clever fellows" at home are hard cases here there are amongst us a desperate set of men capable of anything.   and shows them up in all their native deformity. what a set of jackasses the best of men are—*the best.*   I have never despised human nature as I now do.   Nearly all of our men have turned out to be perfectly use- less.   Some of my men seem to be perfectly stupid and childish, and it is with difficulty I can make them attend to certain duties for their own welfare   dress they think nothing of money plenty

Such profanity I never dreamed existed in the world as I have heard since we have been amongst the emigrants.   The amount of profane language is surprising, and from a general view, one might come to the conclusion that a strict search had been made, and that all the profane swearers in the Union had been sought out and brought together upon this expedition . . . thousands seem to tax their inventive powers in originating new forms of vulgar or blas- phemous language.   a greater amount of swearing hollowing shouting and cussing for one mile of road, I never heard of   Mis- sourians, it seemed, were unusually fertile in oral persuasion.   the presence of our Heavenly Father is less realized here than in any other place. His holy name is never heard except to be profaned.

On Sabbath we have nothing but swearing   addressed us with the Word of the Lord to repent our sins and folleys wich we was giltey of before the Lord sitch as Dansing and Dice playing and card playing with jumping Loud Lafter and all such habbits wich was a bomation in the sight of god and was a stink in his norstels

I notice many names painted on the high rocks along the river. Some people take great pains to be known.   All the accessible faces of blocks & cliffs, were marked and inscribed with names, initials, & dates. This peculiar vanity has been displayed all along the route, from our frontier down into the valley of the Sacramento. Nothing escapes that can be marked upon.—Buffalo-sculls, stumps, logs, trees, rocks, etc. even the slab at the heads of graves, are all marked by this propensity of *"pencilling by the way."* The singular feature is that of marking initials; for instance A.S.S. as if everyone should know who he was.   I suppose that thare is not less than 2 thousand names riten in diffrin plases.   The names of a great many emmigrants are painted on the rocks, with tar.   a soft sandy rock with thousands of names cut on it and mine among them.

Upon an eight-by-ten shanty on the roadside, which some enterprising individual had erected. and in letters as large as the house itself, was chalked the one word: "WHISKY!"   had foresight enough to order a demijon of the best old Bourbon Whiskey, just to have in case of Sickness, or, in time of *great drought*   Whiskey was 50 cents per pint and a great demand for it.   I have said all kinds of property were thrown away. Who ever saw whiskey thrown away?   One qt. raw alcohol, 1 lb. rank black chewing tobacco, 1 bottle Jamaica ginger, 1 handful red pepper, 1 qt. black molasses, Missouri River water as required.   Missouri skull varnish: a mixture of molasses and opalescent undistilled whiskey. a Mormon and his wife trading in lame cattle, moccasins, whiskey piss

A joyous happy shout was soon after heard . . . "Brandy at $8 a gallon."   This morning everything was wet & cold and the clamor was loud for liquor   The Cap. bored a gimblet hole in a keg of rum   & last night several were corned & oh how funny they were.   tapped a keg of good old brandy, and all hands got gentlemanly tite   More excitement, more fun, more bad whiskey drank at this place   The boys raked & scraped all the brandy they could & they toasted, herrayed & drank till reason was out

Pass'd a tolerable night by the aid of a lot of whiskey.

(here the road forks,
(one leading to California,
(the other to Oregon.

He puts the whole number of wagons at 13,000—pack animals
3,000—about 500 footmen, and three wheelbarrow men—one an
Irishman, another a German, and a third a Scotchman.   Soon
after we stopped tonight a man came along with a wheel barrow
going to California he is a dutchman. He wheels his provisions
and clothing all day and then stops where night overtakes him
sleeps on tile ground in the open air He eats raw meat and bread
for his supper

he again set sail he is now far ahead of us   Well, all kinds of
vehicles employed to get to the "Diggins."   I have not the time,
nor the power to describe the queer outfits and queerer people
who are at present to be found on the Western prairies.   Saw
one poor couple with their personal effects, goods & chattel,
packed on a poor ox,—the man, with shouldered rifle, led the
brute, while the wife, with a stick, followed and urged it ahead.
Two Irishmen passed us with nothing in the world but a milk cow
apiece and a small sack of crackers.   Met a man going to Cali-
fornia afoot all alone carrying what makes a little world within
itself here on the prairie, meat, bread, etc.   and to try grazing
on squirrels and prairie dogs the rest of the way.   A Yankee with
buck pants following ox train said he was from every place but this
& trying to get away from this as fast as possible.

The morning is clear and beautiful. The birds
are singing, wolves are howling, and all hands
are busy   *Just after dark the wolves gave us a
grand symphony.*   They kep up an offul houl
all night.

and the question suggested itself, what on earth, or rather what
in California, had brought us all this way . . . to make ourselves

miserable upon short commons and convict labour in a desert. It
was difficult to find a satisfactory answer to this posing query.
People talk about the erratic predisposition of the Anglo-Saxon race.
If the Anglo-Saxon race have an innate affection for stubborn mules
and rancid ham, the natural consequences of being dissatisfied with
railroads and roast beef, I am perfectly willing to respect their self-
denial, but cannot admire their taste. Certainly, I am an Anglo-
Saxon, and very proud of it too. But with all due deference to the
founders of that respected race, I would repudiate my connexion
with them at once, if I thought they had entailed upon me no more
comfortable legacy, than the faculty of seeking discomfort in every
quarter of the globe. Yet what other reason can I give for being here?

as the American to
unbroken, that is, untraveled
and to cause us too much difficulty
Our four wagons which we
too heavily loaded
seemed not to endure much
itself is not at first
after a few days through
charm. There is nothing but a
between mountains and valleys
true refreshment for the
the view of a river
with which everyone
to bring and take a bath
great fear among
snakes; but these
seem and had killed
slow movement of this
One of our people had
when it was about to
the tail again

was for us there
and, when one

to stay in the wagon and

to help, the slow

the best walker

from morning to night we

15 miles

were so tired as though

had to call. Each

8 days up to the

was explained and then

noon and evening

was, out of

then I was the whole

wherever I wanted, only

to care for the horses

at the Blue Earth River

the woman among them also

much pleasure

in the vicinity of the aforementioned

constant windings

route goes

saw 12 antelope

of which 3 sorts

buffalo and some rabbits

but not a single one

Tues. July 17   Very warm—sand roads. Toilsome as hell.
Wednes J 18   Sand!!! Hot!!! Grass parched & dry—
    P.M.   10 ms of R   Camp 8 P.M.
Thurs July 19   Camped 10 P.M. No grass (wheugh!!!)
Fri. July 20, 10 o'c   Hot!!! No halt at noon.
    Camped 6 o'c P.M. Grass 3 ms. Springs at slough.
Sat. July 21   Staid at slough
Sun. July 22   From slew to Sink (O barrenness)

Slept in the Sun & was near killed.   there was found a mudlake ten miles long and four or five miles wide, a veritable sea of slime . . . an ocean of ooze, a bottomless bed of alkaline poison, which emitted a nauseous odor and presented the appearance of utter desolation.   A melancholy and strange-looking country—one of fracture, and violence, and fire.   Wagons, from which their canvas tops had not been removed, were shrinking in the hot sun. it is getting late and the feed is nearly gone, and every day growing worse, and thousands just behind us.   Our cattle dined on faith. ten or a dozen large springs boiling up in large irregular basins or pools . . . Gas is continually bubbling up. I think this would be a glorious place for scalding hogs.   Mules were braying, horses pawing and men swearing, a wild and crazy orchestra in the desert. we had been about 30 hours without sleep, had walked about 65 miles through a dreadful heavy sand & dust, the water so bad we could hardly drink it & the cattle had been in their yokes for 30 hours without grass or water! This is the greatest victory we have had yet. One more such & we shall be ruin'd!   The sand is dry and mixed with the dung of numerous trains which have preceded us. In this dust the wheels and the cattle sink three or four inches, and clouds of it rise until the air is thick. In breathing, the breath seems impregnated with the powdered excrement of the cattle. Our cattle are getting so poor it takes two to make a shadow.

(Tragedy Spring
(No grass

(it was shurley best for us to push on

I saw three or four lizards, one or two flies; one must pitty them.

Here the dumb brutes suffer as never before. There are drifts of ashy earth in these flats in which the cattle sink to their bellies, and go moaning along their way midst a cloud of dust and beneath a broiling sun   The soil is parched by the sun and the earth is reduced to an impalpable powder   We literally had to eat, drink and breathe it.   finer than flour—so fine that at every step a man was enveloped in a cloud.   we could not see the wagon ahead of us.   The least wind raised it.   it blotched and blistered the lips of nearly everyone.   hell can't pe far from dis place.

Next morning when I went out to look for the cattle, there lay
Jerry, my off wheel ox, stark. He would never carry a yoke again.
Red Tom, one of Dad Ridgely's leaders, was just able to rise. The
others, including the two cows, were in a bad way. We thought
that it must have been the stagnant water. Like most tenderfeet we
knew nothing of alkali or its effects upon stock. Something had to
be done, and done quickly. What to do was the question. We had
brought no stock remedies with us. As we watched the poor crea-
tures writhing in their misery, we were confronted with the possi-
bility that all of them might lay their bones among the skeletons
by the wayside, leaving us stranded out in these wilds. Of the
many suggestions offered one at least seemed feasible, and that
was to give them bacon. Some one remembered hearing that it has
been tried under similar circumstances and found effective. So
bacon it should be. We reached into our load and brought out
slabs of the bacon which we cut into strips and proceeded to
administer. Every "critter" rebelled. We coaxed and patted them.
Still they remained obdurate. Finally, when all attempts at moral
suasion failed, we felt that we must resort to methods of forcible
feeding. Snubbing them up to the wagon wheels, we propped their
mouths open, and poled the slices of fat meat down with sticks,
while the animals reared back, twisted, bucked and bawled simul-
taneously. Mrs. Ridgley thought it was a shame to pester the poor
things that way. The rest of us had mixed feelings about it by that
time. But we managed to get about two pounds down each one
and there was plenty to spare, not including what went outside.
We waited a while to note the effect of our heroic treatment. They
seemed to be holding their own. We then yoked up, putting the
two milch cows in place of Jerry and Tom (who was too weak to
work) and started out. It was as a slow procession that made its
way . . . that day. The oxen staggered a little at times and needed to
be eased along; but when night came again they were noticeably
stronger than when we set out that afternoon. Our remedy had
worked.

Buffalo excrement makes good fuel.   cooked with Buffalo Dung
and Dirty River Water   Buffalo chips, (politely so called) fires of

wild sage & B-Dung.   "Bois de Vache"—pronounced Boys da
Wash.   The chips burn well when dry . . . They emit a
delicate perfume.   Tonight I was browning coffee   Buffalo
Shit.

Our men are becoming emaciated and queralous . . . Rancid bacon
with the grease fried out by the hot sun, musty flour, a little pinoles
and some sacks of pilot bread, broken and crushed to dust and well
coated with alkali, a little coffee without sugar   cords and gristle
and lean, flabby meat.   cold meat, hard bread & water   raw
ham, cold bread & brandy   I have lived on scalded milk and
hard bread mostly today, with cayenne pepper in it on account of
irregularity of my bowels.   When you run out of salt and pep-
per, burn your mule steak when broiling it and sprinkle on gun-
powder; it then tastes both salted and peppered.   More beans
discarded than any other article of provisions.—often disagree with
the bowels, and are heavy freight.   sugar which had been fouled
by the excrement of a man dying with something like the Cholera
As with my hunting knife I sliced the veneer from the old Buffalo
junk its resemblance to Honduras mahogany suggested a wooden
supper.   derangement of the digestive organs   musty hard
bread, and beef bones in a state of *incipient putre-faction*   Bacon
with fat 4 inches thick I can eat raw   Dine off raw ham and
water, without bread.   For days they lived on roasted acorns
for my own part I will eat the lizards which infest the sage bushes
The emigrants, or some of them, cook and eat rattlesnakes. They
call them *bush fish*.   They killed some sweet Black mice to
make a pie.   go out in the woods and smoke the Woud mice
out of the Logs and Rost and Eat them. about the only change we
have from bread and bacon is to bacon and bread   bacon and
flapjacks for breakfast. Flap-jacks and bacon for dinner, and repeat
for supper.   Hundreds are entirely out of provisions   I found
in the small creek just above where we got our water for cooking
and drinking, the carcasses of three horses and two oxen in the
most filthy condition possible, bushels of maggots on them. I sup-
pose we drank the juice of the five   For about ten days the only
water we had was obtained from the pools by which we would

camp These pools were stagnant and their edges invariably lined
with dead cattle that had died while trying to get a drink. Select-
ing a carcass that was solid enough to hold us up, we would walk
out into the pool on it, taking a blanket with us, which we would
swash around and get as full of water as it would hold, then carry-
ing it ashore, two men, one holding each end, would twist the
filthy water out into a pan, which in turn would be emptied into
our canteen, to last until the next camping place. As the stomach
would not retain this water for even a moment, it was only used to
moisten the tongue and throat.   I made soop from the washings
of a number of putrid carcasses.   It requires some little practice to
relish a beverage in which putrescent flesh has been for months
steeping.   Our super was a pise of hard biscuit.
   The camp ground I gave it a naim. I cald it Puke camp for one
sertain reason.

Just before we reached the heavy sand twelve miles from the
Carson, we met a man with a pail of water brought from the
river; he said he had four miles further to go with it (making in
all sixteen miles out and the same distance back) to save a favorite
cow which he had been compelled to leave behind.   one old
cow by the road with a paper pined on her head, it stated that she
had been left to die, but if anyone choose, they might have her,
but requested that they would not abuse her as she had been one
of the best of cows.   This morning old Charley being so weak,
we thought best to shoot him,—he has been a good horse, and
served us well, Peace be to his ashes.—   Left old Mullian's
horse at this bend . . . he was good as long as he lasted . . . drove
him into the Humboldt at noon & pushed him over   Have
seen today 38 dead oxen & two horses. 33 dead cattle today. Have
passed 27 oxen dead. Saw today 12 dead oxen. Today I counted 126
head of horses, mules and oxen, and then got tired of the business
and quit it. three or four bushels of maggots about a carcass. A
myriad of buzzards hovered around, alighting now and then to
pick out the eyes of the prostrate, whether dead or alive   rot
and the ravens have more matter than they can conveniently
consume.

Sand in dead animals' eyes gives them an unearthly glitter.

the air pestilential   Dust very disagreeable, but not to compare with the stench from dead carcasses which lie along the road

Dead animals all the way up the stench intolerable.   As soon as an ox dies he bloats as full as the skin will hold . . . and his legs stick straight out   A tanyard or slaughter house is a flower garden in comparison.   the traveler could find his way with no other compass or guide than his nose alone.

There were instances of persons suspecting at times that the circumstances with which they were surrounded were not real; and that they were deceived by the illusions of the most horrible dreams   one of their party leaped from the wagon, under the influence of a paroxysm of insanity, with loud cries and shrieks, and after describing several times by his movements, a circle, he declared that the destiny of Providence, so far as he regarded himself, was accomplished; that nothing more was expected of him, and he was willing to submit to his fate and die on that spot, and be buried within that circle.   The old man . . . says that he can throw himself into a Mesmeric State and visits his family or that of anyone that desires it, can tell where there are rich deposits of gold, &c. &c.   we found a man who was insane . . . He had a fire over which he performed many strange maneuvers.   It was nothing more than a looney clown of an emigrant dragging a battered handcart behind him. When he came up to any outfit he would whinny like a horse and ask if he would find grass further on. One outfit had two insane men tied in a wagon.   Men often mad   emigrant woman gone berserk   One lady was very much alarmed screaming every breath as loud as she could

About twice a week she had one of these hysterical fits. Sometimes while walking along the road she would throw up her arms and scream, then down in the road she would go; three or four men would pick her up and dump her into the wagon where she would lay for two or three hours. After she recovered she was ready for a fight with the first one who would quarrel with her.   left the Bason Camp or Mad Woman Camp as all the women in Camp were mad with anger and mad   Poor cattle bawled all night.

If the thousands who have gone should find themselves in the
mountains without provender or caught in the snow storm what
would become of them and us? We could not find sustenance
sufficient for all at any of the stations on the road . . . I cannot
keep clear of the blues sometimes when I look at the possible
result of this Expedition   saw another grave by the roadside &
almost threatened to get the melancholies.   the ladies wonder-
fully sick of their romantic journey   Oh, my dear Mother . . . I
thought that I had felt bad when I wrote you . . . from Indepen-
dence, but it was nothing like this.   we have seen some hard
sights, that is shure   O the luxury of a house, a house!   These
past few days I have been so disgusted that if an opportunity
could have offered itself I should have returned home.   Boys, if
I ever get back to Missouri I will never leave that country. I would
gladly eat out of the trough with my hogs.   Saw one man
returning; says he can't go all the way. Has money enough; loves
his wife more than gold.   What misery has not California
brought on individuals?   I wish California had sunk into the
ocean before I had ever heard of it.

The water of the Hot Springs which was used freely by both the
men & animals affected them most singularly . . . It was truly
laughable to see their contortions & twistings after urinating,
which they desired to do every hour. I must have ran at least 15
miles before I got back to camp . . . I ran as fast as I could. This
hard running started my bowels anew and it appeared as if every-
thing in me would run out.   Today I have been taken with the
diarea, common now on the prara, and have been kept quite busy
attending to the wants of nature, having 25 passages today.
passed one man that lived in a rock for 7 days having the
Diarrhoer   Dirarhoea   Some of our men have been sick with
mountain fever   a kind of dumb ague   Purpura Honoragica
    three-fourths of all that are sick are from Missouri I do not
know why it is, but such appears to be the fact.   the changed
voice, the *vox cholerica*, consisting of nothing but a mere whisper
without all tone and strength, the hollow sunken eye with a black
halo, the sharp-pointed ice-cold nose, the continual audible rolling

of the gas in the bowels the cramps in the legs, the asphyate condi-
tion, the paralytic condition of the skin, which will keep standing
if elevated, above all, the unquenchable thirst, with a cold-pointed
tongue, a continual effort to vomit or purge, of what? of a rice-
water stool, colorless, odorless   made my legs acan and swell
and my mouth sore and gooms swell, and an acan pain all
over.   they were in Camp for six weeks waiting for the sick to die
or get well Enough to Travil it was Sourten to die for there was no
Hopes of geten Well   Never did Life and Death hustle each other
on a narrower path.   Glourious day—22 cases of cholera.   Took
a little of Dr. Zoril's medicine to purify blood & did me good.

my comred come in to say what will we do I ust tell him what we
wod git a lon some way or rather he sad he was afraid he was
agont to dy on the plans and he usto frett a good dall about dying.
A.H. Unthank, Died July 2, 1850   often as I passed the fresh
made graves, I have glanced at the side boards of the wagon not
knowing how soon it might serve as a coffin   told her Mother
she wanted . . . a Grave six feet deep for she did not want the
wolves to dig her up and eat her.   our deaf and dumb man died
this morning a few rods from our camp name and place of resi-
dence we could not learn for he was too sick to write

   John Dequire   (was eaten in part by wolves)
   Levi Fredenburg   (accidentally shot July 5th)
   Ellis Russel,   Each of these died of cholera
     Sam'l P. Judson   and were buried in a row.
     N.T. Phillips
   J. Griffith   the wolves had disinterred this
                            body the skull one-quarter
                            mile from the grave

In the morning Miller was as well as any man belonging to the
train . . . At sundown he was dead and buried.   This morning
saw a company that had buried a husband last night burying the
wife this morning.   They died with the diaree.   Hutton is
dead. Others are worse. I am better—   During the night Hi
Dudly, Jake Snider and Ben Ferguson died. The sick and dying are

in every tent ... The Train will scarcely stop long enough to bury
the dead   Turn back you can't; go forward you must.

*   *   *   *   *

July 20, 1846. The Californians were much elated and in fine spir-
its, with the prospect of a better and nearer road to the country of
their destination. Mrs. George Donner, however, was an excep-
tion. She was gloomy, sad and dispirited in view of the fact that
her husband and others could think of leaving the old road, and
confide in the statement of a man of whom they knew nothing,
but was probably some selfish adventurer. it was raining then in
the Vallies and snowing on the mountains it come a storme and
they lost the road & got out of provisions they said they had
attempted to cross and could not we laid down on the ground we
spread one shawl down we laid done on it and spred another over
us and then put the dogs on top it was the coldest night you ever
saw the wind blew and it if haden bin for the dogs we would have
Frosen Monday 30th Snowing fast wind w about 4 or 5 feet deep,
no drifts looks as likely to continue as when it commenced no
liveing thing without wings can get about. Dec. 1.—Still snowing,
wind w.; snow about six or six and a half feet deep; very difficult to
get wood, and we are completely housed up; our cattle all killed
but two or three, and these ... supposed to be lost in the snow; no
hopes of finding them alive. Still snowing; now about three feet
deep; wind west; killed my last oxen today Snow very deep say 9
feet thawing alittle in the Sun Scarce of wood to day chop a tree
down it sinks in the Snow and is hard to be got. That, whereas, the
last detachment of emigrants from the United States to California
have been unable, from unavoidable causes, to reach the frontier
settlements and are now in the California mountains, seventy five
or one hundred miles east from the Sacramento Valley, surrounded
by snow, most probably twenty feet deep, and being about eighty
souls in number, a large proportion of whom are women and chil-
dren, who must shortly be in a famishing condition from scarcity
of provisions A great crying with the children and with the parents
praying crying and lamentations on acct of the cold and the dread

of death from the Howling Storm. The hides were boiled, and the
bones were burned brown and eaten. We tried to eat a decayed
buffalo robe, but it was too tough, and there was no nourishment
in it. Some of the few mice that came into camp were caught and
eaten. it snowed and would cover the cabin all over so we could
not get out for 2 or 3 days we would have to cut pieces of the loges
in sied to make fire with I could hardly eat the hides we had not
the first thing to eat   sad news, Jacob Donner, Samuel Shoe-
maker, Rhinehart, and Smith, are dead the rest of them in a low
situation; snowed all night Ma, I'm not going to starve to death.
I'm going to eat the bodies of the dead. On the twenty-seventh
they took the flesh from the bodies of the dead. some of the
compana was eating from them that Died they would commence
on the dead people I suppose they have done so ere this time
thay was 11 days without anything to eat but the Dead.   The
flesh of starved beings contains little nutriment. It is like feeding
straw to horses. I cannot describe the unutterable repugnance
with which I tasted the first mouthful of flesh. eat baby raw,
stewed some of Jake, and roasted his head, not good meat, taste
like sheep with the rot. The dead child that Keseburg hung on
the wall was not eaten by him alone. A part was given to my
sisters and myself, and Simon Murphy whom I remember so
kindly cut a piece, laid it on the coals, cooked and ate it. The
necessary mutilation of the bodies of those who had been my
friends Mrs. Graves' body was lying there with almost all the
flesh cut away from her arms and limbs. Her breasts were cut off,
and her heart and liver taken out, and were all being boiled in a
pot then on the fire. He ate her body, and found her flesh the
best he had ever tasted. At the mouth of the tent stood a large
iron kettle, filled with human flesh, cut up. It was from the body
of George Donner. The head had been split open, and the brains
extracted therefrom he found the body of young Murphy, who
had been dead about three months, with the breast and skull
cut open, and the brains, liver, and lights taken out the liver and
lights were a great deal better, and the brains made good soup!
There were plenty of corpses lying around the abdomens had
been cut open and the entrails extracted. Strewn around the

cabins were dislocated and broken skulls (in some instances
sawed asunder with care, for the purpose of extracting the
brains) Cannibal Cabins Starved Camp Don't let this letter
dishaten anybody never take no cutofs and hurry along as fast
as you can.

*   *   *   *   *

Only 110 miles to diggings.   my litle Family are in all of my
thoughts I have had their interest in view in all of work in plowing
in planting in hoeing and in reaping and in making fires and if I
should be blest to reach California and should be so lucky as to get
gold they will still be in all of my thoughts . . . I am looking for-
ward to the time when I hope through the blessings of Providence
that I will return to the Bosom of My Swee litle family.   Where
the hell *is* California?   We are here but we don't know where
here is.   How, for God's sake, did I get here? Where, for the love
of Christ, am I going?   This is a country that may captivate
mad poets but

We are now in California; what more could we ask?   I encour-
aged them all to wash their clothes and mend them and then take
a bath.   We are here at the end of our long and weary road, and
it is here that we separate. The bonds that held us together on the
long and toilsome march hold us no longer.   the first mining
town in California. Took dinner there, had variety of vegetables.
   and the luxury of laying under the shade of a tree no one knows
but one that has traveled a thousand miles through the hot sun
   I don't regret my going to California for I believe it to be the
best thing I ever done

> We got to Sutter's the eighth of October,
> Havin' been near five months sober.

> Gimme room, for I'm feelin' horny,
> And this is my greetin' for Californy!

THREE

Marcus Whitman was of the seventh generation "of the descen-
dents of John Whitman who arrived in the Massachusetts Bay
Colony some time prior to December, 1638, and settled at
Weymouth some twelve miles south of Boston. It is believed that
John Whitman came from Norfolk, England . . ."

Narcissa Prentice Whitman, bride of Marcus, was descended of
"Henry Prentice, who came from England and settled at Cam-
bridge, Massachusetts, prior to 1640."

Marcus and Narcissa, missionaries to the Indians, travelled west;
arrived at Fort Vancouver, Hudson's Bay Company, John Mc-
Loughlin in command—near the mouth of the Columbia River,
Oregon Territory. It was September, 1836.

Narcissa was amazed:

"On arriving at Vancouver we were met by several gentlemen who
came to give us a welcome . . . after chatting a little we were
invited to take a walk in the garden. What a delightful place it is,
what a contrast to the rough barren plains through which we had
so recently passed: here we find fruits of every description, apples,
grapes, pears, plums, and fig trees in abundance . . ."

"The grapes are just ripe, and I am feasting on them finely. There
is a bunch now on the table before me, they are very fine. I save
all the seeds of those I eat for planting, and of apples also. This is
a rule . . ."

* * *

"I intend taking some young sprouts of apple, peach and grape . . ."

"No captain knew when he started from London to Fort Vancouver on the Columbia River whether he would be wrecked in rounding the Horn, or be caught in some fearful storm in the South Seas; or even whether, at the entrance of the Columbia, the ship might not be drawn, by the swirl of the current or some adverse wind, on the bar. It was a long, dangerous voyage. So, before the yearly ship left London, a dinner was often given to the captain.

'Captain,' said a lady at a dinner given to Captain Simpson in London, 'when you reach that wilderness on the Northwest Coast of America, plant these apple seeds.'

And then, half in fun, she gave him the seeds she had just taken out of an apple. This was probably about 1825 or 1826. The captain said he would surely plant them. Then he put them in his pocket and forgot all about them.

The next day he started off on that long voyage of seven or eight months. He sailed around the Horn, up the western side of South America and of North America, crossed the terrible bar of the Columbia with its thundering white-capped waves, and sailed up to Fort Vancouver.

Then he sat, in his dress suit, at the right hand of Dr. McLoughlin, at another dinner; but this time it was in 'that wilderness on the Northwest Coast of America.'

Putting his hand into his pocket for something, the captain felt the apple seeds. He took them out and told Dr. McLoughlin how they came to be there. At that time there were no apple trees at all at Fort Vancouver, and those seeds suddenly became very important. They were given to Bruce, the gardener, without delay.

It took four grown men to plant those precious seeds: Dr. McLoughlin, Captain Simpson, Mr. Pambrun, and Bruce. First they were put in small boxes, in good earth, with glass over them. The boxes were put in the store-room where no one would find them or touch them.

The green sprouts, later, were planted in the fort garden by
Bruce and carefully protected. The white-haired Dr. McLoughlin
also watched over them. This powerful man, who controlled thou-
sands of Indians, and governed a country eight hundred miles
long, north and south, and nearly a thousand miles east and
west—this 'King of the Columbia' bent down with great interest
over these tiny green apple shoots. He hoped they would bear
fruit, and they did.

'Now come and see. We are going to have some apples,' he said
to Mr. Harvey one day. Harvey himself tells the story, and he was
afterwards the doctor's son in-law. They went to the tree. One lit-
tle green apple was hanging there. When it was ripe, it was picked
and cut into many slices, for everyone had to have a bit of it.

That first apple was a green one, but the next year there were
more apples and they were red. And the seeds of every apple were
saved, planted, and tended, so that they became valuable apple trees.

When the missionaries came, several years after that first seed
was planted, they found a charming apple orchard at Fort Van-
couver, with many a tree covered in the spring with beautiful,
fragrant pink blossoms, and in the fall with red apples."

*　　*　　*

. . . 1833, peaches were added . . .

> (Narcissa, in a letter home: "When Brother Weld
> comes, please remember and fill his pockets with
> peaches, plums and pear seeds, some of the best
> kinds, and some good apple seeds")

1836, McLoughlin's Vancouver farm had "ten acres of young
orchard in bearing."

. . . English gooseberry, cultivated strawberry, Catawba grape . . .

*　　*　　*

Meshach Lewelling, of Welsh ancestry, was a North Carolina physician—and he cultivated a nursery on the side. His family had emigrated to this country in the eighteenth century. Lewelling was a Quaker, and an abolitionist.

"To his surprise and consternation, Meshach was bequeathed several Negro slaves by a relative. Determined to free these slaves but unwilling to do so in North Carolina, he moved his family to . . . the free state of Indiana in 1825. There he manumitted the slaves and continued both his medical practice and the nursery business."

1836, Meshach's oldest son, Henderson Luelling—changing the name's spelling—"had heard glowing reports about the Black Hawk Purchase in what is now southeastern Iowa . . . he moved his family to the village of Salem in the Purchase where he opened a general store and, the following spring, set out a small nursery and an orchard with some 35 varieties of apples, pears, peaches, plums, cherries, and small fruit." His brother John joined him in 1841, and soon "almost every homestead of the south part of Henry and the north part of Lee County blossomed with trees from their nursery. Salem became the apple-growing center of early Iowa . . . The Luellings made 14 trips to Indiana and other eastern points for new tree stock and other plants."

Henderson built a handsome limestone house, and led the anti-slavery movement through the local Friends church.

But he was also reading:

. . . the travels of Lewis and Clark . . . reports of early Oregon emigrants, 1843 and 4 . . . the journal of Col. John Fremont's expedition . . .

Luelling made plans for yet another move: to Oregon.

"When the next spring came he had procured a stout wagon, made two boxes 12 inches deep and of sufficient length and breadth that set in the wagon box side by side they filled it full. These boxes were filled with a compost consisting principally of charcoal and earth, into which about 700 small trees and shrubs, embracing most, if not all of the best varieties in cultivation in that section of the country, were planted.

The trees were from 20 inches to four feet high and protected from stock by light, though strong strips of hickory, bolted onto posts set in staples on the wagon box.

Three good yoke of oxen were hitched to that wagon. All other arrangements being completed we started from Salem, Iowa, on the 17th day of April, 1847 . . ."

> Sweet June, Golden Sweet,
> Summer Bellflower;
> Golden Russet, Gravenstein,
> Northern Spy,
> Lady Apple
>
> Bartlett Pear,
> Early Butter
>
> Black Heart Cherry,
> Isabelle Grape,
>
> Crawford's Peach
> and Golden Cling,
>
> Siberian Crab,
> Orange Quince . . .

"Father had charge of the nursery wagon and decided to bring it through in his own way and time, for it was already pronounced by some of his friends a very hazardous undertaking to draw that heavy a load across the plains and over the Rocky Mountains.

It was necessary to water the trees every day after the dry weather set in . . . hence the load of that wagon maintained its maximum weight all the way across. But to every discouraging criticism Father invariably answered that as long as he could take that load without endangering the safety of his family he would stick to it."

. . . crossing the backbone of the continent at Pacific Springs . . . over Green River . . . Ham's Fork, to Bear River . . . passed over

Soda Springs, and the Lava district . . . Hot Springs, and over the
Portneuf Mountains . . .

. . . at every stream or spring, stopping to water the 700 plants . . .

. . . two oxen were lost on the Sweetwater . . . a wagon tongue and
axletree broken, but quickly repaired . . .

. . . and a band of hostile Indians halted them; but they "believed
that the Great Spirit lived in trees and seeing a man crossing the
wilderness with a wagonload of them, they thought he must be
under the special care of the Great Spirit, and so they did not
harm him."

Arriving on the Columbia, they were met by Marcus Whitman,
who urged them to settle east of the Cascades. But Luelling was
determined to push on. At the Dalles, "Father joined with others
and constructed two boats . . . The fruit trees were taken out of the
boxes when the boats were ready to start . . . and duly wrapped in
cloths to protect them in the various handlings and the frosty
nights."

November 17, 1847, the family arrived in "the long wished for
'Willamette Valley.'"

". . . we moved onto the claim and immediately commenced clear-
ing off the timber, five acres of which had been felled . . . and lay
in great heaps over the ground. With ax and fire plied almost day
and night, for we kept the fires well tended until ten o'clock at
night and were up and at it again by four in the morning, we soon
had land cleared on which to plant our orchard."

. . . between four and five hundred of the seven hundred grafts,
survived the journey . . .

*   *   *

1848, one William Meek came out from Iowa, with twenty grafted
trees and a sack of apple seeds. Luelling and Meek joined forces,
and "it is related that one root graft in the nursery the first year
bore a big red apple, and so great was the fame of it, and such the
curiosity of the people, that men, women, and children came from
miles around to see it, and made a hard beaten track through the
nursery to this joyous reminder of the old homestead so far away."

Apple Fever!

"It is related of some of the earliest settlers in the Willamette Val-
ley that nothing more thoroughly and painfully accentuated their
isolated condition than the absence of fruit trees on their newly-
made farms."

"You can not understand, for you were never young a thousand
miles away from home in a new country, isolated, without trans-
portation, and without fruit."

". . . in the fall of 1848 and spring of 1849, they came hundreds of
miles from all over the country for scions and young trees to set in
the little dooryard or to start an orchard . . ."

"As the fence around the house was finished, we put in an
orchard, papa going far distant and bringing the trees home on
his back."

"Half the beauty and pleasure that brightens the life of youth and
childhood, it is not too much to say, is found in the orchard of the
old homestead—the sight of the trees in bloom, the waiting and
watching for the first ripe fruit, the in-gathering of the fruit in
the fall, and the storing of it away in bin and cellar for use in the
winter around the ingleside."

"Fruit culture is most fascinating and ennobling, . . . and the
advance of the fruit product is evidence of the culture and civiliza-
tion of a people. It is hard to overestimate the beneficial influence

on health, morals, and manners of a generous fruit supply. The
ornamental grounds and orchards of the homestead do much in
childhood to strengthen that love of home and pride of family . . .
The cherished memories of home thus enriched are, in after life,
the strongest bond of family to bring back the absent and wander-
ing to the roof tree . . ."

"In April and May the valley is a fairyland; apple blossoms, with
their beautiful tints and sweet aroma, contrast with drab hillsides
and the pungent odor of sagebrush."

*   *   *

1829, long before Luelling, and before Whitman, "the brig
Owyhee, Captain Dominis, entered the Columbia, and opened
trade with the natives . . . On his voyage out Captain Dominis
touched at the island of Juan Fernandez and brought thence
peach-trees which were planted in Oregon."

Capt. Nathaniel Wyeth, 1835, "speaks of having grafted trees on
his place, Fort William, on Wapatoo Island, now called Sauvies'
Island. Grafts and stock must have come from the Sandwich
Islands . . ."

Also, from the Sandwich Islands, the cut-leaved Evergreen black-
berry . . .

Etienne Lucier and Achilles Peault obtained seeds from
McLoughlin at an early date, and by 1847 had apple, pear and
peach in bearing, on the French Prairie.

Sam Miller and the Freer brothers grew the first fruits in the
Wenatchee country, raising peach from pits, and apples from trees
packed in from Walla Walla . . . Correll planted the first orchard
north of Chelan . . . southerners settled around Waitsburg, at
Sorghum Hollow, Whiskey, Hogeye and Misery . . . the Coes
planted on Hood River, employing orientals to dig the stumps,

cut and burn slash, till the soil . . . The Yoncalla Valley, 1849, was a wilderness, but at the mouth of Elk Creek the Hudson's Bay Company maintained a trading station, and they had apple trees: "Never in the forty years since then have apples tasted so good" . . . Ralph Geer was one of the first to plant on Waldo Hills; he later remembered, "I bought two bushels of apple and pear seeds. I gave half of them to my father, and they were put out on the Clackamas River. From my pear seeds sprung all the pear orchards in this country" . . . 1850, a Mr. Ladd planted at Butteville, and in the same year, a Mr. Settlemeir on Green Point . . . Joel Palmer lost a nursery on the Deschutes River and was able to salvage only a small number of seeds . . .

The first apples raised in the Rogue River Valley were *Gloria Mundi!*

*   *   *

Delicious, and Winesap
Blue and White Pearmain,
Hubbardston Nonesuch,
Esopus Spitzenberg,
Roxbury Russet and Rambo,

Tewksbury, Waxen
Summer Queen and Fall Beauty,

Rhode Island Greening
Jersey Sweeting,
Ohio Favorite,
Virginia Greening,

Smith's Cider, Red June,
Red Canada,
July Bough,
Red Siberian Crab,

Golden Sweet,

Jennetting, Tulpahockin,
Red Cheek Pippin,
Summer Sweet Paradise
          d'Anjou Pear,
          Bosc and Bloodgood,
          Beurre d'Oeil, Onandaga,
          Urbaniste, Fall Butter,
          Seckle, and
          Winter Nellis

                    Cherries: Bing and Sour,
                    Royal Ann, Oxheart, and
                    May Duke

Indian Peach,
Cling, and
Hale's Early

          Breman and Rhine Prune,
          Coe's Golden Drop

                    Plums: Reine-Claude,
                    Vert, and Merabel,
                    Gage, Coe's Late Red, and
                    Ickwort

                    *   *   *

Big Antoine was a Caribbean Islander, educated in England,
spoke many languages . . . he showed up on the Entiat, tributary
of the Columbia . . . was run out of town, because he was Black . . .
left for Wenatchee, taking with him most of the peach trees he
had planted . . .

                    *   *   *

"The bodies of all apple trees should be washed two or three times
each spring with soap suds and a woolen cloth."

*   *   *

"High above the Columbia River in the opening of the hidden
valley of the Swaukane, there boiled from the ground, in appear-
ance a monster spring flowing more than 100 inches of water. As a
matter of fact it was the reappearance of the creek that disappears
miles above in the same valley. By careful surveys, Mr. Wagner
found that water could be carried by ditch and flume seven miles
to his ranch. Having made secure his title to the land he began the
construction of a canal and flume . . .

In places for some distances the flume was literally suspended
from perpendicular cliffs, which made the work both awkward and
dangerous. Members of the family helped. Mr. Wagner himself in
the longest days of summer, saw darkness at both ends of the day . . .

. . . the ditch was completed and successfully conveyed water to
the burning sands that thirsted for it. The transformation from
desert to bearing orchards is a well known story."

In Yakima County, "Mr. Beck built the first irrigation ditch in
1872. The intake was at the Yakima River one half mile above the
Moxee Bridge."

At Entiat, the Indian Silico "used the Chinese mining ditch to
irrigate his garden. The peach trees the negro had planted were
prolific in bearing, and settlers, steamboat crews and the general
public, generously helped themselves to the luscious fruit."

"The mines have ever been and now are a curse to Oregon . . .
Oregon proves to be, perhaps, the best country for apples, pears
and plums, in North America. . . . What is strange, but yet true,
apples and pears of superior size and flavor are obtained here the
third year from the graft or bud! Yet it is apparent to all close
observers that the science of Pomology here, must be learned
anew. . . . all has to be learned anew!"

("The mining region will never be planted in fruit trees—the population there being too transient, and also, they would soon dig up the trees in their zeal for gold!")

*　　*　　*

Trees planted from seed, 1825 and later, were still standing, and bearing, 1949 . . . some with a height of forty feet, a spread of fifty, and three feet across, at the ground . . . bearing heavily . . .

Bibliography

ONE

Baritz, Loren. *City on a Hill: A History of Ideas and Myths in America.* New York, 1964.

Bercovitch, Sacvan. *The Puritan Origins of the American Self.* New Haven, 1975.

______. *The American Jeremiad.* Madison, 1978.

Breen, T.H. *Puritans and Adventurers.* New York, 1980.

Cotton, John. *God's Promise to His Plantations.* Boston, 1896.

Hanscom, Elizabeth D. *Heart of the Puritan.* New York, 1917.

Johnson, Edward. *Wonder-Working Providence.* Ed. J. Franklin Jameson. New York, 1910.

Mather, Cotton. *Magnalia Christi Americana.* Boston, No Date

Plumstead, A. William, ed. *The Wall and the Garden: Selected Massachusetts Election Sermons.* Minneapolis, 1968.

Segal, Charles M. *Puritans, Indians, and Manifest Destiny.* New York, 1977.

Winthrop, John. *Journal, 1630-49.* Ed. James K. Hosmer. New York, 1908.

Winthrop, Robert C. *Life and Letters of John Winthrop.* Boston, 1864-67.

Young, Alexander, ed. *Chronicles of the Pilgrim Fathers of the Colony of Plymouth.* Boston, 1841.

The poem beginning with "You are using my lips to speak—you!—" and ending with "stare into my head . . ." is original.

TWO

Abbey, James. *California: A trip Across the Plains in the Spring of 1850.* New Albany, Indiana, 1850.

Altrocchi, Julia C. *The Old California Trail.* Caldwell, Idaho, 1945.

Armstrong, J. Elza, *The Buckeye Rovers in the Gold Rush.* Ed. Howard L. Scamehorn. Athens, Ohio, 1965.

Barry, Louise. *The Beginning of the West.* Topeka, 1972.

Berrien, Joseph W. "Overland from St. Louis to the California Gold Field." Ed. Ted and Caryl Hinckley. *Indiana Magazine of History* (1960).

Bidwell, John. *Echoes of the Past about California.* Ed. Milo Quaife. Chicago, 1928.

Billington, Ray A. *Far Western Frontier, 1830-1860.* New York, 1956.

Bruff, J. Goldsborough. *Gold Rush*. New York, 1949.

Bryant, Edwin. *What I Saw in California*. New York, 1848.

Chalmers, Robert. "The Journal." Ed. Charles Kelley. Utah Historical Quarterly (1952).

Christy, Thomas. *Road Across the Plains* . . . Ed. Robert H. Becker. Denver, 1969.

Clapp, John T. *A Journal of Travels to and from California*. Kalamazoo, 1851.

Clark, Keith, and Tiller, Lowell. *Terrible Trail: The Meek Cutoff 1845*. Caldwell, Idaho, 1966.

Coke, Henry J. *A Ride over the Rockey Mountains to Oregon and California*. London, 1852.

Decker, Peter. *The Diaries* . . . Ed. Helen S. Giffen. Georgetown, California, 1966.

Delano, Alonzo. *Life on the Plains and in the Diggings*. Ann Arbor, 1966.

Dickson, Albert Jerome. *Covered Wagon Days*. Cleveland, 1929.

Doetsch, Raymond N. *Journey to the Green and Golden Lands*. Port Washington, New York, 1976.

Dowell, B.F. *Diary*. Ms. (Yale University).

Doyle, Simon. *Diary, 1849*. Ms. (Yale University).

Dutton, Jerome. "Across the Plains in 1850; Journals and Letters . . . ," Ed. Claude W. Dutton. *Annals of Iowa* (1910).

Farnham, Elijah B. "From Ohio to California in 1849." Ed. Merrill J. Mattes and Esley J. Kirk. *Indiana Magazine of History* (1950).

Ferguson, Charles D. *The Experiences of a Forty-Niner in California*. New York, 1973.

Frizzell, Lodisa. *Across the plains to California in 1852*. New York, 1915.

Geiger, Vincent. *Trail to California* . . . Ed. David M. Potter. New Haven, 1945.

Granville, Ohio Company. *Diary, 1849*. Ms. (Yale University).

Gray, Charles Glass. *Off at Sunrise*. Ed. Thomas D. Clark. San Marino, 1976.

Hale, John. *California As It Is*. Rochester, New York, 1851.

Hannon, Jessie G. *The Boston-Newton Company Venture*. Lincoln, Nebraska, 1969.

Hardy, Francis. *Diary, 1850*. Ms. (Yale University).

Harlan, Aaron W. "Journal . . . While Crossing the Plains . . ." *Annals of Iowa* (1913).

Harlan, Jacob W. *California '46 to '88*. San Francisco, 1888.

Hickman, Richard Owen. *An Overland Journey to California in 1852*. Missoula, 1929.

Hill, John B. *Trip by Land from St. Jo to California*. TPS (Yale University).

Hillyer, Edwin. "From Waupun to Sacramento in 1849." Ed. John O. Holzhueter. *Wisconsin Magazine of History* (1966).

Holliday, J.S. *The World Rushed In.* New York, 1982.

Houghton, Eliza P. Donner. *The Expedition of the Donner Party and its Tragic Fate.* Chicago, 1911.

Hulbert, Archer Butler. *Forty-Niners, the Chronicles of the California Trail.* Boston, 1931.

Hutchings, James M. *Seeking the Elephant.* Glendale, 1980.

Ingalls, Eleazer S. *Journal of a Trip to California . . .* Fairfield, Washington, 1979.

Jefferson, T.H. *Map of the Emigrant Road from Independence, Missouri, to San Francisco, California.* New York, 1849.

Johnston, William G. *Experiences of a Forty-Niner.* Pittsburgh, 1892.

Keller, George. *A Trip Across the Plains and Life in California.* Oakland, 1955.

Kilgore, William H. *Journal of an Overland Journey to California . . .* Ed. Joyce R. Muench. New York, 1949.

Langworthy, Franklin. *Scenery of the Plains, Mountains and Mines . . .* Ogdensburg, New York, 1855.

Leeper, David Rhorer. *The Argonauts of 'Forty Nine . . .* South Bend, 1894.

Loomis, Leander V. *A Journal of the Birmingham Emigrating Company.* Ed. Edgar M. Ledyard. Salt Lake City, 1928.

Mattes, Merrill J. *The Great Platte River Road.* Publications of Nebraska State Historical Society (1969).

McGlashan, C.F. *History of the Donner Party; a Tragedy of the Sierra.* Ann Arbor, 1966.

McIlhany, Edward. *Recollections of a Forty-Niner.* Kansas City, Missouri, 1908.

McKinstry, Byron N. *The California Gold Rush Overland Diary.* Ed. Bruce L. McKinstry. Glendale, 1975.

Miller, Joaquin. *Overland in a Covered Wagon.* New York, 1930.

Morgan, Dale L., ed. "The Mormon Ferry on the North Platte . . ." *Annals of Wyoming* (July-October, 1949).

______. *Overland in 1846.* Georgetown, California, 1963.

Myres, Sandra L., ed. *Ho for California!* San Marino, 1980.

Nusbaumer, Louis. *Valley of Salt, Memories of Wine . . .* Ed. George Koenig. Berkeley, 1967.

Paden, Irene. *The Wake of the Prairie Schooner.* New York, 1943.

Page, Elizabeth. *Wagons West.* New York, 1930.

Perkins, Elisha D. *Gold Rush Diary.* Lexington, 1967.

Pigney, Joseph. *For Fear We Shall Perish.* New York, 1961.

Price, Joseph. "The Road to California . . ." Ed. Thomas Marshall. *Mississippi Valley Historical Review* (1924).

Pritchard, James A. *The Overland Diary . . . from Kentucky to California.* Ed. Dale L. Morgan. Denver, 1959.

Reid, John Phillip. *Law for the Elephant.* San Marino, 1980.

Robinson Zirkle D. *The Robinson-Rosenberger Journey to the Gold Field of California, 1849-1850.* Ed. Francis C. Rosenberger. Iowa City, 1966.

Rothwell, William R. *Diary.* Ms. (Yale University).

Sawyer, Lorenzo. *Way Sketches . . .* Ed. Edward Eberstadt. New York, 1926.

Schlissel, Lillian. *Women's Diaries of the Westward Journey.* New York, 1982.

Searls, Niles. *The Diary of a Pioneer . . .* Ed. Robert M. Searls. San Francisco, 1940.

Shaw R.C. *Across the Plains in Forty-Nine.* Farmland, Indiana, 1896.

Shepherd, J.S. *Journal of Travel Across the Plains . . .* Racine, 1851.

Steele, John. *Across the Plains in 1850.* Chicago, 1930.

Stewart, George R. *The California Trail.* New York, 1962.

_____. *Ordeal by Hunger: The Story of the Donner Party.* Boston, 1960.

Swain, William. *Diary and Letters, 1849.* Ms. (Yale University).

Tappan, Henry. *Gold Rush Diary . . .* Ed. Everett Walters and George B. Strother. Annals of Wyoming (1953).

Thissel, G.W. *Crossing the Plains in '49.* Oakland, 1902.

Thornton, J. Quinn. *The California Tragedy.* Oakland, 1945.

_____. *Oregon and California in 1848.* New York, 1849.

Turnbull, Thomas. T. *Turnbull's Travels.* Madison, 1914.

Unruh, John David. *The Plains Across.* Urbana, 1979.

Ward, Harriett Sherrill. *Prairie Schooner Lady.* Los Angeles, 1959.

Webb, Todd. *The Gold Rush Trail and the Road to Oregon.* New York, 1963.

Webster, Kimball. *The Goldseekers of '49.* Manchester, New Hampshire, 1917.

Williams, Joseph. *Narrative of a Tour from the State of Indiana . . .* Cincinnati, 1843.

Wistar, Isaac J. *Autobiography . . .* New York, 1937.

Wood, Jolm. *Journal . . . from Cincinnati to the Gold Diggings.* Chillicothe, Ohio, 1852.

Woodward, Thomas. "Diary . . . While Crossing the Plains to California." *Wisconsin Magazine of History* (1934).

Wyman, Walker D., ed. *California Emigrant Letters.* New York, 1952.

THREE

Allen, Opal S. *Narcissa Whitman*. Portland, 1959.

American Guide Series. *Oregon: End of the Trail*. Portland, 1940.

______. *The New Washington: A Guide to the Evergreen State*. Portland, 1950.

Bancroft, H.H. *History of the Northwest Coast*. San Francisco, 1886. Vol. II.

Bowen, William A. *The Willamette Valley*. Seattle, 1978.

Cardwell, J.R. "The First Fruits of the Land." *Oregon Historical Society Quarterly*. Vol. 7.

Drury, Clifford M. *Marcus Whitman, M.D., Pioneer and Martyr*. Caldwell, Idaho, 1937.

Duruz, Willis P. "History of Horticulture in the Pacific Northwest." *Agricultural History* (April 1941).

Ellison, Joseph W. "The Beginning of the Apple Industry in Oregon." *Agricultural History* (October 1937).

Farquhar, Frank S. "Historical Sketches of Yakima County." *Washington Historian* (July 1901).

Freeman, Otis. *The Pacific Northwest* New York and London, 1942.

Hull, Lindley M. *A History of Central Washington*. Spokane, 1929.

Judson, Katherine. *Early Days in Old Oregon*. Portland, 1944.

Long, S.A. "Mrs. Jesse Applegate." *Oregon Historical Society Quarterly*. Vol. 9.

Lyman, Horace S. *History of Oregon*. New York, 1903.

McClintock, Thomas C. "Henderson Luelling, Seth Lewelling and the Birth of the Pacific Coast Fruit Industry." *Oregon Historical Society Quarterly*. Vol. 68.

Newsom, David. *The Western Observer 1805-1882*. Portland, 1972.

Sargent, Alice A. "A Sketch of the Rogue River Valley." *Oregon Historical Society Quarterly*. Vol. 22.

Whitman, Narcissa. *My Journal, 1836*. Fairfield, Washington, 1982.

FIREBIRD

Thanks are due to:

Charles Alexander, for introducing me to John Wolff;

John Wolff, for invaluable research assistance at the Wisconsin State Historical Society;

Don Byrd, for extending to me his research privileges at the State University of New York (Albany), and the New York State Library;

Mark Hurlbert, from whom I have stolen one line (only he knows which one it is!); and

My anonymous fellow hawk-watchers, who shared with me their expertise—and offered even their lunch!—on a glorious autumn morning observing the Broad-wings.

ONE

"Northern Wisconsin, as a rule, is not subject to drought. But the season of 1871 was an exception. The winter . . . was comparatively without snow, a calamity to the lumbermen. Although a wet spring was prophesied, there was no unusual amount of rain. The last heavy rain had fallen on July 8th but left little trace of it. The swamps even were so dry that one could walk over the surface."

"Not a drop of rain fell in northern Wisconsin from July 8 until October 9, 1871 . . ."

". . . the very atmosphere seemed to pant."

". . . particularly with regard to the continuing, dangerous operation of setting fire to huge mounds of wood chips, sawdust and slash. After which, as he pointed out, these fires were allowed to burn unattended, even though the long dry spell had made the bush in Northern Wisconsin as dangerous as a tinder box.

The prevailing westerly winds carried the roaring slash fires into huge stands of virgin timber, but because there was no human habitation between the railroad and Lake Michigan shoreline, no one seemed to bother about the destruction. The fires were set as soon as each slash pile, which consisted of a huge mound of dead wood and branches, reached thirty to forty feet into the air. With a thunderous roar, the slash would dissolve into white heat, scattering fire brands for miles ahead of its path, would travel eastward and attenuate on the shore.

Settlers on the peninsula between Green Bay and Lake Michigan complained to the state that jump fires had crossed the bay, and were endangering their settlements, mostly lumber camps. But communication was bad, the railroad could do no harm, and the forest were full of trees. The wanton burning of slash continued, augmenting the fires that were constantly started by settlers clearing their land, and the fires that raced out of control which were caused by careless trappers and hunters."

"The raw air of autumn is being well cooked by fire."

"The whole air is filled with a dense, suffocating smoke, almost obscuring the vision, over a tract of hundreds of square miles. The sun shone down through the smoke with a red, angry glare."

". . . the smoke was dense and overpowering. It was almost impossible to distinguish a face the width of the street in distance. But the church goers went to church and listened to the preaching . . ."

"By day, flakes of white ashes were continually falling in the streets like snow."

". . . the air was so dry that if a man'd touch a match to it, it'd burn."

"This gloom . . . continued for a week over Green Bay."

"Why the hell don't it rain?"

"Our heaviest hawk flights are generally preceded by meteorological disturbances in the northern Appalachian regions. Low pressure areas advancing across these regions appear to start the hawks off . . ."

". . . the maximum stimulus for migration appears to occur when a period of rain not only ceases but is accompanied by clearing skies, following winds of low speed and a temperature rise or fall according to the season . . ."

It was October 8, 1871 (the same date as the Great Chicago Fire) . . .

"September is noted for Broad-winged Hawk flights which frequently peak about the middle of the month. Such fights, which sometimes contain many thousands of hawk, invariably occur between 11 and 24 September often producing exceptional flights."

"In addition to September's spectacular Broad-wing flights, Bald Eagles also migrate southward in small numbers during late August and throughout September, with occasional stragglers appearing as late as early December. Ospreys also are notable components of the September hawk flights, largest numbers appearing mid- to late September."

"October forms the second major period in the autumn hawk flights. Sharp-shinned Hawks are the most abundant migrants from early to mid-October, but they become less numerous later in the month. Adding zest to the season, however, are lesser numbers of other species including Goshawks, Cooper's Hawks, Golden Eagles, Marsh Hawks, Peregrine Falcons, Merlins, and American Kestrels."

"Toward the end of October and continuing into November, the largest and most majestic hawks reach peaks of abundance in their southward migration. Pick any cold day with northwest winds in early November and goodly numbers of Red-tailed Hawks are likely to be seen at many of the mountain lookouts. Adding more excitement to these flights are lesser numbers of Goshawks, Red-shouldered Hawks, Rough-legged Hawks, and occasionally other species. Golden Eagles, in particular, are the highlights of the hawking season."

There was a theory that the fires "resulted from the passage of a great atmospheric stream, which arose in longitude sixty-two degrees, swept with a cyclone Antigua and the Virgin Isles on 21st August, the Bahamas on 23rd, and then moved slowly to the Northwest, striking Chicago and the forests . . ."

"These handsome small hawks usually travel in loose groups of twenty or more, which come into sight off to the east well strung out and gliding at different levels toward a point somewhere between the river and the Notch."

"A bright light shot across the eastern sky and the whole heavens seemed ablaze . . ."

" . . through the gathering smoke he could see the sky in the west light up brilliant red, turning colour until it was almost blinding and then it subdued slightly and began to glow again like the sun."

*"... a quiet, windless day; a light curtain of mist
hung over the terrain. There was scarcely a move-
ment of any kind of bird life, till nearly eleven o'clock,
when 32 broad-wings appeared, very low ..."*

" .. the smouldering fires in the pineries ..."

"... a tiny tongue of fire that ran along the ground,
in and out, among the trunks of the trees, leaving
the pines untouched but burning up the dry leaves
and pine needles on the woods floor."

"The flames would insidiously work their way
into the swamps and here develop almost a fur-
nace heat, actually burning from one to three feet
into the ground and completely burning out the
peat, roots and alluvial soil, leaving nothing but
ashes and the subsoil of sand. Thus the fires lived
and increased for weeks ..."

"... the flames pursued the roots of the trees into
the very depths of the earth ..."

"... the fires would reach a clump of cedars or
tamarac and dance around the roots. There would
be a hiss as the sap turned to steam, a flash like
that of burning powder as the leaves took fire, and
in an instant the tree would be in flame ..."

black hawk			*white hawk*

		blue hawk				*blue darter*

	little blue darter

			bullet hawk

					big blue darter

	striker		*red hawk*

			singing hawk		*brown hawk*

				squalling hawk

	blue bullet

".. . a low, sullen rumbling began to be heard far away . . ."

". . . a sound similar to that caused by the falling of some mighty water or the roar of ocean waves dashing up against a rocky shore, or the rumbling noise of a train of cars coming at a distance . . ."

			"Most of the hawk species progress along the ridge in absolute silence."

". . . the far-off rumbling had increased to a steady roar like distant thunder, or the coming of heavy freight trains at full speed . . ." ". . . the sound of the cataract, the thunder, and the roar of the sea combined . . ."

"The momentum with which this bird passed through the atmosphere produced a sound not very unlike that of the rush of distant water."

". . . it was grand, it was fearfully sublime . . ."

"During direct flight the tail is usually closed, but, when soaring, it is spread open like a fan."

"Even the very earth seemed to quake and tremble."

"When soaring, the wings are spread to their greatest extent and the outer primaries are curved upward slightly and are separated like the fingers of an open hand."

"Venerable pines, towering over their offspring, were wrapped in flame. The trunk of a hundred-year-old giant would burn fiercely for a time, the flames shooting higher to catch the top branches, then flashing out along them to form a blazing canopy. When the tree had been sufficiently weakened, it would crash down in a shower of sparks and embers."

"The woods were flaming behind them. Pieces of gray ash swirled through the air. The wind gusted. A shower of sparks passed over their heads and suddenly the field was ablaze around them, the hay catching fire in a dozen places at once."

"At one point, the wind began to blow hard. He noticed some dead tree trunks blaze up 'as if the wind had been a breath of fire, capable of kindling them into a flame by its mere contact.'"

"Then would the flames leap from tree to tree, borne on the wings of the wind . . . and in a few minutes the beautiful grove would be a blackened, dismal forest of dry poles."

"There were two fires, one flying across the treetops, the other burrowing among the peaty stumps and roots."

"Migrating flocks often move along in a series of long ellipses."

". . . broad-wings streaming over at every elevation, some just over the treetops."

"The fire spread from tree to tree, in some instances twenty to thirty rods in advance of the fire on the ground."

"Great volumes of fire would rise up, fifty feet from the top of the trees, leap over thirty acres of clearing and, in an instant, flame up in the forests beyond."

". . . the fire crawling along like a snake . . . in the tops of the trees . . ."

". . . there were currents of air on fire. The atmosphere seemed saturated with inflammable gases from the pitchpine forests which had been burning for weeks."

"... the wind came in gusts almost hot enough to burn the skin."

"Not only was the air filled with smoke, but also with sand, which beat against us with blinding fury."

black hawk   *white hawk*

blue hawk   *blue darter*

"The forests in the Sugar Bush, which were largely composed of maple trees, give evidence of the tremendous force of the winds—the heaviest trees being uprooted or twisted off. A tree remaining standing in the central track of the storm is an exception to the general rule. They lay piled up in every conceivable shape, and not more than fifteen or twenty remain standing on an acre. The smaller limbs are burned to ashes and the trunks are charred and blackened. But notwithstanding this evidence of the great force of the wind, it is evident from the time the tornado struck the Sugar Bush . . . that its forward motion did not exceed five to seven miles per hour. The inference is, therefore, that the wind moved in a circling eddy, slowly advancing."

little blue darter

bullet hawk

big blue darter

"The fire appeared to break out spontaneously in pockets or dart forward in tortuous flashes instead of progressing with uniform pace . . ."

"The heat seemed to have moved in gusts or currents with such irregularity . . ."

striker   *red hawk*

     singing hawk   *brown hawk*

"The hurricane moved in a circle, advancing slowly, as if to give time to prepare for its coming."

squalling hawk

"At this time the direction of the wind changed rapidly, blowing from several points of the compass alternately. First from the southwest, then from the northwest, then back again to the south, during which time we were visited by a series of whirlwinds which showered cinders and sparks in every conceivable direction."

"The wind had at last settled to blowing steadily from the southwest, but still it blew with tremendous fury, and the flames in the swamp immediately in the rear of the town, raged with corresponding fearfulness."

blue bullet

The fire was absolutely coming . . .

TWO

"Along the west side of Green Bay there were thousands of acres of swamp, heavily timbered with cedar, pine, and tamarack, with extremely pitchy roots. The soil for a depth of two or three feet was solid peat, dry as powder. For weeks fire had been smoldering in this peat bed, burning beneath the surface for miles, and the roots of this timber had been literally red hot, during all this time, throwing off a highly inflammable gas. Three thousand acres of swamp land was turned into a gigantic gas factory, with no means of controlling the output. There being little or no air moving, the gas settled and remained near the surface of the ground. Those who came through the fire will tell of how they could smell, and even taste the gas for days previous to the conflagration. On Oct. 8, 1871, a tornado swept across the gas field in the direction of Peshtigo. It rolled the gas into billows, balls and streaks, and fanned it into flames . . ."

". . . the hawks concentrate in migration along the windward side of places like our Kittatinny Ridge, to ride the air currents. Without the wind striking against the flanks of the ridge, there can be no powerful updrafts of air upon which the birds coast . . ."

"The cold, brisk northwest surface winds which usually occur after the passage of a strong cold front create excellent flight conditions for migrating hawks because they strike the sides of mountains and are deflected upward. It is these updrafts or deflective air currents which are perfect for the soaring flight . . ."

"The heat rising and the wind rebounding off the mountains provides lift . . ."

". . . it is this dependence upon thermals which causes hundreds of Broad-wings to mass together in milling flocks called 'kettles' . . ."

". . . sheets of rising air, row upon row of combers in the sky . . ."

". . . with the howling of a tornado, against which seemingly nothing could stand, came a storm of fire, which an eyewitness likened to the heaviest snowfall of winter, with each flake of snow a coal of fire."

". . . a compact, whirling mass of broad-wings . . ."

". . . a whirling chimney of superheated air . . ."

". . . they mounted up and up in a gyrating, globular mass . . ."

". . . a towering wall of fire, higher than Niagara, and rolling over and over engulfing everything in its path."

". . . a swirling mass of broad-wings boiled over the mountain . . ."

"The great sheets of fire curled and rolled over the ground like breakers on a reef."

". . . a level sheet of moving birds . . ."

". . . a waterfall of fire rolling and tumbling toward him."

". . . a kettle, a boil, a storm of broad-wings . . ."

"He saw a solid wall of fire, less than a mile away, and it was churning and flowing directly toward Peshtigo."

". . . spiraling together, weaving in and out . . ."

". . . a river of fire . . ."

". . . like words swarming up a page . . ."

". . . an avalanche of fire . . ."

". . . this avalanche of hawks . . ."

"... a large black object, resembling a balloon, which revolved in the air with great rapidity, advancing above the summits of the trees toward a house which it seemed to single out for destruction. Barely had it touched the latter when the balloon burst with a loud report, like that of a bombshell, and at the same moment rivulets of fire streamed out in all directions. With the rapidity of thought, the house chosen was enveloped in flames ..."

"... a boiling mass of hawks milling within the confines of an invisible balloon."

"... a great black, balloon-shaped object whirling through the air over the tops of trees, and which seemed to explode."

"... lifting and ducking, volplaning and diving ..."

"... great balls of fire like flaming missiles shot from unseen artillery ..."

"... a batch of dry leaves lifted and tossed and whirled ..."

"The ball had by this time reached the house and exploded with a loud noise, filling the air with great sheets of flame. A stream of fire entered his house through the crack under the back door, and swept through the house to the front door."

*". . . a seemingly interminable, densely straggling
line . . ."*

"In seconds the pine sidewalks were afire. Then
the dry sawdust of the streets mushroomed into
flame."

*". . . the sky was literally black with the passage of
many thousands of hawks."*

"Cameron leaped up. He gave a yell of warning
and fear and defiance as fire rained down on Pesh-
tigo. The pine sidewalks blazed up. The top of a
house leaped into flame. Seeming close at hand,
the booming crash of great trees falling was heard
over the crackle of the flames. Cameron ran for
the river."

THREE

"As if by a common instinct, all seemed to rush toward the river."

"The air was no longer fit to breathe, full as it was of sand, dust, ashes, cinders, sparks, smoke, and fire. It was almost impossible to keep one's eyes unclosed, to distinguish the road, or to recognize people, though the way was crowded with pedestrians, as well as vehicles crossing and crashing against each other in the general flight. Some were hastening towards the river, others from it, whilst all were struggling alike in the grasp of the hurricane. A thousand discordant deafening noises rose on the air together. The neighing of horses, falling of chimneys, crashing of uprooted trees, roaring and whistling of the wind, crackling of fire as it ran with lightning-like rapidity from house to house—all sounds were there save that of the human voice. People seemed stricken dumb by terror. They jostled each other without exchanging look, word or counsel. The silence of the tomb reigned among the living . . ."

". . . at The Lookout, an outcrop of tumbled boulders, one looks down upon the packed gliding wings."

"I resolved then to cross to the other side though the bridge was already on fire. The latter presented a scene of indescribable and awful confusion, each one thinking he could attain safety on the other side of the river. Those who lived in the east were hurrying towards the west, and those who dwelt in the west were wildly pushing on to the east so that the bridge was thoroughly encumbered with cattle, vehicles, women, children, and men, all pushing and crushing against each other so as to find an issue from it."

> *"There was no sign of any flocking. Each bird seemed independent of the others, each traveling alone on this great natural highway of the air."*

"Down the steep banks tumbled men, women and children followed by horses, cows and pigs all of them clawing for help among the wildly flowing logs."

". . . the flames darted over the river as they did over land, the air was full of them, or rather the air itself was on fire. Our heads were in continual danger. It was only by throwing water constantly over them and our faces, and beating the river with our hands that we kept the flames at bay."

> *". . . dives and sails . . ."*

"The river was as bright, brighter than by day, and the spectacle presented by these heads rising above the level of the water, some covered, some uncovered, the countless hands employed in beating the waves, was singular and painful in the extreme."

*". . . in the forms of arcs and a series of dips and
rises . . ."*

"Cattle, too, rushed into the river and swam
bewildered, sometimes rolling over the logs to
which human beings were clinging."

". . . only to side-skip, arc, dive, and rise again . . ."

"Even the very fishes were reached by some
mysterious agency and killed . . ."

*". . . another repeating the maneuver, then another,
and another."*

*   *   *

"Wherever a building seemed to resist the fire, the
roof would be sent whirling into the air, breaking
into clouds of flame as it fell."

"Alfred Phillip's house, in the upper Sugar Bush,
was destroyed, but the family escaped. They state
that two opposite currents of air apparently struck
the house . . . and carried it bodily into the air,
about 100 feet. It then burst into flames, and in a
few minutes was entirely destroyed. The house
was not on fire when it left the ground."

*"Round and round it goes—a short sweep into the
wind and a long one to leeward—no movement of*

*wings or tail beyond a constant small adjustment of
their planes—up, and up, and up."*

"Not long after Father Pernin arrived at the river,
the Peshtigo Company's woodenware factory
began burning, sending flames high into the air.
As the wind picked up, the roof blew off and a
great cargo of burning tubs and wooden buckets
exploded through the open top of the building,
soaring high in the air in flaming arcs . . ."

"The wooden ware factory was perhaps the largest
institution of its kind under one roof in the
United States. It run two hand shingle machines,
a large circular saw, a small circular (siding mill),
two cross-cut cut-off saws, two bench saws, a bot-
tom saw, three pail stave saws,

On the thirteenth day of September, nineteen

two tub stave saws,two kannakin stave saws,

hundred and eighty-three, on Wachusett Mountain

two tub lathes, one kitt lathe, one kannakin lathe,

in eastern Massachusetts, an official count of

one churn lathe, three pail lathes, three broom

hawks was taken.

handle lathes, four clothes-pin lathes, one planer, one hoop planer, one hoop saw, two button sizing saws, one bottom planer, two jointers, five bottom lathes, three hoop rollers, five hoop cutters, two broom handle saws, one cross-cut saw, one churn cover saw, two pail bail machines, and two paint mills. . . .

The capacity of the wooden ware factory was about as follows: 600 pails, 170 tubs, 200 kanna

In the space of one hour—from twelve noon to

kins 250 fish kitts, 200 keelers, 5,000 broom

one P.M.—a total of sixteen thousand two hundred

handles,50 boxes clothes pins, 45,000 shingles,

and sixteen broad-wing hawks were recorded.

8 dozen barrel covers, 260 tobacco pails, 200 paint pails per day. Over two hundred hands were employed, and the work turned out was famous for its excellence."

". . . vomiting a dragon's breath of exploding tubs, buckets and clothespins, which flew through the air like bullets."

FOUR

"But the fire finally struck the building [the Congregational Church] and gradually crawled up towards the spire. When it was well on fire, a blast of wind blew off the spire, and it fell point downward to the ground. The point entered the ground, and the spire burned there, standing inverted by the side of the church."

FIVE

". . . at the boarding house, a strange hallucination seemed to prevail that it would be saved, and a large number of people took refuge there."

"When the flames struck the building the whole front was on fire in an instant."

"A heap of undistinguishable calcined bones and charred flesh in the ruins of the building, giving no clue to sex or number, was all that remained."

*   *   *

"Peshtigo is burnt clean as a prairie."

SIX

"Schwartz the hermit, a one-eyed German, lived alone on a farm just outside Peshtigo. He and his animals survived by plunging into Trout Brook."

"The Hill family, consisting of ten persons, lived near by. They had working for them a half grown Indian boy, who was ordered down to hitch up the team. The barn getting on fire, the master ordered him to return. Not coming as fast as Hill desired, the order was repeated in a more peremptory manner, when the Indian looked up and said, 'It's everybody for himself now,' and off he started with the speed of the deer. Rushing through the fire, he reached a clearing half a mile and was saved, while the entire Hill family perished."

"In the Upper Bush country there is only one house left, the home of 'old man' Place. Many years ago this man settled here, soon afterwards married a squaw, by whom he has had many children. He has always engaged in trading with the Indians, who have had his house as their headquarters. When the fire came about twenty Indians covered the house with their blankets, which they kept wet down, and thus saved the house. One great big fellow stood at the pump for nine hours, showing an endurance possessed by very few white men. Strange as it may now seem, while there are about as many Indians as whites in this section, at least one thousand of the latter perished, and not a single Indian. This may seem strange, but it is vouched for by the very best persons here. Whether the Indians could smell the fire sooner than their more refined white brethren and escaped in time, I know not, but I do know that they were all saved. And the only ones I heard of being injured were the half-breed children."

*   *   *

"Six days after the fire a searching party was startled when a body crashed to the ground from high in a tree. It was that of a young logging camp foreman who had either forgotten his woods lore or preferred death high on a pyre to death on the ground."

*   *   *

"Sparrow Hawks are often seen circling and diving about the edge of grass or brush fires, flying in and out of the smoke to catch insects disturbed by the flames."

Bibliography

PESHTIGO

Brown, Elton T. *A History of the Great Minnesota Forest Fires.* St. Paul, 1894.

Goodspeed, E.J. *History of the Great Fires in Chicago and the West.* New York, 1871.

Holand, H.R. *Old Peninsula Days.* Ephraim, Wisconsin, 1943.

Holbrook, Stewart. *Burning an Empire.* New York, 1945.

Luzerne, Frank. *The Lost City!* New York and Chicago, 1872.

Martin, Charles I. *History of Door County.* Sturgeon Bay, Wisconsin, 1881.

McClement, Fred. *The Flaming Forests.* Toronto and Montreal, 1969.

Pernin, Peter. *The Great Peshtigo Fire.* State Historical Society of Wisconsin, Madison, 1971.

Stephenson, Isaac. *Recollections of a Long Life.* Chicago, 1915.

Tilton, Frank. *Sketch of the Great Fires in Wisconsin.* Green Bay, 1871.

Tuttle, Charles R. *An Illustrated History of the State of Wisconsin.* Boston and Madison, 1875.

Wells, Robert W. *Fires at Peshtigo.* Englewood Cliffs, 1968.

Newspaper accounts:

Marinette Eagle-Star, October 8, 1923.

Marinette Eagle-Star, October 8, 1934.

Marinette-Peshtigo Eagle Extra, October 9, 1871.

Marinette-Peshtigo Eagle, October 14, 1871.

Marinette Star, October 14, 1921.

Milwaukee Journal, October 9, 1921.

Milwaukee Journal, October 9, 1928.

Peshtigo Times, October 6, 1921.

Shawano Journal, September 17, 1931.

Sturgeon Bay Advocate, October 14, 1921.

HAWKS

Austing, G. Ronald. *The World of the Red-Tailed Hawk.* Philadelphia and New York, 1964.

Bent, Arthur C. *Life Histories of North American Birds of Prey.* U.S. National Museum, 1937.

Broun, Maurice. *Hawks Aloft.* New York, 1949.

Brown, Leslie. *Eagles, Hawks and Falcons of the World.* New York, 1968.

Eastwood, Eric. *Radar Ornithology.* London, 1967.

Hagar, J.A. "Hawks at Mt. Tom." *Bulletin of the Massachusetts Audubon Society* (April 1937).

Harwood, Michael. *The View from Hawk Mountain.* New York, 1973.

Heintzelman, Donald S. *A Guide to Eastern Hawkwatching.* University Park, 1976.

__________. *A guide to hawk watching in North America.* University Park, 1979.

__________. *Autumn Hawk Flights.* New Brunswick, 1975.

May, John B. *The Hawks of North America.* New York, 1935.

Pough, Richard H. "A Glider Highway." *Bird Lore* (Sept.-Oct. 1935).

Sprunt, Alexander. *North American Birds of Prey.* New York, 1955.

THREE PLAYS

AN AMERICAN CHRONICLE

A TWO-ACT DOCUMENTARY DRAMA

Act One

Act Two

ACT ONE

SCENE ONE: CHRISTOPHER COLUMBUS

(Lights come up, revealing the basic set. There is a platform upstage, perhaps 12″-16″ high. Flats left and right, to mask the entrances and exits. The four actors are to be simply and similarly dressed, for all scenes—say slacks and sport shirts or sweatshirts. Makeup is to be minimal. There are to be no props, except those specifically mentioned in the text.)

(Enter right a SPEAKER, *who addresses audience.)*

SPEAKER: At the age of fourteen, Christopher Columbus went to sea.

(Enter right COLUMBUS. *He moves down-center, faces audience, and bows deeply. Exit* SPEAKER.*)*

COLUMBUS: Most exalted Sovereigns: At a very early age I entered upon the sea navigating, and I have continued doing so until today. The calling in itself inclines whoever follows it to desire to know the secrets of this world. Forty years are already passing which I have employed in this manner: I have traversed every region which up to the present time is navigated.

During this time I have seen, and in seeing, have studied all writings, cosmography, histories, chronicles, and philosophy and those relating to other arts, by means of which our Lord made me understand with a palpable hand, that it was practicable to navigate from here to the Indies and inspired me with a will for the execution of this navigation. And with this fire, I came to your highnesses.

It might be that your Highnesses and all the others who knew me, either in secret or in public would reprove me in divers manners, saying that I am not learned in letters and calling me a crazy sailor, a worldly man, etc.

I say that the Holy Spirit works in Christians, Jews, Moors, and in all others of all sects, and not only in the wise but the ignorant: for in my time I have seen a villager who gave a better account of the heavens and the stars and their courses than others who expended money in learning of them.

I always read that the world, land and water, was spherical. Now I observed so much divergence, that I began to hold different views about the world and I found that it was not round but pear-shaped, round except where it has a nipple, for it is taller, or as if one had a round ball and, on one side, it should be like a woman's breast, and this nipple part is the highest and closest to heaven.

(Blackout.)

SCENE TWO: CHEROKEE MYTHS

The lights come up and four Indians are discovered, seated down left, in a close semicircle, warming their hands over a campfire.

FIRST INDIAN: In the beginning there were Kanati, The Lucky Hunter, and Selu, The Corn. Kanati brought in game and Selu washed it in the streams. They had a son and the son played with a strange boy who came from the blood of the game that Selu washed in the stream. Kanati, Selu, The Son, and The Wild Boy.

(As the FIRST INDIAN *continues, the others get up and mime the action, stage center.)*

FIRST INDIAN: Selu went into a little cabin and shut the door. The boys pushed out a chink of clay between the logs and watched her. She stood before an empty basket. She rubbed her belly and the basket was half full of corn. She rubbed her armpits and the basket was full with beans.

SECOND INDIAN *(as The Son)*: We must kill her, for she is a witch.

THIRD INDIAN *(as Selu)*: So you know, and you must kill me. Well, when I am dead you will drag my body over the ground and sit up and watch all night. Wherever you drag my body, corn will spring up, and will be ripe before morning.

FIRST INDIAN: The Son and The Wild Boy killed her with clubs. They cut off her head and put it on a stick on the housetop so that Kanati would know when he returned from hunting. They dragged her body over the ground as she had told them and they watched through the night. The green shoots sprang up, and in the morning there was corn.

(The miming actors return to the campfire and regroup themselves in a semicircle.)

SECOND INDIAN: There is the Snake Boy. He left the cabin one morning without breakfast, went into the woods, and was gone all day.

(The THIRD *and* FOURTH INDIANS *get up and begin to mime the action, stage center.)*

SECOND INDIAN: He returned in the evening with a pair of deer horns, and went to a hut where his grandmother was waiting for him. He told her he must be alone all night, and she left, but at day-break she went in the hut, and no boy was there, but an immense green serpent with horns in its head, still with human legs instead of a serpent's tail. It spoke to her, told her to leave, and she went away, and when the sun was well up, it began to crawl out, but it was not free of the hut until full noon. It made a terrible hissing noise, striking through the air like a vibrant wind, reverberant and omnipresent, and the people fled as it crawled among the cabins, leaving a broad trail behind it, until it came to the river, to a deep bend in the river, where it plunged in and went under the water and was never seen again.

(The miming actors return to the campfire and regroup themselves in a semicircle. The FIRST INDIAN *rises, moves stage center, and mimes the following actions:)*

THIRD INDIAN: Utlunta the Spear-finger may still wander in the mountains. A woman monster with powers over stone, she could lift great rocks and join them without mortar. Her skin was of rock that no weapon could wound or penetrate. The stony forefinger of her right hand was of bone, like an awl or spearhead, and she sang a pretty song about human liver, for this was her food; she would stab a hunter with the spear-finger.

(The FIRST INDIAN *returns to the semicircle. During the following, all the* INDIANS *mime the story, or respond to it, from their seated positions.)*

FOURTH INDIAN: The hunters were camping in the mountains one night when they saw two lights moving along a distant ridge. They watched and wondered. They saw them the next night, and the next. On the third morning, they crossed to the ridge. They found two creatures, round and large, with fine gray fur, and little heads like those of terrapins. When the breeze played upon the fur, showers of sparks flew out. The hunters kept them several days. At night they would grow bright and shine, by day they were balls of gray fur, except when the wind stirred and the sparks flew out. They were quiet and no one thought of their trying to escape, but on the seventh night they rose from the ground like balls of fire, above the treetops, climbing higher and higher and higher, until they were only bright points. The hunters then knew they were stars.

(Blackout.)

SCENE THREE: TRAVELING WITH INDIANS

(In this scene, two actors are pioneers, two are Indians. The two pioneers alternate speaking the lines, while the Indians, and the pioneer who is not speaking at the moment, mime the action. Discovered, PIONEER ONE *down-left, and two Indians and* PIONEER TWO

stage-center, the two Indians miming the action of paddling a canoe, while the second pioneer is seated between them. Subsequent action is to be worked out in rehearsal.)

PIONEER ONE: In order to practice patience in good earnest and to endure hardships beyond the limit of human strength it is only necessary to make journeys with the savages, and long ones especially, such as we did; because, besides the danger of death on the way, one must make up one's mind to endure and suffer more than could be imagined, from hunger, from the stench that those dirty disagreeable fellows emit almost constantly in their canoes, from walking with great labour in water and bogs and rain on one's back and all the evils that the season and weather can inflict, and from being bitten by a countless swarm of mosquitos and midges . . .

Add to these difficulties that one must sleep on the bare earth, or on a hard rock, for lack of a space ten or twelve feet square on which to place a wretched hut; that one must endure continually the stench of tired-out savages; and must walk in water, in mud, in the obscurity and entanglement of the forest . . .

Be with whom you like, you must expect to be, at least, three or four weeks on the way, to have as companions persons you have never seen before; to be cramped in a bark canoe in an uncomfortable position, not being free to turn yourself to one side or the other; in danger fifty times a day of being upset or of being dashed upon the rocks. During the day, the sun burns you, during the night, you run the risk of being a prey to mosquitos. You sometimes ascend five or six rapids in a day; and, in the evening, the only refreshment is a little corn crushed between two stones and cooked in fine clear water; the only bed is the earth, sometimes only the rough, uneven rocks, and usually no roof but the stars; and all this in perpetual silence.

PIONEER TWO:
    It is a strange thing when victualls are wanting,
    worke whole nights & dayes,
    lye downe on the bare ground,
       & not allwayes that hap,

the breech in the water,
    the feare in ye buttocks . . .

PIONEER ONE: . . . harden thy soul, resist hunger; thou wilt be sometimes two, sometimes three or four days without food, do not let thyself be cast down, take courage . . .

PIONEER TWO: There is no safety in crossing the rivers of this country by fording unless one knows them well, because there are a great many quicksands, in which one sinks so far that it is impossible to get out.

PIONEER ONE: It was snowing hard; but, with necessity urging us on, the bad weather could not stop us.

PIONEER TWO: We ftayed 14 dayes in this place moft miserable, like to a churchyard; ffor there did fall fuch a quantity of fnow and froft, and wth fuch a thick mift, that all the fnow ftoocke to thefe trees that are there fo ruffe, being deal trees, pruffe cedars, and thorns, that caufed yt darkneffe uppon ye earth that it is to be believed that the fun was eclipfd . . .

PIONEER ONE: In some places where the current is not less strong than in these rapids, although easier at first, the Savages get into the water, and haul and guide by hand their canoes with extreme difficulty and danger; for they sometimes get in up to the neck and are compelled to let go their hold, saving themselves as best they can from the rapidity of the water, which snatched from them and bears off their canoe.

PIONEER TWO:
    We left the Iroquoits in his fort
    and the feare in our breeches,
    for wthout apprenhenfion
        we rowed from friday to tuefday
    wthout intermiffion.

    We had fearce to eat
    a bitt of fault meat.

It was pitty to fee our feete & leggs in blood
by drawing our boats through the frift ftreames,
where the rocks have fuch fharp points
that there is nothing but death
could make men doe what we did.

PIONEER ONE: If you go to visit them in their cabins . . . you will find there a miniature picture of Hell—seeing nothing, ordinarily, but fire and smoke, and on every side naked bodies, black and half-roasted, mingled pell mell with the dogs, which are held as dear as the children of the house, and share the beds, plates, and food of their master. Everything is in a cloud of dust, and if you go within you will not reach the end of the cabin, before you are completely befouled with soot, filth, and dirt.

Instead of being a great master and great Theologian as in France, you must reckon on being here a humble Scholar, and then, good God! with what masters!—women, little children, and all the Savages—and exposed to their laughter. The Huron language will be your Saint Thomas and your Aristotle; and clever man as you are, and speaking glibly among learned and capable persons, you must make up your mind to be for a long time mute among the Barbarians. You will have accomplished much, if, at the end of a considerable time, you begin to stammer a little.

PIONEER TWO: . . . to tell the truth, the life of missionaries in this country is the most dissipating life that can be imagined. Scarcely anything is thought of but bodily necessities, and the constant example of the savages, who think only of satisfying their flesh, brings the mind into an almost inevitable enervation . . .

PIONEER ONE:
As to the matter of food,
it is such as to cause all the books to be burned
that cooks have ever made

The ordinary diet is Indian corn . . .
the seasoning with meat or fish,
when you have any.

PIONEER TWO: Now when they were in the open country and the hour for encamping arrived, they would seek some fitting spot on the bank of a river for a camp, or in another place where dry wood could easily be found to make a fire; then one of them set himself to look for it and collect it, another to put up the lodge and find a stick on which to hang the kettle at the fire, another look for two flat stones for crushing the Indian corn over a skin spread out on the ground, and afterwards to put it into the kettle and boil it . . . there was always dirt and refuse, partly because they used fresh stones every day, and very dirty ones, to crush the corn. Besides, the bowls could hardly have a pleasant smell, for when they were under the necessity of making water in their canoes they usually use the bowl for the purpose . . .

PIONEER ONE:

    . . . a Beaver in the morning,
    and in the evening of the next day
    a porcupine as big
    as a sucking Pig.

    . . . we were forc'd to feafon our *Indian* Corn . . . with
    little Frogs that the Natives gather'd in the Meadows

PIONEER ONE: . . . we lived on wild garlick, which we were obliged to grub up from under the snow.

PIONEER TWO: . . . the entrails of deer, full of blood and half-putrefied excrement, boiled fungus, decayed oysters, frogs eaten whole, head and feet, unskinned, uncleaned . . .

PIONEER ONE: Then they offered us some of their sagamite to eat, as they often have some remains of it in the pot; but for my part I very rarely took it, both because it usually smelt too strong of stinking fish and because the dogs frequently put their nose into it and children their leavings.

PIONEER TWO: . . . the women savages eating the lice from their own bodies . . .

PIONEER ONE: . . . mingling some yallowiſh meale in the breath of that infected ſtinking meate . . .

PIONEER TWO: . . . they feeded me wth their hodpot, forcing me to ſwallow it in a manner . . .

PIONEER ONE: . . . unſavoury and clammie by reaſon of the ſcume that was upon the meat . . .

PIONEER TWO: . . . their filthy meate that I could not digeſt, but muſt ſuffer all patiently.

PIONEER ONE: . . . the stink worse even than sewers.

PIONEER TWO: . . . I ate old Moose skins, tougher than those of the Eel; I went through the woods biting the ends of the branches, and gnawing the more tender bark.

PIONEER ONE: As we went backe uppon our ſtepps for to gett any thing to fill our bellyes, we were glad to gett the boans and carcaſſes of the beasts that we killed.

PIONEER TWO: . . . in the next place, the ſkins that were reſerved to make us ſhooſe, cloath, and ſtokins, yea, moſt of the ſkins of our cottages, the caſtors ſkins, where the children beſhit them above a hundred times. We burned the hair on the coals; the reſt goes downe throats . . .

PIONEER ONE: Every one cryes out for hunger; the women become baren, and drie like wood. You men muſt eate the cord, being you have no more ſtrength to make uſe of the bow. Children, you muſt die. French, you called yourſelves Gods of the earth, that you ſhould be feared, for your intereſt; notwithſtanding you shall taſt of the bitterneſſe, and too happy if you eſcape. Where is the time paſt? Where is the plentyneſſe that yee had in all places and countreys?

PIONEER TWO:

> We were out of provisions,
> and found only some dried meat
> . . . which we took to appease our hunger;
>
> but soon after perceiving it to be human flesh,
> we left the rest to our Indians.

PIONEER ONE: (It was very good and delicate.)

(Blackout.)

SCENE FOUR: INDIAN TORTURE

(In this scene, one actor is the victim, two are torturers. The fourth is the SPEAKER. *The* SPEAKER, *off-right, reads the lines as the others mime the action, with shouts and groans.)*

SPEAKER: For they cut off both his thumbs, and through the stump of the left one they drove a pointed stake up to his very elbow.

The first thing they did to him afterward was that one of them cut with a knife across his scalp, which he stripped off in order to carry away the hair, and, according to their custom, to preserve it as very precious.

After such treatment one would hardly believe that there could remain any sensation of life in a body so worn out with tortures. But lo! he suddenly rises, and takes in his hand, which were all in shreds, a firebrand, that he might not die as a captive, and that he might defend the brief liberty he had recovered a little while before death. The rage and the cries of his enemies redouble at this sight; they rush towards him with pieces of red-hot iron in their hands. His courage gives him strength; he puts himself on the defensive; he hurls his firebrands upon those who come nearest him; he throws down the ladders, to cut off their way, and avails himself of the fire;

and flame, the severity of which he has just experienced, to repel their attack vigorously. The blood that streamed down from his head over his entire body would have rent with pity a heart which had any remnant of humanity; but the fury of our barbarians found therein its satisfaction. Some throw upon him coals and burning cinders; others underneath the scaffold find open places for their firebrands. He sees on all sides almost as many butchers as spectators; when he escapes one fire, he encounters another, and takes not one step without falling into the evil that he flees.

While defending himself thus for a long time, a false step causes him to fall backward to the ground. At the same time, his enemies pounce upon him, burn him anew, then throw him upon the fire. This invincible spirit, rising again from the midst of the flames—all covered with cinders that were imbued in his blood, two flaming firebrands in his hands—turns towards the mass of his enemies, to inspire them with fear once more before he dies. Not one is so hardy as to touch him; he makes a way for himself, and walks towards the Village, as if to set it on fire. He advances about a hundred paces, when some one throws a club which fells him to the ground; before he can rise again, they are upon him; they cut off his feet and hands, and, having seized the rest of this mangled body, they turn it round and round over nine different fires, which he almost entirely extinguished with his blood. Finally they thrust him under an overturned tree-trunk, all on fire, so that, at the same time, there may be no part of his body, which is not cruelly burned . . . and, having fallen outside of them, he moved more than ten paces, upon his elbows and knees, in the direction of his enemies, who fled from him, dreading the approach of a man to whom nothing remained but courage.

(Blackout.)

SCENE FIVE: A FORTUNATE VOYAGEUR

*(In this scene, the first actor is a pioneer, the other three are Indians. The
pioneer speaks the lines, and all mime the action, with much laughter,
singing, etc.)*

PIONEER: . . . the young men tooke delight in combing my head,
greaſing and powdering out a kinde of redd powder, then tying my
haire wth a redd ſtring of leather like to a coard, wch cauſed my
haire to grow longer in a ſhort time.

They tooke a fancy to teach mee to ſing; and as I had already a
beginning of their hooping, it was an eaſy thing for me to learne . . .

In this place they cutt off my hair in the front and upon the
crowne of the head, and turning up the locks of ye haire they dab'd
mee wth ſome thicke greaſe. So done, they brought me a looking-
glaſſe. I viewing myſelfe all in a pickle, ſmir'd with redde and black,
covered with ſuch a cappe, and locks tyed up wth a peece of leather
and ſtunked horribly, I could not but fall in love wth myſelfe . . .

The women were tender and delicate . . . the weather lovely . . .
the wind fayre . . . and nature satisfied. Friends, I must confess, I
loved those poor people entirely well.

(Blackout.)

SCENE SIX: ROGER WILLIAMS

*(In this scene, the four actors are stationed across the stage, and they
alternate speaking the lines.)*

#1:

    "But for their later Descent,
    and whence they came into thoſe pars,
    if ſemes as harde to finde,
    as to finde the *Well-head* of some freſh *Streame,*

which running many miles out of the *Countrey*
to the ſalt *Ocean,*
hath met with many mixing *Streames*
by the way.
They ſey themſelves,
that they have *ſprung* and *growne* up
in that very place,
like the very *trees* of the *Wilderneſſe.*"

#2:

(. . . they are so exquiſitely skilled
in all the body and bowels of the
Countrey . . .)

#3: ". . . I humbly pray your consideration, whether it be not only
possible, but very easy, to live and die in peace with all the natives of
this country."

#4: ". . . that the whole land, English and natives, might sleep in
peace securely."

#1: ". . . for the establiſhing of peace through all the bowels of the
country . . ."

#2:

"Yet I have found leſſe noyſe, more peace
In wilde *America* . . ."

#3: I desire not to sleepe in security & dreame of a nest which no
hand can reach. I cannot but expect changes . . .

#4: There is so much sound and noise of purchase and purchasers.

1: Having brought Truth deare, we must not sell it cheape . . .

#2: If riches, if children, if friends, if cattle, if whatsoever increase,
let us watch that the heart fly not loose upon them.

#3: P.S. My love to all my Indian friends.

(Blackout.)

SCENE SEVEN: JOHN MARR (HERMAN MELVILLE)

(In this scene, a SPEAKER, *off-right, reads the text, while two actors, side-by-side, slowly inch their way across the stage, from up-right to down-left.)*

SPEAKER: Save the prairie-hen, sometimes startled from its lurking place in the rank grass, and, in their migratory season, pigeons, high overhead on the wing, in dense multitudes eclipsing the day like a passing storm-cloud; save these—there being no wide woods with their underwood—birds were strangely few.

"Blank stillness would for hours reign unbroken on this prairie. 'It is the bed of a dried-up sea,' said the companionless sailor—no geologist—to himself, musing at twilight upon the fixed undulations of that immense alluvial expanse bounded only by the horizon, and missing there the stir that, to alert eyes and ears, animates at all times the apparent solitudes of the deep.

"But a scene quite at variance with one's antecedents may yet prove suggestive of them. Hooped round by a level rim, the prairie was to John Marr a reminder of ocean.

"With some of his former shipmates, chums on certain cruises, he had contrived, prior to this last and more remote removal, to keep up a little correspondence at odd intervals. But from tidings of anybody of any sort he, in common with the other settlers, was now cut off; quite cut off, except from such news as might be conveyed over the grassy billows by the last-arrived prairie-schooner—the vernacular term, in those parts and times, for the emigrant-wagon arched high over with sailcloth, and voyaging across the vast champaign. There was no reachable post-office as yet; not even the rude little receptive box with lid and leather hinges, set up at convenient intervals on a stout stake along some solitary green way, affording a perch for birds, and which, later in the unremitting advance of the frontier, would perhaps decay into a mossy monument, attesting yet another successive overleaped limit of civilized life; a life which in America can to-day hardly be said to have any western bound but the ocean that washes Asia. Throughout these plains, now in places overpopulous with towns overopulent; sweeping plains, elsewhere fenced off in every direction into flourishing farms—pale townsmen and hale farmers alike, in part, the descendants of the first sallow settlers; a region that half a century ago produced little for the sustenance of men; but to-day launching its superabundant wheat-harvest on the world;—of this prairie, now everywhere intersected with wire and rail, hardly can it be said that at the period here written of there was so much as a traceable road. To the long-distance traveller the oak-groves, wide apart, and varying in compass and form; these, with recent settlements, yet more widely separate, offered some landmarks; but otherwise he steered by the sun. In early midsummer, even going but from one log encampment to the next, a journey it might be of hours or good part of a day, travel was much like navigation. In some more enriched depressions between the long, green, graduated swells, smooth as those of ocean becalmed receiving and subduing to its own tranquility the voluminous surge raised by some far-off hurricane of days previous, here one would catch the first indication of advancing strangers either in the distance, as a far sail at sea, by the glistening white canvas of the wagon, the wagon itself wading through the rank vegetation and hidden by it, or, failing that, when near to, in the ears of the team, peeking, if not above the tall tiger-lilies, yet above the yet taller grass.

"Luxuriant, this wilderness; but, to its denizen, a friend left behind anywhere in the world seemed not alone absent to sight, but an absentee from existence.

"Though John Marr's shipmates could not all have departed life, yet as subjects of meditation they were like phantoms of the dead. As the growing sense of his environment threw him more and more upon retrospective musings, these phantoms, next to those of his wife and child, became spiritual companions, losing something of their first indistinctness and putting on at last a dim semblance of mute life; and they were lit by that aureole circling over any object of the affections in the past for reunion with which an imaginative heart passionately yearns."

(Blackout.)

ACT TWO
SCENE ONE: DER BLACK GUINEA

(Enter the SPEAKER *and three actors. The speaker recites the text, while the actors cross and recross the stage, impersonating the various types described. With the introduction of the Black Guinea, one of the actors assumes this role. A second actor assumes the role of the Drover, and they speak the dialogue.)*

SPEAKER: "Natives of all sorts, and foreigners; men of business and men of pleasure; parlour men and backwoodsmen; farmhunters, bee-hunters, happiness-hunters, truth-hunters, and still keener hunters after all these hunters. Fine ladies in slippers, and moccasined squaws; Northern speculators and Eastern philosophers; English, Irish, German, Scotch, Danes; Sante Fe traders in striped blankets, and Broadway bucks in cravats of cloth of gold; fine-looking Kentucky boatmen, and Japanese-looking Mississippi cotton planters; Quakers in full drab, and United States soldiers in full regimentals; slaves, black, mulatto, quadroon, modish young Spanish Creoles, and old-fashioned French Jews; Mormons and Papists; Dives and Lazarus; jesters and mourners, teetotallers and convivialists, deacons and blacklegs; hard-shelled Baptists and clay-eaters; grinning negroes, and Sioux chiefs solemn as high-priests. In short, a piebald parliament, an Anacharsis Cloots congress of all kinds of that multiform pilgrim species, man.

"As pine, beech, birch, ash, hackmatack, hemlock, spruce, basswood, maple, interweave their foliage in the natural wood, so these varieties of mortals blended their varieties of visage and garb. A Tartar-like picturesqueness, a sort of pagan abandonment and assurance. Here reigned the dashing and all-fusing spirit of the West, whose type is the Mississippi itself, which, uniting the streams of the most distant and opposite zones, pours them along, helter-skelter, in one cosmopolitan and confident tide.

"In the forward part of the boat, not the least attractive object, for a time, was a grotesque negro cripple, in towcloth attire and an old coal-sifter of a tambourine in his hand, who, owing to something wrong about his legs, was, in effect, cut down to the stature of a New Foundland dog; his knotted black fleece and good-natured, honest black face rubbing against the upper part of people's thighs as he made shift to shuffle about, making music, such as it was, and raising a smile even from the gravest. It was curious to see him, out of his very deformity, indigence, and houselessness, so cheerily endured, raising mirth in some of that crowd, whose own purses, hearths, hearts, all their possessions, sound limbs included, could not make gay.

DROVER: What is your name, old boy?

GUINEA: Der Black Guinea dey calls me, sar.

DROVER: And who is your master, Guinea?

GUINEA: Oh, sar, I am der dog widout massa.

DROVER: A free dog, eh? Well, on your account, I'm sorry for that, Guinea. Dogs without masters fare hard.

GUINEA: So dey do, sar; so dey do. But you see, sar, dese here legs? What ge'mmen want to own dese here legs?

DROVER: But where do you live?

GUINEA: All 'long shore, sar; dough now I'se going to see brodder at der landing; but chiefly I libs in der city.

DROVER: St. Louis, ah? Where do you sleep there of nights?

GUINEA: On der floor of der good baker's oven, sar.

DROVER: In an oven? Whose, pray? What baker, I should like to know, bakes such black bread in his oven, alongside of his nice white rolls, too. Who is that too charitable baker, pray?

GUINEA: Dar he be.

DROVER: The sun is the baker, eh?

GUINEA: Yes, sar, in der city dat good baker warms der stones for dis ole darkie when he sleeps out on der pabements o' nights

DROVER: But that must be in the summer only, old boy. How about winter, when the cold Cossacks come clattering and jingling? How about winter, old boy?

GUINEA: Den dis poor old darkie shakes werry bad, I tell you, sar. Oh, sar, oh! don't speak ob der winter.

(Blackout.)

SCENE TWO: JOHN BROWN

(Lights come up on a bare stage. Enter SPEAKER, *down-right.)*

SPEAKER: May 8, 1858, Chatham, Ontario, the Provisional Constitutional Convention was held: there was a reading of the Provisional Constitution and Ordinance for the People of the United States: "Whereas, slavery throughout its entire existence in the United States is none other than a most barbarous, unprovoked, and unjustifiable war of one portion of its citizens upon another portion . . ."

(Enter JOHN BROWN. *He moves stage-center.)*

SPEAKER: Commander-in-chief: John Brown.

BROWN: I wish to say, furthermore, that you had better—all you people at the South—prepare yourselves for a settlement of that question that must come up for settlement sooner than you are prepared for it . . . this question is still to be settled—this negro question I mean; the end of that is not yet.

(*Enter two other actors, associates of* BROWN.)

SPEAKER: July, 1859, Brown, with 22 associates, rented the Kennedy farm, on the Maryland side, not far from Harper's Ferry.

BROWN: And now gentlemen, let me impress this one thing upon your minds. You all know how dear life is to you, and how dear your life is to your friends. And in remembering that, consider that the lives of others are as dear to them as yours are to you. Do not, therefore, take the life of anyone, if you can possibly avoid it; but if it is necessary to take life in order to save your own, then make sure work of it.

SPEAKER: October 16, 1859, after dark:

BROWN: Men, get your arms; proceed to the Ferry.

(*Exit* BROWN *and associates, in marching order.*)

SPEAKER: Brown believed that upon the first intimation of a plan formed for the liberation of the slaves, they would immediately rise all over the Southern states.

(*Enter* BROWN, *and two associates.*)

BROWN: These mountains are the basis of my plan. God has given the strength of the hills to freedom; they are placed here for the emancipation of the negro race; they are full of natural forts, where one man for defence will be equal to a hundred for attack; they are also full of good hiding places, where large numbers of brave men could be concealed, and baffle and elude pursuit for a long time. I know these mountains well, and could take a body of men into them and keep them there, despite of all the efforts of Virginia to dislodge them.

1ST ASSOCIATE: There was, indeed, always a sort of thrill in John Brown's voice when he spoke of mountains. I shall never forget the quiet way in which he once told me that "God had established the Allegheny Mountains from the foundation of the world that they might one day be a refuge for fugitive slaves."

2ND ASSOCIATE: Captain Brown was a grim, farmer-like-looking man, with a long gray beard and glittering, gray-blue eyes which seemed to me to have a little touch of insanity about them.

BROWN: I may be very insane, and I am so, if insane at all. But if that be so, insanity is like a very pleasant dream to me.

1ST ASSOCIATE: And they are themselves mistaken who take him to be a madman. He is a bundle of the best nerves I ever saw. He is cool, collected, and indomitable, and it is but just to him to say that he was humane to his prisoners. He is a fanatic, vain and garrulous, but firm, truthful, and intelligent.

(Exit TWO ASSOCIATES. BROWN *sits on the floor, stage-center. He seems to be writing a letter, and turns to* SPEAKER.*)*

BROWN: Have you any objection to my writing to my wife to tell her that I am to be hanged on the second of December at noon?

(Returns to writing, and reads from letter.)

Dear Wife and Children, every one: I can trust God with both the time and the manner of my death, believing, as I now do, that for me at this time to seal my testimony for God and humanity with my blood will do vastly more toward advancing the cause I have earnestly endeavored to promote, than all I have done in my life before. I feel no consciousness of guilt in the matter. Already dear friends at a distance, with kindest sympathy, are cheering me with the assurance that posterity, at least, will do me justice.

(Enter two other actors as soldiers. During the following, they escort BROWN *to the platform, up-center, where* BROWN *sits, under their guard.)*

SPEAKER: As he came out, the six companies of infantry and one troop of horse, with General Teliaferro and his entire staff, were deploying in front of the jail, whilst an open wagon with a pine box, in which was a fine oak coffin, was waiting for him.

BROWN: I had no idea that Governor Wise considered my execution so important.

SPEAKER: Brown looked around and spoke to several persons he recognized, and, walking down the steps, took a seat on the coffin box along with the jailer, Avis. He looked with interest on the fine military display. The wagon moved off, flanked by two files of riflemen in close order.

BROWN: This is a beautiful country. I never had the pleasure of seeing it before.

SPEAKER: On reaching the field where the gallows was erected, the prisoner said:

BROWN: Why are none but military allowed in the enclosure? I am sorry citizens have been kept out.

SPEAKER: On reaching the gallows, he observed Mr. Hunter and Mayor Green standing near, to whom he said:

BROWN: Gentlemen, good-bye.

(The soldiers step aside, and BROWN *pantomimes being hanged, us described by the* SPEAKER.*)*

SPEAKER: He was swung off at fifteen minutes past eleven. A slight grasping of the hands and twitching of the muscles were seen.

(At the same instant, one of the soldiers appears to faint, and is aided by the other.)

SPEAKER: As the trap was sprung, a private of the Richmond Grays turned pale, his knees weak. Those near him asked if he felt ill, and he asked for a stiff drink of whiskey. It was John Wilkes Booth, who had come along for the show.

(Blackout.)

SCENE THREE: FIRST MANASSAS (WALT WHITMAN)

(The stage remains dark.)

SPEAKER *(offstage)*: First Manassas.

(Lights come up. Enter WALT WHITMAN *and three straggling, defeated soldiers. They mime the action, and* WHITMAN *moves among them as he speaks the lines.)*

WHITMAN: "The defeated troops commenced pouring into Washington over the Long Bridge at daylight on Monday, 22nd—day drizzling all through with rain. The Saturday and Sunday of the battle (20th, 21st) had been parched and hot to an extreme—the dust, the grime and smoke, in layers, sweated in, follow'd by other layers again sweated in, absorb'd by those excited souls—their clothes all saturated with the clay-powder filling the air—stirr'd up everywhere on the dry roads and trodden fields by the regiments, swarming wagons, artillery, etc.—all the men with this coating of murk and sweat and rain, now recoiling back, pouring over the Long Bridge—a horrible march of twenty miles, returning to Washington baffled, humiliated, panic-struck . . .

. . . Sidewalks of Pennsylvania Avenue, Fourteenth Street, etc., crowded, jamm'd with citizens, darkies, clerks, everybody, lookers-on;

women in the windows, curious expressions from faces . . . During the forenoon, Washington gets all over motley with these defeated soldiers—queer-looking objects, strange eyes and faces, drench'd (the steady rain drizzles on all day) and fearfully worn, hungry, haggard, blister'd in the feet . . . Amid the deep excitement, crowds and motion, and desperate eagerness, it seems strange to see many, very many, of the soldiers sleeping—in the midst of all, sleeping sound. They drop down anywhere, on the steps of houses, up close by the basements of fences, on the sidewalk, aside on some vacant lot, and deeply sleep. A poor seventeen- or eighteen-year-old boy lies there, on the stoop of a grand house; he sleeps so calmly, so profoundly. Some clutch their muskets . . ."

SCENE FOUR: ANTIETAM

(The stage remains dark.)

SPEAKER *(offstage)*: Antietam.

(Lights come up, and a soldier is discovered, standing dejectedly, as though in a trance. His jaw has been shot off.)

SPEAKER *(offstage)*: The poor fellow's whole lower jaw had been knocked off; carrying tongue and teeth with it, leaving the moustache, clotted with blood; arching over a frightful chasm of tangled muscles and arteries! The dripping from the aperture ran down over his bosom in a sheet of gelid, clotted gore.

SCENE FIVE: GETTYSBURG

(The stage remains dark.)

SPEAKER *(offstage):* Gettysburg.

(Lights come up, discovering three soldiers, lolling on the ground, resting. As they speak the lines, they mime the action, lazily.)

#1: Eleven o'clock came. The noise of battle has ceased upon the right; not a sound of a gun or musket can be heard on all the field; the sky is bright, with only the white fleecy clouds floating over from the west. The July sun streams down its fire upon the bright iron of the muskets in stacks upon the crest and the dazzling brass of the Napoleons. The Army lolls and longs for the shade . . . The silence and sultriness of a July noon are supreme.

#2: Shortly after eleven o'clock the firing ceased, and, for over an hour, there was hardly a picket shot heard. It was a queer sight to see men look at each other without speaking; the change was so great men seemed to go on tiptoe, not knowing how to act . . . I began looking around for something to eat . . .

#3: While we are resting here we amuse ourselves by pelting each other with green apples.

#1: As the sun climbed towards the meridian, many of the men drew out their "corn dodgers" and bits of bacon, to make their frugal dinner . . . Others spread their blankets on the gravelly hillside and stretched themselves for a nap. Everything looked quiet, dull and lazy—as one sees the harvest-hands lolling under the trees at noontime.

#2: We dozed in the heat, and lolled upon the ground, with half-open eyes. Our horses were hitched to the trees munching some oats. A great lull rests upon all the field. Time was heavy . . .

#3: At noon all Longstreet's dispositions were made. His troops for attack were deployed into line, and lying down in the woods: his batteries were ready to open. The general then dismounted and went to sleep . . .

#1: There was not wanting to the peacefulness of the scene the singing of a bird, which had a nest in the peach tree . . .

(Blackout.)

SCENE SIX: PICKETT'S CHARGE

(This entire scene is played in the dark. There is a sudden, explosive drum roll, from offstage. The actors shout the lines, from offstage, in alternation, over a continuing drumroll.)

#1: In an instant . . . the report of gun after gun in rapid succession smote our ears and their shells plunged down and exploded all around us. We sprang to our feet. In briefest time the whole Rebel line to the West was pouring out its thunder and its iron upon our devoted crest. The wildest confusion for a few moments obtained sway among us. The shells came bursting all about. The servants ran terror-stricken for dear life and disappeared. The horses, hitched to the trees or held by the slack hands of the orderlies, neighed out in fright and broke away and plunged riderless through the fields.

#2: . . . the ground roar of nearly the whole artillery of both armies burst in on the silence, almost as suddenly as the full notes of an organ would fill a church.

#3: The armies seemed like mighty wild beasts growling at each other. . . .

#4: The men did not cheer or shout—they growled.

#1: We thought that at the second Bull Run, at the Antietam, and at Fredericksburg . . . we had heard heavy cannonading; they were but holiday salutes compared with this. Besides the great ceaseless roar of the guns, which were but the background of the others, a million various minor sounds engaged the ear. The projectiles shriek long and sharp. They hiss, they scream, they growl, they sputter; all sounds of life and rage; and each has its different note . . .

#2: The enemy shot hurled among us and clipped off the clover heads by our side.

#3: The very earth shook as from a mighty quake. So intense were its vibrations that loose grass, leaves, and twigs arose from six to eight inches above the ground, hovered and quivered as birds about to drop . . .

#4: Large limbs were torn from the trunks of the oak trees under which we lay and precipitated down upon our heads.

#1: The sun . . . was now darkened . . . In any direction might be seen guns, swords, haversacks, heads, limbs, flesh and bones in confusion or dangling in the air or bounding on the earth . . .

#2: A small boy of twelve years was riding with us at the time. This urchin took a diabolical interest in the bursting of the shells, and screamed with delight when he saw them take effect.

#3: Riderless horses galloping madly through the fields . . . Mules with ammunition, pigs wallowing about, cows in the pasture . . .

#4: . . . a shell at our right exploded and a piece cut through the bowels of the off wheel horse, another striking the nigh swing horse . . . on the gambrel joint, breaking the off leg . . . We continued on, the wheel horse trampling on his bowels all the time . . .

#1: When the cannonade was at its height, a Confederate band of music, between the cemetery and ourselves, began to play polkas and waltzes, which sounded very curious . . .

#2: Alfred B. Gardner was struck in the left shoulder, almost tearing his arm from his body. He lived a few minutes and died shouting, "Glory to God! I am happy! Hallelujah!"

(Blackout.)

SCENE SEVEN: A CONFEDERATE PRISONER

(The lights come up, discovering a Confederate prisoner, sitting on the floor, writing in his diary, and reading from it.)

THE DIARY OF BARTLETT YANCEY MALONE: Bartlett Y. Malone was borned and raised in North Carolina Caswell County in the Year of our Lord 1838. And was Gradguated in the corn field and tobacco patch: and inlisted in the war June the 18th 1861. And was a member of the Caswell Boys Company . . .

> His purpose will ripen fast
> Unfolding evry hour
> The bud may have a bitter taste
> But sweet will be the flower
>
> May your days be days of pleasure
> May your nites be nites of rest
> May you obtain lifes sweetest pleasure
> And then be numbered with the blest.

> Whar ere you rome
> What ere your lot
> Its all I ask
> Forget me not.

Remember me when I am gon
Dear friend remember me
And when you bow befour the throne
O then remember me.

Candy is sweet
It is very clear
But not half so sweet
As you my dear

One day amidst the plas
Where Jesus is within
Is better than ten thousand days
Of pleasure and of Sin

O for grace our hearts to soften
Teach us Lord at length to love
We alas forget too often
What a friend we have above.
All I like of being a Whale
Is a water Spout and a tail.

A certain cewer for the Toothack if the tooth is hollow take a pease
of the scale that is on a horses leg and put it in the hollow of the
tooth. It is a serten cewer so sais J.H. Lyon.

B.Y.M....

THIS IS THE YEAR 1863: . . . we was then cutoff and had to Surender;
was then taken back to the rear and stied thir untell next morning.
The morning of the 8th we was marched back to Warrenton Junc-
tion and got on the cars and about day next morning we got to
Washington we then staid in Washington untel 3 o'clock in the
eavning of the 8th then was marched down to the Warf and put on
the Stemer *John Brooks* and got to Point Lookout about one o'clock
on the eavning of the 10th day of November 1863 . . .

Our rations at Point Lookout was five crackers and a cup of coffee for breakfast. And for dinner a small ration of meat two crackers three Potatoes and a cup of Soup. Supper we have non. We pay a dollar for eight crackers or a chew of tobacco for a cracker.

A Yankey shot one of our men the other day wounded him in the head shot him for peepen threw the cracks of the planken . . .

The 24th day of Dec. 63 was a clear day but very cool. And Generl Butler the Yankey beast reviewed the prisners camp:

The 25th was Christmas day and it was clear and cool and I was both coal and hungry all day only got a peace of Bread and a cup of coffee for Breakfast and a small Slice of Meat and a cup of Soup and five Crackers for Dinner and Supper I had non:

The 26th was clear and cool and dull for Christmas.

The 28th was cloudy and rained a littel. The 28th was a raney day.

The 29th was cloudy in the morning and clear in the eavning. And Jefferson Walker died in the morning he belonged to the 57th N.C. Regt. The 30th was a beautyful day

The 31st which was the last day of 63 was a raney day. And mayby I will never live to see the last day of 64. And theirfour I will try to do better than I have. For what is a man profited if he shall gain the whole world and loose his one Soul: Or what Shal one give in exchange for his Soul: B.Y. MALONE

B.Y. MALONE'S BOOK FOR THE YEAR 1864: I spent the first day of January 64 at Point Lookout M.D. The morning was pleasant but toward eavning the air changed and the nite was very coal. Was so coal that five of our men froze to death before morning. We all suffered a great deal with coal and hunger too of our men was so hungry to day that they caught a Rat and cooked him and eat it. Thir names were Sergt. N.W. Hester & I.C. Covington.

The 6th was coal and cloudy and we had nine men to die at the Hospital to day. Our beds at the place is composed of Sea feathers that is we geather the small stones from the Bay and lye on them. The 7th was very cool a small Snow fell after nite

The 10 was a nice day and I saw the man to day that makes Coffens at this plaice for the Rebels and he sais that twelve men dies here every day that is averidgs twelve

The Commander at this point is named Marsto

The 22th day of January 64 was a very pritty And it was my birth day which maid me 25 years of age I spent the day at Point Lookout. M.D. And I feasted on Crackers and Coffee. The two last weeks of January was beautyfull weather . . .

The 18th it was so coal that a mans breath would freeze on his beard going from the Tent to the Cookhouse. O, it was so coal the 18th . . .

(Blackout.)

SCENE EIGHT: JOHN WILKES BOOTH

(Lights come up. Enter JOHN WILKES BOOTH. *He recites the lines dramatically, and moves all over the stage, grossly overplaying.)*

BOOTH: Right or wrong, God judge me, not man. For be my motive good or bad, of one thing I am sure, the lasting condemnation of the North. I love peace more than life. Have loved the Union beyond expression. For four years I have waited, hoped, and prayed for the dark clouds to break and for a restoration of our former sunshine. To wait longer would be a crime. All hope for peace is dead. My prayers have proved as idle as my hopes, God's will be done. I go to see and share the bitter end.

I have ever held the South were right. The very nomination of Abraham Lincoln four years ago, spoke plainly war, war, upon southern rights and institutions. His election proved it. "Await an overt act." Yes, till you are bound and plundered. What folly. The South was wise. Who thinks of argument or pastime when the finger of his enemy presses the trigger?

The country was formed for the white, not for the black man. And looking upon African slavery from the same standpoint held by the noble framers of our constitution, I, for one, have ever considered it one of the greatest blessings (both for themselves and us) that God ever bestowed upon a favored nation. Witness heretofore our wealth and power; witness their elevation and enlightenment above their race elsewhere. I have lived among it most of my life, and have seen less harsh treatment from master to man than I ever beheld in the North from father to son . . .

When I aided in the capture and execution of John Brown (who was a murderer on our western border and who was fairly tried and convicted, before an impartial judge and jury, of treason, and who, by the way, has since been made a god), I was proud of my little share in the transaction, for I deemed it my duty that I was helping our common country to perform an act of justice. But what was a crime in poor John Brown is now considered (by themselves) as the greatest and only virtue of the whole Republican party. Strange transmigration. Vice so becomes a virtue, simply because more indulged in . . .

Alas, poor country. Is she to meet her threatened doom? Four years ago I would have given a thousand lives to see her remain (as I had always known her) powerful and unbroken. And even now I would hold my life as naught to see her what she was. O, my friend, if the fearful scenes of the past four years had never been enacted, or if what has been was a frightful dream, from which we could now awake, with what overflowing hearts could we bless our God . . .

My love, (as things stand to-day) is for the South alone. Nor do I deem it a dishonour in attempting to make for her a prisoner of this man to whom she owes so much misery. If success attends me, I go penniless to her side. They say she has found that "last ditch" which the North has so long derided, and been endeavoring to enforce her in, forgetting they are our brothers, and that it is impolite to goad an enemy to madness . . .

A Confederate doing duty upon his own responsibility.

J. WILKES BOOTH

(*Blackout.*)

SCENE NINE: THE END OF THE BEOTHUK

(Lights come up, discovering all four actors, stationed at different points on the stage. They read the lines from manuscripts.)

#1: WHEREAS it has been represented to the King, that the subjects residing in the said Island of Newfoundland, instead of cultivating such a friendly intercourse with the savages inhabiting that island as might be for their mutual benefit and advantage, do treat the said savages with the greatest inhumanity, and frequently destroy them without the least provocation or remorse. In order, therefore, to put a stop to such inhuman barbarity, and that the perpetrators of such atrocious crimes may be brought to due punishment, it is His Majesty's royal will and pleasure, that I do express his abhorrence of such inhuman barbarity, and I do strictly enjoin and require all His Majesty's subjects to live in amity and brotherly kindness with the native savages of the said island of Newfoundland. I do also require and command all officers and magistrates to use their utmost diligence to discover and apprehend all persons who may be guilty of murdering any of the said native Indians, in order that such offenders may be sent over to England, to be tried for such capital crimes . . .

#2: . . . they secrete themselves in the woods, keep an unremitting watch, and are seldom seen; a conduct which their defenseless condition . . . have compelled them to adopt.

#3: 1770, the beothuk quarrelled with the micmac, fought a disastrous battle at grand pond . . . the french offered the micmac a reward for every head of a beothuk.

#4: I fear that the race will be totally extinct in a few years . . .

#1: What number of these Indians may still be left, no person can even hazard a conjecture, but it must decrease annually: for our people murder all they can . . .

#2: . . . at the East end of Badger Bay Great Lake, at a portage known as the Indian path, we found traces made by the Red Indians . . .

#3: . . . the chance of finding even a single family now . . . is very small indeed.

#4: . . . the native Indians have not been seen on the coast this year.

#1: The good work should be continued, until it becomes morally certain that none remain . . . The prospect of success seems clouded, but however late the effort, it will be a consolation to have done all that was now possible.

#2: They had totally deserted their favorite Rendezvous . . .

#3: The banks of the noble river of Exploits we afterwards also found abandoned.

#4: 1827, the beothuk institution for the civilization of the native savages sent out an expedition:

#1: . . . but discovering nothing which indicated that any of the living tribe had recently been there, Mr. Cormack rafted about seventy miles down the river, touching at various places in his way, and again reached the mouth of the Exploits after an absence of thirty days, and having traversed two hundred miles of the interior, encompassing most of the country which is known to have been hitherto the favourite resort of the Indians.

#2: . . . the race has emigrated, or become extinct.

#3: Although we may infer where the remnant of the Red Indians would most likely be found, yet from the certainty of the smallness of their number, if any really do exist, it would not be prudent again to send an armed . . . (the remainder of the MS. is torn off.)

#4:

on some of the old french charts
of the north of the island,
le petit nord,
a track or path is shown,
along the low flat shore
forming the south side of
the strait of the belle isle,
and facing the coast of labrador:

it is called
chemin de sauvage
and may mark the last of the beothuk,
emigrating to the north . . .

#1:

they feared
a powerful monster,
who was to appear
from the sea . . .

#2:

the micmacs
thought them witches:

#3:

they could raise
a fog,

#4:

through which

#1:

to escape

THE CONFIDENCE MAN
by Herman Melville

ADAPTED FOR THE STAGE BY PAUL METCALF

Cast

IN ORDER OF APPEARANCE

Confidence Man	Man with Cane
Captain	Episcopal Minister
Deaf Mute	Methodist Minister
Barber	Lady
First Porter	Business Man
Second Porter	Invalid
First Passenger	Country Bumpkin
Second Passenger (Mr. Roberts)	Cripple in Audience
Third Passenger	Cripple on Crutches

PROLOGUE

Down-left is the CONFIDENCE MAN's *dressing room with no wall on the side facing the audience. The* CONFIDENCE-MAN *is seated within, applying makeup. Down-right there is a section of riverboat railing. A riverboat is painted in close-up on the backdrop, so that the stage may be conceived as part of the deck. The place where the boat's name might appear is blank.*

The CAPTAIN, *a big clownish figure, enters left, carrying a banner furled up. He prances about, mugging with the audience—a burlesque, a caricature of a riverboat captain. Going to the backdrop, he unfurls the banner and tacks it up in the appropriate place. The lettering says* FIDELE. *The* CAPTAIN *winks roguishly at the audience.*

Enter left the CONFIDENCE MAN. *He is dressed in gray, a sombre, religious figure. He displays a placard:* APRIL FOOLS' DAY.

The CAPTAIN *spies him, draws a whistle from his pocket, such as might announce the boat's departure. He blows a blast on it, salutes the other figure, and capers out left, followed by the other.*

(Blackout.)

ACT ONE

All the action in this scene should be performed very much as a dance. Enter the CAPTAIN, *left, carrying a placard. He is more serious this time. He goes to the backdrop and tacks up his placard, which shows a picture of a criminal type, with big letters, WANTED. Exit* CAPTAIN, *left. Offstage we hear crowd noises, a sort of low rumble of conversation. Enter, left, a blond* YOUNG MAN *in cream-colored suit and fleecy hat, carrying a number of signs. He makes his way, jostling and being jostled, through an imaginary crowd. He holds up a sign: CHARITY THINKETH NO EVIL, and is at once jostled by the crowd. He changes to another sign: CHARITY SUFFERETH LONG, AND IS KIND. Again he is jostled. He changes again: CHARITY ENDURETH ALL THINGS; and finally, CHARITY NEVER FAILETH. With this last one, he is almost knocked off his feet. While this is going on, enter right the* BARBER, *carrying the chair for his customers, and a sign. He tacks the sign up on the backdrop—NO TRUST—stands behind his chair, takes a straight edge razor from his pocket, and runs his thumb over the edge. At the same time, enter left two* PORTERS *carrying a trunk. The crowd noises increase in volume. The* PORTERS *make their way through the imaginary crowd, shouting incoherent imprecations. They come to the young blond man, who is now fairly recovered but has his back to them. They shout at him, but he pays no attention to them. They finally shove him aside, roughly, and as he goes to his knees, he holds up a final sign: DEAF MUTE. The* PORTERS, *grumbling and mumbling, exit right with the trunk. The* YOUNG MAN *huddles himself into a ball, as if to sleep, the DEAF MUTE sign displayed in front of him. The* BARBER *continues to study his razor.*

(Blackout.)

ACT TWO

(The BARBER *and his chair are gone. Otherwise the scene is the same, with the young man asleep. Enter right three* PASSENGERS *who circle around the* YOUNG MAN *as they speak.)*

FIRST: Odd fish!

SECOND: Poor fellow!

THIRD: Who can he be?

FIRST: Casper Hauser.

SECOND: Bless my soul!

THIRD: Uncommon countenance.

FIRST: Green prophet from Utah.

SECOND: Humbug!

THIRD: Singular innocence.

FIRST: Means something.

SECOND: Spirit-rapper.

THIRD: Moon-calf.

FIRST: Piteous.

SECOND: Trying to enlist interest.

THIRD: Beware of him.

FIRST: Fast asleep here, and doubtless, pickpockets on board.

SECOND: Kind of daylight Endymion.

THIRD: Escaped convict, worn out with dodging.

FIRST: Jacob dreaming at Luz.

(The CAPTAIN'*s whistle is heard again, offstage. The crowd noise recurs, a soft rumble, followed by the churning of the paddle wheels. The three* PASSENGERS *turn their backs to the* YOUNG MAN, *stare out over the audience, leaning on the riverboat railing.)*

(Blackout.)

ACT THREE

(The three PASSENGERS *are center stage, conversing. The* YOUNG MAN *is gone. Enter the* CONFIDENCE MAN, *left. He wears a blackface mask, black gloves, and a white wig, and he pushes himself along in a little cart. He approaches the* PASSENGERS, *holding out a tambourine for coins.)*

FIRST: What is your name, old boy?

CONFIDENCE MAN: Der Black Guinea dey calls me sar.

FIRST: And who is your master, Guinea?

CONFIDENCE MAN: Oh sar, I am der dog widout massa.

FIRST: A free dog, eh? Well, on your account, I'm sorry for that, Guinea. Dogs without masters fare hard.

CONFIDENCE MAN: So day do, sar; so dey do. But you see, sar, dese here legs? What ge'mman want to own dese here legs?

FIRST: But where do you live?

CONFIDENCE MAN: All 'long shore, sar; dough now I'se going to see brodder at der landing; but chiefly I libs in der city.

FIRST: St. Louis, eh? Where do you sleep there of nights?

CONFIDENCE MAN: On der floor of der good baker's oven, sar.

FIRST: In an oven? whose, pray? What baker, I should like to know, bakes such black bread in his oven, alongside of his nice white rolls, too. Who is that charitable baker, pray?

CONFIDENCE MAN *(raising his tambourine over his head)*: Dar he be.

FIRST: The sun is the baker, eh?

CONFIDENCE MAN: Yes sar, in der city dat good baker warms der stones for dis old darkie when he sleeps out on der pabements o'nights.

FIRST: But that must be in the summer only, old boy. How about winter, when the cold Cossacks come clattering and jingling? How about winter, old boy?

CONFIDENCE MAN: Den dis poor old darkie shakes werry bad, I tell you, sar. Oh sar, oh! don't speak ob der winter.

(Blackout.)

ACT FOUR

Standing left is a LITTLE MAN *with a severe limp—walks with a cane. The* PASSENGERS *are tossing coins at the* CONFIDENCE MAN, *some of which he catches in the tambourine, others in his mouth. They applaud when he accomplishes the latter. Standing right is an* EPISCO-PAL MINISTER.

LITTLE MAN: He's a fraud, I tell ye! An imposter! They ain't a thing wrong with his legs!

FIRST PASSENGER: Well, Guinea, what do you say for yourself?

CONFIDENCE MAN: Oh, sar . . .

SECOND PASSENGER: What about it? Do you have any papers?

LITTLE MAN: That's it! The papers! The papers! Ask him to show you his papers!

(Enter left a METHODIST MINISTER.*)*

CONFIDENCE MAN: No no, dis poor old darkie hain't none of dem waloable papers.

EPISCOPAL: But is there not someone who can speak a good word for you?

CONFIDENCE MAN: Oh yes, oh yes, ge'mmen, yes, dar is aboart here a werry nice, good ge'mman wid a weed, and a ge'mman in a gray coat and white tie, what knows all about me; and a ge'mman in a yaller west; and a ge'mman wid a brass plate; and a ge'mann in a wiolet robe; an a ge'mman as is a sodjer; and ever so many good, kind, honest ge'mmen more aboard what knows me and will speak for me, God bress 'em; yes and what knows me as well as dis poor old darkie knows hisself, God bress him! Oh, find 'em, find 'em, and let 'em come quick, and show you all, ge'mmen, dat dis poor old darkie is werry well wordy of all you kind ge'mmen's kind confidence.

THIRD PASSENGER: But how are we to find all these people?

EPISCOPAL: Where are we to find them? I will go find one to begin with.

(EPISCOPAL MINISTER *exits left.*)

LITTLE MAN: Wild goose chase! Don't believe there's a soul of them aboard. Did ever a beggar have such heaps of fine friends? He can walk fast enough when he tries, a good deal faster than I; but he can lie yet faster. He's some white operator, betwisted and painted up for a decoy. He and his friends are all humbugs.

METHODIST: Have you no charity, friend?

LITTLE MAN: Charity is one thing, and truth is another. He's a rascal, I say.

METHODIST: But why not, friend, put as charitable a construction as one can upon the poor fellow? He looks honest, don't he?

LITTLE MAN: Looks are one thing, and facts are another. And as to your constructions, what construction can you put upon a rascal, but that a rascal he is?

METHODIST: Be not such a Canada thistle. Charity, man, charity.

LITTLE MAN: To where it belongs with your charity! to heaven with it! Here on earth, true charity dotes, and false charity plots. Who betrays a fool with a kiss, the charitable fool has the charity to believe is in love with him, and the charitable knave on the stand gives charitable testimony for his comrade in the box.

METHODIST: Surely, friend, to say the least, you forget yourself. Apply it home. Suppose, now, I should exercise no charity in judging your own character by the words which have fallen from you. What sort of vile, pitiless man do you think I would take you for?

LITTLE MAN: No doubt some such pitiless man as had lost his piety in much the same way that the jockey loses his honesty.

METHODIST: And how is that, friend?

LITTLE MAN: Never mind how it is; but all horses ain't virtuous, no more than all men kind; and come close to, and much dealt with, some things are catching. When you find me a virtuous jockey, I will find you a benevolent wise man.

METHODIST: Some insinuation there.

LITTLE MAN: More fool that you are puzzled by it.

METHODIST: Reprobate! Godless reprobate! If charity did not restrain me, I could call you by names you deserve.

LITTLE MAN: Could you, indeed?

METHODIST: Yes, and teach you charity on the spot. *(He grabs the* LITTLE MAN *by the coat collar).* You took me for a noncombatant, did you? Thought, seedy coward that you are, that you could abuse a Christian with impunity. You find your mistake!

FIRST: Well said and better done, church militant!

SECOND: The white cravat against the world!

FIRST, SECOND, and THIRD PASSENGERS *(together)*: Bravo! Bravo!

LITTLE MAN *(breaking loose)*: You fools! You flock of fools, under this captain of fools, in this ship of fools!

METHODIST: There he shambles off on his one good leg, emblematic of his one-sided view of humanity.

LITTLE MAN (*pointing to the* CONFIDENCE MAN): But trust your painted decoy, and I have my revenge.

FIRST: But we ain't agoing to trust him!

LITTLE MAN: So much the better. Look you: I have been called a Canada thistle. Very good. And a seedy one; still better. And the seedy Canada thistle has been pretty well shaken among ye; best of all. Dare say some seed has been shaken out; and won't it spring through? And when it does spring, do you cut down the young thistles, and won't they spring the more? It's encouraging and coaxing 'em. Now, when with my thistles your farms shall be well stocked, why then—you may abandon 'em!

(The LITTLE MAN *exits left.)*

SECOND: What does all that mean, now?

METHODIST (*speaking as though preaching*): Nothing. The foiled wolf's parting howl. Spleen, much spleen, which is the rickety child of his evil heart or unbelief: it has made him mad. I suspect him for one naturally reprobate. Oh, friends, oh beloved, how are we admonished by the melancholy spectacle of the raver. Let us profit by the lesson; and is it not this: that if, next to mistrusting Providence, there be aught that man should pray against, it is against mistrusting his fellow-man. I have been in mad-houses full of tragic mopers, and seen there the end of suspicion: the cynic, in the moody madness muttering in the corner; for years a barren fixture there; head lopped over, gnawing his own lip, vulture to himself; while, by fits and starts, from the corner opposite came the grimace of the idiot at him.

SECOND: What an example!

THIRD: Might deter Timon.

CONFIDENCE MAN: Oh, oh, good ge'mmen, have you no confidence in dis poor ole darkie?

SECOND: Confidence in you? That remains to be seen.

THIRD: I tell you what it is, Ebony. Yonder churl is, no doubt, a churlish fellow enough, and I would not wish to be like him; but that is no reason why you may not be some sort of black Jeremy Diddler.

CONFIDENCE MAN: No confidence in dis poor old darkie, den?

THIRD: Before giving you our confidence, we will wait the report of the kind gentleman who went in search of one of your friends who was to speak for you.

FIRST: Very likely, in that case, we shall wait here till Christmas. Shouldn't wonder did we not see that kind gentleman again. After seeking a while in vain, he will conclude he has been made a fool of, and so not return to us for pure shame. Something queer about this darkie, depend on it.

CONFIDENCE MAN: No confidence in dis poor ole darkie . . .

SECOND: Yes, my poor fellow, I have confidence in you. And here, here is some proof of my trust. Here, here, my poor fellow.

(The SECOND PASSENGER *reaches into his pocket and hands the* CONFIDENCE MAN *a large silver coin, and, as he does so, a business card accidentally slips out of his pocket. The* CONFIDENCE MAN *deftly gathers it in.)*

CONFIDENCE MAN *(pushing his cart toward the exit)*: Oh, whar, whar is dat good friend of dis darkie's, dat good man wid to weed?

(Blackout.)

ACT FIVE

(The stage is bare. The CONFIDENCE MAN *enters, from his dressing room. He is now white, dressed like a business man, with a piece of black crepe around his hat. He stands beside the* BARBER'S *NO TRUST sign. Enter the* SECOND PASSENGER, *right. The* CONFIDENCE MAN *approaches him. A low murmur of crowd noise can be heard.)*

CONFIDENCE MAN: How do you do, Mr. Roberts?

SECOND: Eh?

CONFIDENCE MAN: Don't you know me?

SECOND: No, certainly.

CONFIDENCE MAN: Is it possible, my dear sir, that you do not recall my countenance? Why, yours I recall distinctly as if but half an hour, instead of half an age, had passed since I saw you. Don't you recall me, now? Look harder.

SECOND: In my conscience—truly—I protest—bless my soul, sir, I don't know you—really, really. But stay, stay—yes—seems to me, though I have not the pleasure of personally knowing you, yet I am pretty sure I have at least *heard* of you, and recently, too, quite recently. A poor negro aboard here referred to you, among others, for a character, I think.

CONFIDENCE MAN: Oh, the cripple. Poor Fellow, I know him well. They found me. I have said all I could for him. I think I abated their distrust. Would I could have been of more substantial service. And apropos, sir, now that it strikes me, allow me to ask, whether the circumstances of one man, however humble, referring for a character to another man, however afflicted, does not argue more or less of moral worth in the latter? *(Pause.)* Still you don't recall my countenance?

SECOND: Still does truth compel me to say that I cannot, despite my best efforts.

CONFIDENCE MAN: Can I be so changed? Look at me. Or is it I who am mistaken? Are you not, sir, Henry Roberts, forwarding merchant, of Wheeling, Pennsylvania? Pray, now, if you use the advertisement of business cards, and happen to have one with you, just look at it, and see whether you are not the man I take you for.

SECOND: Why, I hope I know myself.

CONFIDENCE MAN: And yet self-knowledge is thought by some not so easy. Who knows, my dear sir, but for a time you may have taken yourself for somebody else? Stranger things have happened. To come to particulars, my dear sir, I met you, now some six years back, at Brade Brothers & Co.'s office, I think. I was traveling for a Philadelphia house. The senior Brade introduced us, you remember; some business-chat followed, then you forced me home with you to a family tea, and a family time we had. Have you forgotten about the urn, and what I said about Werter's Charlotte, and the bread and butter, and that capital story you told of the large loaf? A hundred times since, I have laughed over it. At least you must recall my name—Ringman, John Ringman.

SECOND: Large loaf? Invited you to tea? Ringman? Ringman? Ring? Ring?

CONFIDENCE MAN: Ah sir, don't ring the changes that way. I see you have a faithless memory, Mr. Roberts. But trust in the faithfulness of mine.

SECOND: Well, to tell the truth, in some things my memory ain't of the very best. But still—still I—

CONFIDENCE MAN: Oh sir, suffice it that it is as I say. Doubt not that we are all well acquainted.

SECOND: But—but I don't like this going dead against my own memory; I—

CONFIDENCE MAN: But didn't you admit, my dear sir, that in some things this memory of yours is a little faithless? Now, those who have faithless memories, should they not have some little confidence in the less faithless memories of others?

SECOND: But of this friendly chat and tea, I have not the slightest—

CONFIDENCE MAN: I see, I see; quite erased from the tablet. Pray, sir, about six years back, did it happen to you to receive any injury on the head? Surprising effects have arisen from such a cause. Not alone unconsciousness as to events for a greater or less time immediately subsequent to the injury, but likewise—strange to add—oblivion, entire and incurable, as to events embracing a longer or shorter period immediately preceding it; that is when the mind at the time was perfectly sensible of them, and fully competent also to register them in the memory, and did in fact so do; but all in vain, for all was afterwards bruised out by the injury. *(Pause.)* In my boyhood I was kicked by a horse, and lay insensible for a long time. Upon recovering, what a blank! No faintest trace in regard to how I had come near the horse, or what horse it was, or where it was, or that it was a horse at all that had brought me to that pass. For the knowledge of those particulars I am indebted solely to my friends, in whose statements, I need not say, I place implicit reliance, since particulars of some sort there must have been and why should they deceive me? You see, sir, the mind is ductile, very much so: but images, ductilely received into it, need a certain time to harden and bake in their impressions, otherwise such a casualty as I speak of will in an instant obliterate them, as though they had never been. We're but clay, sir, potter's clay, as the good book says, clay, feeble, and too-yielding clay. But I will not philosophize. Tell me, was it your misfortune to receive any concussion upon the brain about the period I speak of? If so, I will with pleasure supply the void in your memory by more intimately rehearsing the circumstances of our acquaintance.

SECOND: Well, now—come to think—there was, about that time— a bout with brain fever . . .

CONFIDENCE MAN: There now, you see, I was not wholly mistaken. The brain fever accounts for it all.

SECOND: Nay; but—

CONFIDENCE MAN: Pardon me, Mr. Roberts, but time is short, and I have something private and particular to say to you. If I remember, you are a mason, Mr. Roberts?

SECOND: Yes, yes.

CONFIDENCE MAN: And would you not loan a brother a shilling if he needed it?

(The SECOND PASSENGER *steps back, astonished.)*

CONFIDENCE MAN: Ah, Mr. Roberts, I trust you are not one of those business men, who make a business of never having to do with unfortunates. For God's sake, don't leave me. I have something on my heart—on my heart. Under deplorable circumstances thrown among strangers, utter strangers. I want a friend in whom I may confide. Yours, Mr. Roberts, is almost the first known face I've seen for many weeks. I need not say, sir, how it cuts me to the soul, to follow up a social salutation with such words. I know that I jeopardize your good opinion. But I can't help it; necessity knows no law, and heeds no risk. Sir, we are masons, one more step aside; and I will tell you my story.

(The crowd noise becomes much louder. The CONFIDENCE MAN *takes the* SECOND PASSENGER *by the elbow, guides him up-right, and*

appears to engage him in honest conversation. Twice during this sequence the SECOND PASSENGER *takes out his wallet and hands the* CONFIDENCE MAN *a bill. They shake hands, and prepare to part. The crowd noise diminishes. As an apparent afterthought, the* CONFIDENCE MAN *turns again to the other.)*

CONFIDENCE MAN: I am just reminded that the president, who is also transfer agent, of the Black Rapids Coal Company, happens to be on board here, and has his transfer-book with him. A month since, in a panic contrived by artful alarmists, some credulous stockholders sold out. The Company, I hear, is now ready, but not anxious to redispose of those shares, offering to one in funds a rare chance for investment. For, the panic subsiding more and more every day, it will daily be seen how it originated; confidence will be more than restored; there will be a reaction from the stock's descent: its rise will be higher than from no fall; the holders trusting themselves to fear no second fate.

SECOND: Pray, do you think that upon a pinch anything could be transacted on board here with the transfer agent?

CONFIDENCE MAN: The gentleman might not object to doing a little business on board. Along the Mississippi, you know, business is not so ceremonious as at the East.

SECOND: True. This would seem a rare chance indeed. Why, upon first hearing it, did you not snatch at it? I mean for yourself.

CONFIDENCE MAN: I? Would it had been possible!

SECOND: Ah, yes, I had forgotten.

CONFIDENCE MAN: Forgetfulness. Charity will impute this to some lingering effect of the brain-fever.

SECOND: As to that, I am not—

CONFIDENCE MAN: But enough. My object, sir, in calling your attention to this stock, is by way of acknowledgement of your goodness. I but seek to be grateful. *(They shake hands.)*

(Blackout.)

ACT SIX

(The CONFIDENCE MAN, *dressed as the religious-looking figure from the Prologue, is center-stage, with one hand out, appealing to the* FIRST PASSENGER.*)*

FIRST: You—pish! *(To the audience:)* Why will the captain suffer these begging fellows on board?

(The FIRST PASSENGER *exits right, and, at the same moment, the* EPISCOPAL MINISTER *enters left. He approaches the* CONFIDENCE MAN.*)*

EPISCOPAL: Your pardon, but shortly since I was all over looking for you.

CONFIDENCE MAN: For me?

EPISCOPAL: Yes, for you. Do you know anything about the negro, apparently a cripple, aboard here? Is he, or is he not, what he seems to be?

CONFIDENCE MAN: Ah, poor Guinea! Have you, too, been distrusted? You, upon whom Nature has placarded the evidence of your claims?

(Enter left the LITTLE MAN *with the crippled leg and cane. He stands by the others unobserved, eavesdropping.)*

EPISCOPAL: Then you really do know him, and he is quite worthy? It relieves me to hear it—much relieves me. Come, let us go find him, and see what can be done.

CONFIDENCE MAN: Another instance that confidence may come too late. I am sorry to say that at the last landing I myself—just happening to catch sight of him on the gangway plank—assisted the cripple ashore.

LITTLE MAN: Ha, ha, ha! *(Pause.)* Wouldn't think it was I who laughed, would you?

EPISCOPAL: But who was it you laughed at? or rather, tried to laugh at?

LITTLE MAN: Neither you nor any one within a thousand miles of you.

CONFIDENCE MAN *(to* EPISCOPAL*):* Who is that scoffer? Who is he, who even were truth on his tongue, his way of speaking it would make truth about as offensive as falsehood? Who is he?

EPISCOPAL: He who I mentioned to you as having boasted his suspicion of the negro. In short, the person to whom I ascribe the origin of my own distrust. He maintained that Guinea was some white scoundrel, betwisted and painted up for a decoy. Yes, these were his very words, I think.

CONFIDENCE MAN: Impossible! He could not be so wrongheaded. *(Approaches the* LITTLE MAN.*)* The reverend gentleman tells me, sir, that a certain cripple, a poor negro, is by you considered an ingenious imposter. Would you tell me now, whether you were not merely joking in this notion? Would you be so kind?

LITTLE MAN: Well, he's just what I said he was.

CONFIDENCE MAN: A white masquerading as a black?

LITTLE MAN: Exactly.

CONFIDENCE MAN *(to the* EPISCOPAL MINISTER*):* I thought you represented your friend here as a very distrustful sort of person, but he appears endued with a singular credulity. *(To the* LITTLE MAN:*)* Tell me, sir, do you really think that a white could look the negro so? For one, I should call it pretty good acting.

LITTLE MAN: Not much better than any other man acts.

CONFIDENCE MAN: You trifle. I ask again, if a white, how could he look the negro so?

LITTLE MAN: Never saw the negro-minstrels, I suppose?

CONFIDENCE MAN: But his limbs, if not a cripple, how could he twist his limbs so?

LITTLE MAN: How do other hypocritical beggars twist theirs?

CONFIDENCE MAN: The sham is evident, then?

LITTLE MAN: To the discerning eye.

CONFIDENCE MAN: Well, where is Guinea? Where is he? Let us at once find him, and refute beyond cavil this injurious hypothesis.

LITTLE MAN: Do so. I'm just in the humor now for having him found, and leaving the streaks of these fingers on his paint. Yes, find him, I'll make wool fly, and him after.

EPISCOPAL: You forget that you yourself helped poor Guinea ashore.

CONFIDENCE MAN: So I did, so I did; how unfortunate.

(The LITTLE MAN *laughs jeeringly, and withdraws up-right.)*

CONFIDENCE MAN: A bad man, a dangerous man; a man to be put down in any Christian community. And this was he who was the means of begetting your distrust? Ah, we should shut our eyes to distrust!

EPISCOPAL: With me at the time his ill words went for nothing; the same as now; afterwards they had effect; and I confess this puzzled me.

CONFIDENCE MAN: Strangle the least symptom of distrust, of any sort, which hereafter, upon whatever provocation, may arise in you.

EPISCOPAL: I will do so. Ah, but the poor negro! You see him occasionally, perhaps?

CONFIDENCE MAN: No, not often; though in a few days, as it happens my engagements will call me to the neighborhood of his present retreat; and, no doubt, honest Guinea, who is a grateful soul, will come to see me there.

EPISCOPAL: Take this mite. Hand it to Guinea when you see him; say it comes from one who has full belief in his honesty, and is sincerely sorry for having indulged, however transiently, in a contrary thought.

CONFIDENCE MAN: I accept the trust. And, by the way, since you are of this truly charitable nature, you will not turn away an appeal in behalf of the Seminole Widow and Orphan Asylum?

EPISCOPAL: I have not heard of that charity.

CONFIDENCE MAN: But recently founded. *(Pause.)* Ah, well, if that subtle bane, we were speaking of just now, is so soon beginning to work, in vain my appeal to you.

EPISCOPAL: Nay, you do me an injustice; instead of indulging present suspicions, I had rather make amends for previous ones. Here is something for your asylum. Not much; but every drop helps. Of course, you have papers?

CONFIDENCE MAN: Of course.

(Blackout.)

ACT SEVEN

(There are two deck chairs, against the back drop. One is occupied by a well-dressed LADY, *reading her bible. The* CONFIDENCE MAN, *dressed as before, is seated in his dressing room, checking his makeup. He turns and sees the* LADY, *leaves the dressing room, and approaches her.)*

CONFIDENCE MAN: Madam, pardon my freedom, but there is something in that face which strangely draws me. May I ask, are you a sister of the church?

LADY: Why—really—you—

CONFIDENCE MAN: It is very solitary for a brother here. I find none to mingle souls with. It may be wrong—I know it is—but I cannot force myself to be easy with the people of the world. I prefer the company, however silent, of a brother or sister in good standing. By the way, madam, may I ask if you have confidence?

LADY: Really, sir—why, sir, really—I—

CONFIDENCE MAN: Could you put confidence in me, for instance?

LADY: Really, sir—as much—I mean, as one may wisely put in a— a—stranger, an entire stranger, I had almost said.

CONFIDENCE MAN: Entire stranger! Ah, who would be a stranger? In vain, I wander; no one will have confidence in me.

LADY: You interest me. Can I any way befriend you?

CONFIDENCE MAN: No one can befriend me, who has not confidence.

LADY: But I—I have—at least to that degree—I mean that—

CONFIDENCE MAN: Nay, nay, you have none, none at all. Pardon, I see it. No confidence. Fool, fond fool that I am to seek it!

LADY: You are unjust, sir. But it may be that something untoward in your experiences has unduly biased you. Not that I would cast reflections. Believe me, I—yes, yes—I may say—that—that—

CONFIDENCE MAN: That you have confidence? Prove it. Let me have twenty dollars.

LADY: Twenty dollars!

CONFIDENCE MAN: There, I told you, madam, you had no confidence.

LADY: Tell me, sir, for what you want the twenty dollars.

CONFIDENCE MAN: For the widow and the fatherless. I am traveling agent of the Widow and Orphan Asylum, recently founded among the Seminoles.

LADY: And why did you not tell me your object before? Poor souls—Indians, too—those cruelly-used Indians. Here, here; how could I hesitate? I am so sorry it is no more.

CONFIDENCE MAN: Grieve not for that, madam. Good-bye; you have confidence.

(Blackout.)

ACT EIGHT

ROBERTS: Ah, wine is good, and confidence is good; but can wine or confidence percolate down through all the stony strata of hard considerations, and drop warmly and ruddily into the cold cave of truth? Truth will not be comforted. Led by dear charity, lured by sweet hope, fond fancy essays this feat; but in vain; mere dreams and ideals, they explode in your hand, leaving naught but the scorching behind!

BUSINESS MAN *(grasping the bottle)*: Why, why, why! If *In vino veritas* be a true saying, then, for all the fine confidence you professed with me, just now, distrust, deep distrust, underlies it; and then thousand strong, like the Irish Rebellion, breaks out in you now. That wine, good wine, should do it! Upon my soul, you shall drink no more of it. Wine was meant to gladden the heart, not grieve it; to heighten confidence, not depress it.

ROBERTS *(retrieving the bottle)*: I repent calling for the champagne. To a temperament like yours, champagne is not to be recommended. Pray, my dear sir, do you feel quite yourself again? Confidence restored?

BUSINESS MAN: I hope so; I think I may say it is so. But we have had a long talk, and I think I must retire now.

(Blackout.)

ACT NINE

CONFIDENCE MAN: You tell me, that by advice of an eminent physiologist in Louisville, you took tincture of iron. For what? To restore your lost energy. And how? Why, in healthy subjects iron is naturally found in the blood, and iron in the bar is strong; ergo, iron is the source of animal invigoration. But you being deficient in vigor, it follows that the cause is deficiency of iron. Iron, then, must be put into you. What is iron in the vial will prove iron in the vein.

(The INVALID *makes a gesture, as though wishing to be left alone. The* CONFIDENCE MAN *ignores him.)*

CONFIDENCE MAN: But this notion, that science can play farmer to the flesh, making there what living soil it pleases, seems not so strange as that other conceit—that science is nowadays so expert that, in consumptive cases, as yours, it can, by prescription of the inhalation of certain vapors, achieve the sublimest act of omnipotence, breathing into all but lifeless dust the breath of life. For did you not tell me, my poor sir, that by order of the great chemist in Baltimore, for three weeks you were never driven out without a respirator, and for a given time of every day sat bolstered up in a sort of gasometer, inspiring vapors generated by burning of drugs? As if this concocted atmosphere of man were an antidote to the poison of God's natural air. Try to rid my mind of it as I may, yet still these chemical practitioners with their tinctures, and fumes, and braziers, and occult incantations, seem to me like Pharaoh's vain sorcerers, trying to beat down the will of heaven. Day and night, in all charity, I intercede for them, that heaven may not, in its own language, be provoked to anger with their inventions; may not take vengeance of their inventions. A thousand pities that you should ever have been in the hands of these Egyptians.

(Again, the INVALID *gestures, and the* CONFIDENCE MAN *ignores him.)*

CONFIDENCE MAN: How different we herb doctors! who claim nothing, invent nothing; but staff in hand, in glades, and upon hillsides, go about in nature, humbly seeking our cures. True Indian doctors, though not learned in names, we are not unfamiliar with essences—successors of Solomon the Wise, who knew all vegetables from the cedar of Lebanon, to the hyssop on the wall. *(He withdraws a packet from his pocket).* A few vials of my Omni-Balsamic Reinvigorator would, I am certain, give you some strength.

INVALID *(rousing himself with difficulty)*: Begone! You are all alike. The name of doctor, the dream of helper, condemns you. For years I have been but a gallipot for you experimentizers to rinse your experiments into, and now, in this livid skin, partake of the nature of my contents. Begone! I hate ye.

CONFIDENCE MAN: I were inhuman, could I take affront at a want of confidence, born of too bitter an experience of betrayers. Yet, permit one who is not without feeling . . .

INVALID: Begone! Just in that voice talked to me, not six months ago, the German doctor at the water cure, from which I now return, six months and sixty pangs nigher my grave.

CONFIDENCE MAN: The water-cure? Oh, fatal delusion of the well-meaning Breisnitz! Sir, trust me—

INVALID: Begone!

CONFIDENCE MAN: Nay, an invalid should not always have his own way. Ah, sir, reflect how untimely this distrust in one like you. How weak you are; and weakness, is it not the time for confidence? Yes, when through weakness everything bids despair, then is the time to get strength by confidence. Turn not away. This may be the last time of health's asking. Work upon yourself; invoke confidence, though from ashes; rouse it; for your life, rouse it, and invoke it, I say.

INVALID *(eyeing the package)*: What does it contain?

CONFIDENCE MAN: Herbs.

INVALID: What herbs? And the nature of them? And the reason for giving them?

CONFIDENCE MAN: It cannot be made known.

INVALID: Then I will have none of you.

CONFIDENCE MAN: I give up.

INVALID: How?

CONFIDENCE MAN: You are sick, and a philosopher.

INVALID: No, no—not the last.

CONFIDENCE MAN: A sick philosopher is incurable.

INVALID: Then you give me no hope?

CONFIDENCE MAN: Hope is proportioned to confidence. How much confidence you give me, so much hope do I give you. *(He holds up the box)*. For this, if all depended on this, I should rest. It is nature's own. Trust me, nature is health; for health is good, and nature cannot work ill. As little can she work error. Get nature, and you get well.

INVALID: Then you do really think that if I take this medicine I shall regain my health? *(He accepts the box, holds it at arm's length.)*

CONFIDENCE MAN: Not in a day, nor a week, nor perhaps a month, but sooner or later; I say not exactly when, for I am neither prophet nor charlatan. Still, if, according to the directions in your box there, you take my medicine steadily, without assigning an especial day, near or remote, to discontinue it, then may you calmly look for some eventual result of good. But again I say, you must have confidence.

INVALID: But to one like me, it is so hard, so hard. The most confident hopes so often have failed me, and as often have I vowed never, no, never, to trust them again. Oh, you do not know, you do not know.

CONFIDENCE MAN: Time is short. You hold your cure, to retain or reject.

INVALID *(handing over money)*: I retain.

(*Blackout.*)

ACT TEN

(The CONFIDENCE MAN, *as Herb Doctor, is discovered. During the following, he addresses the audience, coming as close to them as the staging will permit.)*

CONFIDENCE MAN: Ladies and gentlemen, I hold in my hand here the Samaritan Pain Dissuader, thrice-blessed discovery of that disinterested friend of humanity whose portrait you see. Pure vegetable extract. Warranted to remove the acutest pain within less than ten minutes. Five hundred dollars to be forfeited on failure. Especially efficacious in heart disease and tic-douloureux. Observe the expression of this pledged friend of humanity.

(Enter, left, a COUNTRY BUMPKIN, *a great giant of a man. The* CONFIDENCE MAN *approaches him.)*

CONFIDENCE MAN: Excuse me, but, if I err not, I was speaking to you the other day—on a Kentucky boat, wasn't it?

BUMPKIN: Never to me.

CONFIDENCE MAN: Ah! But I am again mistaken, or don't you go a little lame, sir?

BUMPKIN: Never was lame in my life.

CONFIDENCE MAN: Indeed? I fancied I had perceived not a limp, but a hitch, a slight hitch—some experience in these things—divined some hidden cause of the hitch—buried bullet, may be—some dragoons of the Mexican war discharged with such, you know. Surely you have pain, strong pain, somewhere; in strong frames pain is strongest. Try, now, my specific. Do but look at the expression of this friend of humanity. Trust me, certain cure for any pain in the world.

BUMPKIN: No! *(Turns away.)*

CONFIDENCE MAN *(addressing audience)*: The Samaritan Pain Dissuader, which I here hold in my hand, will either cure or ease any pain you please, within ten minutes after its application.

BUMPKIN: What was that you last said?

CONFIDENCE MAN: I was saying what, since you wish it, I cheerfully repeat, that the Samaritan Pain Dissuader, which I here hold in my hand, will either cure or ease any pain you please, within ten minutes after its application.

BUMPKIN: Does it produce insensibility?

CONFIDENCE MAN: By no means. Not the least of its merits is, that it is not an opiate. It kills pain without killing feeling.

BUMPKIN: You lie!

CONFIDENCE MAN *(addressing audience)*: Only three bottles, faithfully taken, cured a Louisiana widow (for three weeks sleepless in a darkened chamber) of neuralgic sorrow for the loss of her husband and child, swept off in one night by the last epidemic. For the truth of this, a printed voucher was produced, duly signed.

(The BUMPKIN suddenly strikes the CONFIDENCE MAN with his fist, knocking him to the floor.)

BUMPKIN: Profane fiddler on heart-strings! Snake!

(The BUMPKIN exits. The CONFIDENCE MAN rises unsteadily, feeling his jaw. He uncorks the medicine, applies a little of it to his jaw, and is instantly restored.)

CONFIDENCE MAN: No, no, I won't seek redress; innocence is my redress. But if that man's wrathful blow provokes me to no wrath, should his evil distrust arouse you to distrust? I do devoutly hope, for the honor of humanity, that, despite this cowardly assault, the Samaritan Pain Dissuader stands unshaken in the confidence of all who hear me!

(Blackout.)

ACT ELEVEN

(The stage is bare. Enter the CONFIDENCE MAN, *as Herb Doctor, left. Enter the* SECOND PASSENGER, *right. He stands apart.)*

CONFIDENCE MAN *(addressing audience)*: Is the agent of the Seminole Widow and Orphan Asylum within here? *(Pause.)* Is there here any agent or any member of any charitable institution whatever? *(Pause.)* If there be within here any such person, I have in my hand two dollars for him. *(Pause.)* I was called away so hurriedly, I forgot this part of my duty. With the proprietor of the Samaritan Pain Dissuader it is a rule to devote, on the spot, to some benevolent purpose, the half of the proceeds of sales. Eight bottles were disposed of among this company. Hence, four half-dollars remain to charity. Who, as steward, takes the money? *(Pause.)* Does diffidence prevail over duty? If, I say, there be any gentleman, or any lady, either, here present, who is in any connection with any charitable institution whatever, let him or her come forward. He or she happening to have at hand no certificate of such connection, makes no difference. Not of a suspicious temper, thank God, I shall have confidence in whoever offers to take the money. *(Pause.)* Is it to be believed that, in this Christian company, there is no charitable person? I mean, no one connected with any charity? Well, then, is there no object of charity here? *(Pause.)* Are there none here who feel in need of help, and who, in accepting such help would feel that they, in their time, have given or done more than may ever be given or done to them? Man or woman, is there none such here?

(A poorly dressed woman in the audience begins to sob, rises to her feet, and then sits back down. A crippled man, heavily bandaged, rises, and makes his way to the stage. The CONFIDENCE MAN *hands him the coins.)*

CONFIDENCE MAN: Ah, poor wounded hazzar!

(Exit the CONFIDENCE MAN. *The* SECOND PASSENGER *approaches the* CRIPPLE.*)*

SECOND PASSENGER: Don't be frightened, you; but I want to see those coins. Yes, yes; good silver, good silver. There, take them again.

(The CRIPPLE *takes the coins and exits.)*

SECOND PASSENGER *(to audience)*: Strange! The money was good money.

(Blackout.)

ACT TWELVE

(Discovered are the CONFIDENCE MAN, *as Herb Doctor, and another* CRIPPLE, *this one on crutches.)*

CONFIDENCE MAN: To mere reason, your case looks something piteous, I grant. But never despond; many things—the choicest— yet remain. You breathe this bounteous air, are warmed by this gracious sun, and, though poor and friendless, indeed, nor so agile as in your youth, yet, how sweet to roam, day by day, through the groves, plucking the bright mosses and flowers, till forlornness itself becomes a hilarity, and, in your innocent independence, you skip for joy.

CRIPPLE: Fine skipping with these 'ere horse-posts—ha ha!

CONFIDENCE MAN: Pardon; I forgot the crutches. My mind, figuring you after receiving the benefit of my art, overlooked you as you stand before me.

CRIPPLE: Your art? You call yourself an herb doctor and a bonesetter —a natural bone-setter, do ye? Go bone-set the crooked world, and then come bone-set crooked me.

CONFIDENCE MAN: Truly, my honest friend, I thank you for again recalling me to my original object. Let me examine you. *(He bends down).* Ah, I see, I see; much such a case as the negro's. Did you see him? Oh, no, you came aboard since. Well, his case was a little something like yours. I prescribed for him, and I shouldn't wonder at all if, in a very short time, he were able to walk almost as well as myself. Now, have you no confidence in my art?

CRIPPLE: Ha, ha!

CONFIDENCE MAN: I will not force confidence on you. Still, I would fain do the friendly thing by you. Here, take this box; just rub that liniment on the joints night and morning. Take it. Nothing to pay. God bless you. Good-bye.

CRIPPLE: Stay, stay—thank'ee—but will this really do me good? Honor bright, now; will it? Don't deceive a poor fellow.

CONFIDENCE MAN: Try it. Good-bye.

CRIPPLE: Stay, stay! *Sure* it will do me good?

CONFIDENCE MAN: Possibly, possibly; no harm in trying. Good-bye.

CRIPPLE: Stay, stay; give me three more boxes, and here's the money.

CONFIDENCE MAN: My friend, I rejoice in the birth of your confidence and hopefulness. Believe me that, like your crutches, confidence and hopefulness will long support a man when his own legs will not. Stick to confidence and hopefulness, then since how mad for the cripple to throw his crutches away. You ask for three more boxes of my liniment. Luckily, I have just that number remaining. Here they are. I sell them at half-a-dollar apiece. But I shall take nothing from you. There, God bless you again; good-bye.

CRIPPLE: Stay, stay, stay! You have made a better man of me. You have borne with me like a good Christian, and talked to me like one, and all that is enough without making me a present of these boxes. Here is the money. I won't take nay. There, there; and may Almighty goodness go with you.

(The CONFIDENCE MAN *takes the money, bows, and exits. The* CRIP-PLE *is left holding the liniment, leaning on his crutches, a saturnine expression on his face.)*

(Blackout.)

ACT THIRTEEN

(The BUSINESS MAN *in the tasseled cap and the* SECOND PASSENGER *(the country merchant,* MR. ROBERTS*) are seated at the table, as before, with champagne. Both appear asleep.)*

BUSINESS MAN *(awaking)*: Wine, you know, opens the heart.

ROBERTS *(awaking)*: Opens it! It thaws it right out. Every heart is ice-bound till wine melt it, and reveal the tender grass and sweet herbage budding below, with every dear secret, hidden before like a dropped jewel in a snowbank, lying unsuspected through winter till spring.

BUSINESS MAN: And in just that way, my dear friend, is one of my little secrets now to be shown forth.

ROBERTS: Ah! What is it?

BUSINESS MAN: Be not so impetuous. Let me explain. You see, naturally, I am a man not overgifted with assurance; in general, I am, if anything, diffidently reserved; so, if I shall presently seem otherwise, the reason is, that you, by the geniality you evinced in all your talk, and especially the noble way in which, while affirming your good opinion of men, you intimated that you never could prove false to any man—in short, in short, how shall I express what I mean, unless I add that by your whole character you impel me to throw myself upon your nobleness; in one word, put confidence in you, a generous confidence?

ROBERTS: I see, I see, something of moment you wish to confide. Now, what is it, my good friend? Love affair?

BUSINESS MAN: No, not that.

ROBERTS: What then? Speak—depend upon me to the last. Out with it.

BUSINESS MAN: Out it shall come, then. I am in want, urgent want of money.

ROBERTS *(suddenly sober, leaps from his chair)*: In want of money!

BUSINESS MAN *(rising, also sober)*: Yes, and you are going to loan me fifty dollars. I could almost wish I was in need of more only for your sake. Yes, for your sake; that you might the better prove your noble kindness, my dear friend.

ROBERTS: None of your dear friends!

BUSINESS MAN: Why, why, why?

ROBERTS: None of your why, why, why! Go to the devil, sir! Beggar, imposter! Never so deceived in a man in my life.

(The BUSINESS MAN *takes ten gold coins from his pocket, which he places in a circle around* MR. ROBERTS, *where the latter stands.* MR. ROBERTS *becomes mesmerized, transfixed.)*

BUSINESS MAN: Reappear, reappear, reappear, oh, my former friend! Replace this hideous apparition with thy blest shape, and be the token of thy return the words, "My dear friend."

ROBERTS: My dear friend! (*He steps out of the ring of coins.*) My dear friend, what a funny man you are; full of fun as an egg of meat. How could you tell me that absurd story of your being in need? But I relish a good joke too well to spoil it by letting on. Of course, I humored the thing; and, on my side, put on all the crude airs you would have me. Come, this little episode of fictitious estrangement will but enhance the delightful reality. Let us sit down again and finish our bottle.

BUSINESS MAN: With all my heart. Yes, I am something of a funny man now and then; while for you, what you say about your humoring the thing is true enough; never did man second a joke better than you did just now. You played your part better than I did mine; you played it to the life.

ROBERTS: You see, I once belonged to an amateur play company; that accounts for it. But come, fill up, fill up!

(Blackout.)

ACT FOURTEEN

(Scene the same as before, with BUSINESS MAN *and* MR. ROBERTS. *The gold coins have been removed.)*

BUSINESS MAN: Really, early as it is, I think I must retire; my head feels unpleasantly; this confounded elixir of logwood, little as I drank of it, has played the deuce with me.

ROBERTS: Little as you drank of it? Why, good friend, you are losing your mind. To talk so for the genuine, mellow champagne. Yes, I think that by all means you had better away, and sleep it off. There—don't apologize—don't explain—go, go—I understand you exactly. I will see you tomorrow.

(Exit ROBERTS, *unsteadily.)*

ROBERTS: *(addressing audience)*: If ever, in days to come, you shall see ruin at hand, and, thinking you understand mankind, shall tremble for your friendships, and tremble for your pride; and, partly through love for the one and fear for the other, shall resolve to be beforehand with the world, and save it from a sin by prospectively taking that sin to yourself, then will you do as one I now dream of once did, and like him will you suffer; but how fortunate and grateful should you be, if like him, after all that had happened, you could be a little happy again.

(Blackout.)

ACT FIFTEEN

(The BARBER *is discovered, asleep in his chair, beneath the NO TRUST sign. The* CONFIDENCE MAN, *as Philanthropist, emerges from his dressing room.)*

CONFIDENCE MAN: Bless you, barber!

(The BARBER *awakens suddenly, his arms thrashing about.)*

CONFIDENCE MAN: Why, barber, are you reaching up to catch birds there with salt?

BARBER: Ah, it is only a man . . .

CONFIDENCE MAN: Only a man? As if to be but a man were nothing. But don't be too sure what I am, barber. You can conclude nothing absolute from the human form. But enough. It is my desire that you conclude to give me a good shave. Are you competent to a good shave, barber?

BARBER: No broker more so, sir.

CONFIDENCE MAN: Broker? What has a broker to do with lather? A broker I have always understood to be a worthy dealer in certain papers and metals.

BARBER: He, he? You understand well enough, sir. Take this seat, sir.

CONFIDENCE MAN: Thank you.

(The CONFIDENCE MAN *sits down, and the* BARBER *begins to prepare the lather, with mug and brush. The* CONFIDENCE MAN *suddenly sees the sign, and rises again.)*

CONFIDENCE MAN: But look, look—what's this? *No Trust?* No trust means distrust; distrust means no confidence, Barber. What fell suspiciousness prompts this scandalous confession? My life! if but to tell a dog that you have no confidence in him be matter for affront to the dog, what an insult to take that way the whole haughty race of man by the beard? By my heart, sir!

BARBER: Your sort of talk is not exactly in my line, sir.

CONFIDENCE MAN: But the taking of mankind by the nose is; a habit, barber, which I sadly fear has insensibly bred in you a disrespect for man.

(The CONFIDENCE MAN *sits again. During the following conversation the* BARBER *repeatedly approaches to lather the other's face, and the* CONFIDENCE MAN *repeatedly prevents him, at the last instant, with his gestures.)*

CONFIDENCE MAN: But, tell me, though I, too, clearly see the import of your notification, I do not, as yet, perceive the object. What is it?

BARBER: Now you speak a little in my line, sir. That notification I find very useful, sparing me much work which would not pay. Yes, I lost a good deal, off and on, before putting that up.

CONFIDENCE MAN: But what is its object? Surely, you don't mean to say, in so many words, that you have no confidence? For instance, now, suppose I say to you, "Barber, my dear barber, unhappily I have no small change by me to night, but shave me, and depend upon your money tomorrow"—suppose I should say that now, you would put trust in me, wouldn't you? You would have confidence?

BARBER: Being that it is you, sir, I won't answer that question. No need to.

CONFIDENCE MAN: Of course, of course—in that view. But, as a supposition—you would have confidence in me, wouldn't you?

BARBER: Why—yes, yes.

CONFIDENCE MAN: Then why that sign?

BARBER: Ah, sir, all people ain't like you.

CONFIDENCE MAN: All people ain't like me. Then I must be either better or worse than most people. Worse, you could not mean; no, barber, you could not mean that; hardly that. It remains, then, that you think me better than most people. But that I ain't vain enough to believe; though from vanity, I confess, I could never yet, by my best wrestlings, entirely free myself; nor, indeed, to be frank, am I at bottom overanxious to—this same vanity, barber, being so harmless, so useful, so comfortable, so pleasingly preposterous a passion.

BARBER: Very true, sir; and upon my honor, sir, you talk very well. But the lather is getting a little cold, sir.

CONFIDENCE MAN: Better cold lather, barber, than a cold heart. Why that cold sigh? Ah, I don't wonder you try to shirk the confession. You feel in your soul how ungenerous a hint is there. And yet, barber, now that I look into your eyes—which somehow speak to me of the mother that must have so often looked into them before me—I dare say, though you may not think it, that the spirit of that notification is not one with your nature. For look now, setting business views aside, regarding the thing in an abstract light; in short, supposing a case, barber; supposing, I say, you see a stranger, his face accidentally averted, but his visible part very respectable-looking; what now, barber—I put it to your conscience, to your charity—what would be your impression of that man, in a moral point of view? Being in a signal sense a stranger, would you for that signally set him down for a knave?

BARBER: Certainly not, sir; by no means.

CONFIDENCE MAN: You would upon the face of him—

BARBER: Hold, sir, nothing about the face; you remember, sir, that is out of sight.

CONFIDENCE MAN: I forgot that. Well then, you would, upon the back of him, conclude him to be, not improbably, some worthy sort of person; in short, an honest man; wouldn't you?

BARBER: Not unlikely I should, sir.

CONFIDENCE MAN: Well now—don't be so impatient with your brush, barber—suppose that honest man meet you by night in some dark corner of the boat where his face would still remain unseen, asking you to trust him for a shave—how then?

BARBER: Wouldn't trust him, sir.

CONFIDENCE MAN: But is not an honest man to be trusted?

BARBER: Why—why—yes, sir.

CONFIDENCE MAN: There! Don't you see, now?

BARBER: See what?

CONFIDENCE MAN: Why, you stand self-contradicted, barber; don't you?

BARBER: No.

CONFIDENCE MAN: Barber, the enemies of our race have a saying that insincerity is the most universal and inveterate vice of man—the lasting bar to real amelioration, whether of individuals or of the world. Don't you now, barber, by your stubborness on this occasion, give color to such a calumny?

BARBER: Hity-tity! Stubborness? Will you be shaved or won't you?

CONFIDENCE MAN: Barber, I will be shaved, and with pleasure; but pray, don't raise your voice that way. Why, now, if you go through life gritting your teeth in that fashion, what a comfortless time you will have.

BARBER: I take as much comfort in this world as you or any other man.

CONFIDENCE MAN: To resent the imputation of anything like unhappiness I have often observed to be peculiar to certain orders of men, just as to be indifferent to that imputation, from holding happiness but for a secondary good and inferior grace, I have observed to be equally peculiar to other kinds of men. Pray, barber, which think you is the superior creature?

BARBER: All this sort of talk is, as I told you once before, not in my line. In a few minutes I shall shut up this shop. Will you be shaved?

CONFIDENCE MAN: Shave away, barber. What hinders?

(The BARBER *begins to lather the* CONFIDENCE MAN's *face.)*

(Blackout.)

ACT SIXTEEN

(The scene is the same, except that the shaving is finished, and the CONFIDENCE MAN *is standing, with paper and pen in his hand.)*

CONFIDENCE MAN: First down with that sign, barber. Down with it.

(Reluctantly, the BARBER *takes down the NO TRUST sign.)*

CONFIDENCE MAN: Now, then, for the writing. Ah, I shall make a poor lawyer, I fear. Ain't used, you see, barber, to a business which, ignoring the principle of honor, holds no nail fast till clinched. *(He holds up the paper.)* Strange, barber, that such flimsy stuff as this should make such strong hawsers; vile hawsers, too. *(Pause.)* Barber, I won't put it in black and white. It were a reflection upon our joint honor. I will take your word and you shall take mine.

BARBER: But your memory may be none of the best, sir. Well for you, on your side, to have it in black and white, just for a memorandum like, you know.

CONFIDENCE MAN: That, indeed! Yes, and it would help your memory, too, wouldn't it, barber. Yours, on your side, being a little weak, too, I dare say. Ah, barber! how ingenious we human beings are; how kindly we reciprocate each other's little delicacies, don't we? What better proof, now that we are kind, considerate fellows, with responsive fellow-feelings—eh, barber? But to business. Let me see. What's your name, barber?

BARBER: William Cream, sir.

CONFIDENCE MAN: "AGREEMENT Between FRANK GOODMAN, Philanthropist, and Citizen of the World, and WILLIAM CREAM,

Barber of the Mississippi steamer, *Fidele*. The first hereby agrees to make good to the last any loss that may come from his trusting mankind, in the way of his vocation, for the residue of the present trip; PROVIDED that William Cream keep out of sight, for the given term, his notification of 'NO TRUST,' and by no other mode convey any, the least hint of intimation, tending to discourage men from soliciting trust from him, in the way of his vocation, for the time above specified; but on the contrary, he do, by all proper and reasonable words, gestures, manners, and looks evince a perfect confidence in all men, especially strangers; otherwise, this agreement to be void. Done, in good faith, this first day of April, eighteen hundred, etc. in the shop of William Cream, on board the said boat, *Fidele*." There barber, will that do?

BARBER: That will do. Only now put down your name.

(*Both sign, and the* CONFIDENCE MAN *hands the paper to the* BARBER.)

BARBER: Very good. And now nothing remaining but for me to receive the cash.

CONFIDENCE MAN: You speak of cash, barber; pray in what connection?

BARBER: Why in this paper here, you engage, sir, to insure me against a certain loss, and—

CONFIDENCE MAN: Certain? Is it so certain you are going to lose?

BARBER: Well, sir, what use your mere writing and saying you will insure me, unless beforehand you place in my hands a moneypledge, sufficient to that end?

CONFIDENCE MAN: I see; the material pledge.

BARBER: Yes, and I will put it low; say fifty dollars.

CONFIDENCE MAN: Now what sort of a bargaining is this? You, barber, for a given time engage to trust man, to put confidence in men, and, for your first step, make a demand implying no confidence in the very man you engage with. But fifty dollars is nothing, and I would let you have it cheerfully, only, I unfortunately happen to have but little change with me just now.

BARBER: But you have money in your trunk, though?

CONFIDENCE MAN: To be sure. But you see—in fact, barber, you must be consistent. No, I won't let you have the money now; I won't let you violate the inmost spirit of our contract, that way. So good night, and I will see you again.

BARBER: Stay, sir—the—the shaving.

CONFIDENCE MAN: Ah, I *did* forget that. But now that it strikes me, I shan't pay you at present. Look at your agreement; you must trust. Tut! against loss you hold the guarantee. Goodnight, my dear barber.

(The CONFIDENCE MAN *exits to his dressing room. The* BARBER *starts to follow him, then stops, stares at the paper. He suddenly crumples it, throws it away. He retrieves the* NO TRUST *sign, and hangs it in its original position.)*

(Blackout.)

EPILOGUE

In the darkness the crowd noise is heard, a low rumble of conversation. The lights come up, discovering the CONFIDENCE MAN *in his dressing room, applying makeup, and the blond* YOUNG MAN *in cream-colored suit and fleecy hat, carrying a number of signs. He makes his way, jostling and being jostled, through the imaginary crowd. He holds up a sign:* CHARITY THINKETH NO EVIL, *and is at once jostled by the crowd. He changes to another sign:* CHARITY SUFFERETH LONG, AND IS KIND. *Again he is jostled. He changes again:* CHARITY ENDURETH ALL THINGS, CHARITY BELIEVETH ALL THINGS; *and finally,* CHARITY NEVER FAILETH. *With this last one he is almost knocked off his feet. Enter the* BARBER, *carrying his chair and the* NO TRUST *sign. He hangs the latter on the wall, takes his razor from his pocket, and stands behind his chair. While this is going on, enter two* PORTERS *carrying a trunk. The crowd noises increase in volume. The* PORTERS *make their way through the crowd, shouting incoherent imprecations. They come to the blond* YOUNG MAN, *who is now fairly recovered, but has his back to them. They finally shove him aside, and, as he goes to his knees, he holds up a final sign:* DEAF MUTE. *The* PORTERS, *grumbling and mumbling, exit right with trunk. The* YOUNG MAN *huddles himself into a ball, as if to sleep, the* DEAF MUTE *sign displayed in front of him. While this is going on, enter the* CAPTAIN, *clowning about, mugging with the audience. He points to the three signs on the wall:* WANTED, FIDELE, *and* NO TRUST. *The* CONFIDENCE MAN *steps just outside his dressing room, dressed in gray. He holds up a sign:* APRIL FOOL'S DAY. *The* CAPTAIN *spies him, takes out his whistle, and blows a blast on it. The two salute each other, and the* CAPTAIN *capers out.*

(Blackout.)

THE PLAYERS

A DOCUMENTARY COMEDY-DRAMA

Scene One

(The stage is bare, except for four straight chairs, randomly placed, but all more or less facing front. Enter the NARRATOR, *stage-left. He is a tall, genial master-of-ceremonies type.)*

NARRATOR: Good evening. And welcome. Allow me to introduce the cast for our little play. *(He turns and faces left).* First . . .

(Enter JOHN BURROUGHS, *left.)*

NARRATOR: . . . the eminent American naturalist, bird-watcher, bird lover and all-around celebrant of Nature, John Burroughs—known familiarly as John O'Birds.

*(*BURROUGHS *is of medium build, with an earnest expression, seldom smiling. As he enters, he is busy putting in place and adjusting a set of false whiskers, giving him a full gray beard. He and the* NARRATOR *nod to each other as* BURROUGHS *crosses and sits in the chair farthest right.)*

NARRATOR *(facing left again)*: A man known to all of us—he needs no introduction—the good gray poet, Walt Whitman.

(Enter WHITMAN, *left. Like* BURROUGHS, *he is putting on and adjusting a set of false whiskers, as he acknowledges the* NARRATOR, *and saunters to the chair next to* BURROUGHS.*)*
NARRATOR: May I introduce to you now a man with a brief but meteoric career, erstwhile major league pitcher Mark "The Bird" Fidrych?

(Enter FIDRYCH, *left. He carries a can of beer in one hand and a baseball in the other. Nodding rather insolently to the* NARRATOR, *he slouches to the chair next to* BURROUGHS. *Throughout the scene, he may be seen from time to time sipping his beer and/or tossing and catching the baseball.)*

NARRATOR: And finally, a colorful character in his own right, former major league umpire Ron Luciano.

(Enter LUCIANO, *left. He is tall and heavyset, but moves rapidly and gracefully, and seems to be perpetually smiling. He strides to the* NARRATOR *and shakes his hand, and then does the same with the other characters, in order, before taking the final seat. Throughout the play the* NARRATOR *moves about freely, but he generally works up-stage.)*

NARRATOR: Let us turn first to John Burroughs—John O'Birds. Born early April, early spring time, the year 1837, on a hard-scrabble farm in the Catskills . . .

BURROUGHS: Take the farm-boy out of my books and you have robbed them of something vital!

NARRATOR: . . . he grew up on intimate terms with an America long vanished.

BURROUGHS: In my boyhood the vast armies of the passenger pigeons were one of the most notable spring tokens. Often late in March, or early in April, the naked beechwoods would suddenly become blue with them, and vocal with their soft childlike call; or all day the sky would be streaked with the long lines or dense masses of the moving armies. What man now in his old age who witnessed in youth that spring or fall festival and migration of the passenger pigeons would not hail it as one of the gladdest hours of his life if he could be permitted to witness it once more? It was such a spectacle of bounty, of joyous, copious animal life, of fertility in the air and in the wilderness, as to make the heart glad. I have seen the fields and woods fairly inundated for a day or two with these fluttering, piping, blue-and-white hosts. The very air at times seemed suddenly to turn to pigeons.

NARRATOR: The passenger pigeon, of whose millions scarce man or woman alive today can remember a single bird.

BURROUGHS: The birds have always meant much to me; as a farm-boy they were like a golden thread that knit the seasons together.

NARRATOR: Turning now to the good gray poet, Walt Whitman . . .

WHITMAN: I am stuccoed with birds and quadrupeds all over.

BURROUGHS: It might almost be said that the birds are all birds of the poets and no one else, because it is only the poetical temperament that responds to them.

NARRATOR: Whitman's brother George reported that, as a young man, Walt "was inclined toward vigorous exercise and play."

BURROUGHS: The songbirds might all have been brooded and hatched in the human heart. Nearly the whole gamut of human passion and emotion is expressed in their varied songs.

WHITMAN: In fibre, muscle, organically: in build, arm, leg, chest, belly—in physical equipment—I started superbly—no one more so—more gifted, blessed.

BURROUGHS: The mere studying of the birds, seeking more knowledge of them is not enough. You must live with the birds, have daily and seasonal associations with them. Then they are a part of your life, and help give tone and color to your day.

NARRATOR: Peter Doyle reported the Young Walt to be "an athlete —great, great." And Brother George said he was "an old-fashioned ball-player and entered a game heartily enough."

(FIDRYCH *for the first time emerges from his ball-and-beer stupor, and seems to pay attention. And* LUCIANO *fairly leaps from his seat, raises his arms enthusiastically, smiles ever more broadly.)*

WHITMAN: I am feeling hearty and in good spirits—go around more than usual—go to such doings as base-ball matches.

BURROUGHS *(looking disdainfully at others)*: There seems to be a community of mind among birds that there is not among men.

WHITMAN: Thousands go to see them play.

BURROUGHS: People who have not made friends with the birds do not know how much they miss.

WHITMAN: The game played yesterday afternoon between the Atlantic and Putnam clubs, on the grounds of the latter Club, was one of the finest and most exciting games we ever witnessed. The Atlantic beat their opponents by four runs, but the general opinion was that the defeat was as much the result of accident as of superior playing. On the fourth innings the Putnams made several very loose plays, and allowed their opponents to score nine runs . . .

BURROUGHS: When one is fortunate enough to see a line of swans etched upon the sky near sunset, a mile or more high, one has seen something he will not soon forget.

WHITMAN: In our sundown perambulations, of late, through the outer parts of Brooklyn, we have observed several parties of youngsters playing "base," a certain game of ball. We wish such sights were more common among us.

BURROUGHS: The observer of bird-life in the open has heaven and earth thrown in.

WHITMAN: Has God made this beautiful earth—the sun to shine— all the sweet influences of nature to operate—and planted in man a wish for their delights and all for nothing? Let us go forth awhile, and get better air in our lungs. Let us leave our close rooms, and the dust and corruption of stagnant places, and taste some of the good things Providence has scattered around us so liberally.

BURROUGHS: One sees the passing bird procession in his own grounds and neighborhood without pausing to think that in every man's grounds and in every neighborhood throughout the State, and throughout a long, broad belt of States, about several millions of homes, and over several millions of farms, the same flood tide of bird-life is creeping and eddying or sweeping over the land.

WHITMAN: Base-ball is our game: the American game: I connect it with our national character. Sports take people out of doors, get them filled with oxygen—generate some of the brutal customs (so-called brutal customs) which, after all, tend to habituate people to a necessary physical stoicism. We are some ways a dyspeptic, nervous set: anything which will repair such losses may be regarded as a blessing to the race.

BURROUGHS: Shall I ever again be able to hear the song of the oriole without being pierced through and through?

WHITMAN *(ripping off his whiskers)*: We want to go out and howl, swear, jump, wrestle, even fight, if only by doing so we may improve the guts of the people: the guts, vile as guts are, divine as guts are!

BURROUGHS: The live bird is a fellow passenger; we are making the voyage together, and there is a sympathy between us.

WHITMAN: The game of ball is glorious!

BURROUGHS: Just think of it! While the Battle of Gettysburg was being fought, I was in the woods, studying the birds!

WHITMAN: That's beautiful: the hurrah game! . . . America's game: has the snap, go, fling, of the American atmosphere . . .

BURROUGHS: I was pursuing the birds in 1864 when our soldiers were dying in the Battle of the Wilderness!

WHITMAN: Enthusiasm: without that what is a man?

BURROUGHS: To take the birds out of my life would be like lopping off so many branches from the tree: there is so much less surface of leafage to absorb the sunlight and bring my spirits in contact with the vital currents.

WHITMAN: Cheer! Cheer! Is there anything better in this world anywhere than cheer—just cheer? Any religion better?—any art? Just cheer?

BURROUGHS: How much more easily and surely knowledge comes through sympathy than through the knowing faculties! It is as if I had imbibed my knowledge of the birds through the pores of my skin, through the air I have breathed, through the soles of my feet, through the twinkle of the leaves, and the glint of the waters. I have gone a-fishing, and read their secrets out of the corners of my eyes. I have lounged under a tree, and the book of their lives has been opened to me. I have hoed in my garden, and read the histories they write in the air. Studied the birds? No, I have played with them, camped with them, gone berrying with them, summered and wintered with them, and my knowledge of them has filtered into my mind almost unconsciously.

(WHITMAN *restores his whiskers.*)

NARRATOR: When Whitman was living in Camden, late in life, a good friend named Tom Harned came to visit him, and Harned had just been to a baseball game.

(*During the following,* FIDRYCH *sets down his beer, rises from the chair, and haltingly mimes the action described.* LUCIANO *does a limited version of the same, without rising.*)

WHITMAN (*addressing* NARRATOR): Tell me, Tom—I want to ask you a question: in base-ball is it the rule that the fellow pitching the ball aims to pitch it in such a way the batter cannot hit it? Gives it a twist—what not—so it slides off, or won't be struck fairly?

NARRATOR: Harned affirmed that this indeed was the case.

WHITMAN: Eh? That's the rule then, is it? I thought something of the kind—I read the papers about it—it seemed to indicate that there.

NARRATOR: The original rule forbade the throwing of the ball: instead, the ball had to be pitched underhand, smoothly, so that the batter could hit it. This rule had been refined over the years, first requiring that the hand not be raised above the hip, then requiring only that the hand pass below the hip as the ball was pitched, then only below the waist, then the shoulder (allowing for sidearm pitching). Originally, then, the pitcher's function was simply to put the ball in play by allowing the hitter to hit it; one player usually pitched all the games. But as the skills of the players became more refined, the pitcher's role became more strategic. In 1884 the National League removed all restrictions on a pitcher's delivery. The curve ball now became a requisite skill.

WHITMAN: I have made it a point to put the same question to several fellows lately. There certainly seems no doubt but that your version is right, for that is the version everyone gives me.

NARRATOR: Whitman was not impressed with this new skill and saw the rule change as emblematic of the deception and lack of openness he saw creeping everywhere into America.

WHITMAN: The wolf, the snake, the cur, the sneak all seem entered into the modern sportsman—I should call it everything that is damnable!

(FIDRYCH *tosses and catches the ball, smiles at* WHITMAN, *and sits down.)*

BURROUGHS: O to share the great, sunny, joyous life of the earth!

NARRATOR: The Baltimore Orioles, the St. Louis Cardinals, the Toronto Blue Jays . . .

WHITMAN: You must not know too much, or be too precise or scientific about birds.

NARRATOR: One day a benighted Red Sox outfielder let an easy fly ball fall for a double when, instead of chasing the ball, he pursued a pigeon . . .

WHITMAN: A certain free margin, and even vagueness, helps your enjoyment . . .

NARRATOR: And Casey Stengel once emerged from the dugout, bowed to the crowd, doffed his cap—and out flew a sparrow.

BURROUGHS: To be as happy as the birds are!

(FIDRYCH *tosses the ball high in the air.* LUCIANO *leaps from his chair, and gives an exaggerated, flamboyant version of the "out" sign.* FIDRYCH *catches the ball.*)

(*Blackout.*)

Scene Two

(*The four actors and* NARRATOR *are discovered, as at the end of Scene One.* FIDRYCH *and* LUCIANO, *however, have their backs turned to the audience.* BURROUGHS *suddenly leaps from his chair, as though shot from a gun.*)

BURROUGHS: I would gladly chant a paean for the world as I find it. What a mighty interesting place to live in!

(FIDRYCH *and* LUCIANO *turn their heads sharply, and briefly, to stare at* BURROUGHS.)

BURROUGHS: I am in love with this world: by my constitution I have nestled lovingly in it. It has been home. It has been my point of outlook into the universe. I have not bruised myself against it, nor tried to use it ignobly. I have tilled its soil, I have gathered its harvests. I have waited upon its seasons, and always have I reaped what I have sown. While I delved I did not lose sight of the sky overhead. While I gathered its bread and meat for my body, I did not neglect to gather its bread and meat for my soul. I have climbed its mountains, roamed its forests, sailed its waters, crossed its deserts, felt the sting of its frosts, the oppression of its heats, the drench of its rains, the fury of its winds, and always have beauty and joy waited upon my goings and comings. *(Pause.)* The rind of the earth, of this round and delicious globe which has hung so long ripening in the sun, must be sweet. *(Pause.)* The air is full these days of all sweet meadow and woodland smells. The earth seems good enough to eat! *(Pause. He turns and addresses* WHITMAN.*)* Who before Whitman ever drew his poetic, his aesthetic, and ethical standards from the earth, from the sexuality, from the impartiality of the earth, or his laws of creating from the earth? It was my rare good fortune to know this quiet, sympathetic, tolerant man for more than thirty years, and to walk or saunter with him at all seasons and hours. Often at night he would stop and gaze long and silently at the stars, and resume his walk. Whitman opens the doors, and opens them wide . . . he has the quality of things in the open air, the quality of the unhoused, the untamed, the elemental . . . rankly common, like freckles and sweat.

WHITMAN: John's power is in his simplicity. He writes well because he does not try to write.

BURROUGHS: I have studied him as I have studied the birds.

WHITMAN: John is a wood wizard: things come out of their holes —present themselves—ask for orders—when John goes into the woods.

BURROUGHS: It was a poet's life from first to last—free, unhampered, unworldly, unconventional, picturesque, simple, untouched by the craze of money-getting, unselfish, devoted to others, and was, on the whole, joyfully and contentedly lived. It was a pleased and interested saunter through the world—no hurry, no fever, no strife: hence no bitterness, no depletion, no wasted energies.

NARRATOR: Emerson said of Walt, "Unto us a man is born." And Lincoln said, "Well, he looks like a man."

BURROUGHS: No great poet ever appeared except from a race of good fighters, good eaters, good sleepers, good breeders.

WHITMAN: John never slushes . . .

BURROUGHS: We have swarms of little poetlings, producing swarms of soft and sickly little rhymelets.

WHITMAN: Human thought, poetry or melody, must have dim escapes and outlets—must possess a certain fluid, aerial character, akin to space itself.

BURROUGHS: *Leaves of Grass* requires a large perspective, you must not get your face too near the book.

WHITMAN: Most literary men, as you know, are the kind of men a hearty man would not go far to see.

BURROUGHS: Whitman was afraid of what he called "the beauty disease."

WHITMAN: A literary class in America always strikes me with a laugh or with nausea . . .

BURROUGHS: Most authors are parks, handsomely laid out and fenced in, with signs posted to KEEP OFF THE GRASS.

WHITMAN: Literary men learn so little from life—borrow so much from the borrowers.

BURROUGHS: It has been charged by an unfriendly critic that he strikes lower than the intellect.

NARRATOR: Later, Emerson changed his mind, described Walt as "half song thrush and half alligator."

BURROUGHS: Not withstanding the beauty and expressiveness of his eyes, I occasionally see something in them as he bends them upon me, that almost makes me draw back. I cannot explain it—whether it is more, or less, than human. It is as if the Earth looked at me—dumb, yearning, relentless, immodest, unhuman. If the impersonal elements and forces were concentrated in an eye, that would be it. It is not piercing, but absorbing and devouring—the pupil expanded, the lid slightly drooping, and the eye set and fixed. *(Pause.)* I loved him as I never loved any man. I owe more to him than to any other man in the world. He brooded me. *(Pause.)* I have come, not only to love him as a friend, but to look to him as the greatest, sweetest soul I have yet met in this world.

*(*BURROUGHS *becomes more nervous, agitated. He moves about abruptly, hesitates between sentences.)*

BURROUGHS: There is something grainy and saline in him. He always had the look of a man who had just taken a bath. The skin was light and clear, and the blood well to the surface. His body, as I once noticed when we were bathing in the surf, had a peculiar fresh bloom and finesse and delicacy of texture.

WHITMAN: To be surrounded by beautiful, curious, breathing, laughing flesh is enough . . .

BURROUGHS: He bathed today while I was there—such a handsome body, and such delicate, rosy flesh as I never saw before. I told him he looked good enough to eat.
WHITMAN: I do not ask any more delight; I swim in it, as in a sea.

BURROUGHS: I have been much with Walt. Have even slept with him. I love him very much. The more I see and talk with him, the greater he becomes to me. He is as vast as the earth . . . I saw a soldier the other day stop on the street and kiss him. He kisses me as if I were a girl. There was something fine, delicate, womanly in him. *(Pause.)* Did I ever tell you that Oscar Wilde came here once to see me? A splendid talker, and a handsome man, but a voluptuary. As he walked from you, there was something in the motion of his hips and back that was disagreeable.

(FIDRYCH *tosses the ball, and catches it.*)

(*Blackout.*)

Scene Three

(*The setting is the same, except that* WHITMAN *and* BURROUGHS *have turned their backs, and* FIDRYCH *and* LUCIANO *now face the audience.* LUCIANO *suddenly jumps from his seat. During the following speech he is all over the stage, making the most out of what little he has to say.*)

LUCIANO: Baseball changed dramatically from the time I came up to the major leagues in 1969 . . . When I started, it was played by nine tough competitors, on grass, in graceful ballparks. But while I was busy trying to answer the daily "Quiz O-Gram" on the exploding scoreboard—Question: Who in the ballpark today has played for every team in the American League? Answer: the organist—a revolution was taking place around me. By the time I hung up my whisk broom there were ten men on each side, the game was being played indoors, on plastic, and I had to spend half my time watching out for a man dressed in a chicken suit who kept trying to kiss me.

(*During the following dialogue,* FIDRYCH *is alternately up and down, in and out of his seat, as the mood strikes.* LUCIANO *remains standing, a repressed listener.*)

NARRATOR: The coach at Bristol, Jeff Hogan, was he the first person who called you Bird?

FIDRYCH: Yeah. Yeah, that was the first day.

NARRATOR: The first day you were there?

FIDRYCH: No, the first day in spring training, down in Lakeland, Florida. Like, we went down there for a week, then we split for

Bristol. I just ran out on the field—I got my uniform on. I had my white shoes on, and I had my Spag Special glove, y'know. And all these other guys, they had these other things. And I just—I just didn't *buy* equipment, man! I didn't know what kind of equipment to have.

NARRATOR: What kind of glove did you have?

FIDRYCH: Just a Spag Special glove. Spalding, y'know? It was just—I just came with what I had. What I was playing with before. And like, they said, Hey, you can't have white spikes. You can get new ones now. I said, What the hell, where am I gonna get the money? They said, Spend some of the bonus money we hit you with! I go, How can I spend that bonus, you didn't *give* me anything. They hit me with that, y'know? I go, Holy shit, y'know?

(On the word "shit" WHITMAN *and* BURROUGHS *jump in their chairs, and gradually settle back. They jump a little less, and recover, with each repetition of the word.)*

FIDRYCH *(continuing)*: I had to pay for my schoolin', y'know? I mean, Worcester Academy was two thousand bucks. So I gave my dad half of it. And then I got a thousand of it—I bought a stereo system. I had nothin' else left, and I had other bills to pay. Spend that bonus, they're tryin' to hit me with! Shit! Give me forty grand, and I mighta spent my bonus. And I mighta come here with a new glove and all that shit. Right?

NARRATOR: Did you get any new equipment somehow?

FIDRYCH: I lucked out. The week we were there, some little kids broke into the locker room. They stole the equipment! They stole my glove and spikes! So I got new ones—I lucked out.

NARRATOR: You got 'em replaced.

FIDRYCH: Yeah—I actually lucked out. So it was neat, y'know?

NARRATOR: So how come Jeff calls you . . .

FIDRYCH: I just come out on the field and he goes, Bird. And I just turn around. And he goes, that's your nickname I gave you. And, you know, he told me—he goes, If you stick in baseball, that name's gonna stick with you. And you watch what that name's gonna be. And it was weird. And I said, What did you call me that for? And he said, You look like that goofy bird on *Sesame Street*. And I said, Whaddaya mean? He goes, Hey, you just look like the bird on *Sesame Street*. So that's your nickname. I can't—Fidrych is too hard to, y'know, *say*.

NARRATOR: Had you ever seen *Sesame Street?*

FIDRYCH: Huh? Yeah, when I was a kid. My little sister used to watch it once in a while. But it was weird. Like, no one even thought about it, all through the minors. They didn't even talk about it. They just called me Bird, they didn't think anything of it. And you go, *voom*! You hit the majors, man, it's a whole different page. The page just folded right over. The minor leagues is gone, and now—this is what happened.

NARRATOR: And all of a sudden the name comes back, right?

FIDRYCH: Yeah.

NARRATOR: That *is* weird.

FIDRYCH: I mean, y'know, everyone knew me through the ball team as Bird. But *they*—they didn't think it was no big deal.

NARRATOR: They didn't think it was a big deal then, because you weren't a big deal. Things are different now.

FIDRYCH: But I'll clue ya, I don't goof around half as much as I used to.

NARRATOR: You mean in the minors?

FIDRYCH: Yeah. I used to goof around more than I do in the majors. But goofin' around in the majors is different.

NARRATOR: Probably more fun.

FIDRYCH: Yeah. It's more fun in the majors.

NARRATOR: You don't sound too convinced!

FIDRYCH: I mean, but—in the minors, I mean, like goofin' around in this hotel room. Like when I threw that water out. Someone mighta been *down* there. Y'know?

NARRATOR: Oh, when you threw that ice water out?

FIDRYCH: Yeah.

NARRATOR: What's down there, anyway? Just more Hilton?

FIDRYCH: Nothin', but just—but a ceiling. But that don't mean—but that's what we woulda done. Y'know? Or you destroy a guy's room, and you just walk out and laugh your head off, there's just weird things like that. You did more—well, what they'd call, what they'd classify as *immature* things, right? But really they're not immature things, 'cause they *teach* you, y'know?

NARRATOR: Well, that's also called havin' a good time.

FIDRYCH: Yeah. Here you are, makin' five hundred bucks a month—gettin' this paycheck that you never even *thought* of seein', and livin' for a hundred and fifty bucks a month, because this place only cost you a hundred that you're stayin' at, I mean, y'know, and you just—it was *neat*. I had all the beer money I wanted, and I had all my food money. And I was happy, y'know?

NARRATOR: Were any of those guys making big money down at Bristol? The guys who got big bonuses?

FIDRYCH: Oh, you don't! Minor league guys, your first year you all make the same. Five hundred bucks a month. And that's it, y'know? No big deal.

(Blackout.)

Scene Four

*(*FIDRYCH *and* LUCIANO *are seated, with their backs turned.* WHITMAN *is seated, facing the audience, comfortably slumped in his chair, and* BURROUGHS *is standing, facing* WHITMAN. *The* NARRATOR *remains to one side.)*

BURROUGHS: Find Walt sitting in a chair with a long gray-bearded goatskin behind him, a shawl pinned about him, and a chaos of paper, letters, books, mss., and so on, at his feet and reaching far out into the room. Never saw such confusion and litter—bundles of letters, bundles of newspapers, cuttings, magazines, a cushion or two, footrests, books opened and turned down, dust, and above all the grand, serene face of the poet.
WHITMAN: This room is full of lost and found.

*(*BURROUGHS *becomes restless, agitated, and for the remainder of the scene he moves about the stage, from one part to another.)*

BURROUGHS: I hope you are still mending, Walt. I am almost certain you eat too heartily and make too much blood and fat . . .

WHITMAN *(his voice becoming more feeble)*: I really think John thinks I am mostly or mainly the cause of my own ill health. *(Pause.)* John used to be so equable, quiet, buoyant, happy: so like a strong helpful stream of water: all eyes for joyous reassurances— a grown man with a boy's soul.

*(*FIDRYCH *tosses the ball and catches it.)*

WHITMAN *(continuing)*: Now much of that beautiful John is gone: I could not tell why. He was so wise, so gay, though never boisterous, in those times. Why is John's faith less seaworthy than it was then? The material must all be there still—all of it. Why does he put it aside—refuse to make use of it? *(Pause.)* I don't know about John—he stands aloof so much of the time: I have asked myself whether this betokens any change of feeling: I suppose it don't. But he don't come around much—he seems to avoid visiting me. I miss him a lot.

BURROUGHS *(in anguish)*: Without death and decay, how could life go on?

WHITMAN *(more feebly)*: From the medical point of view they tell me I'm getting on all right, but from the point of view of my own comfort I'm in a pretty boggy condition indeed. But so the doctor feels all right about it I don't suppose it matters what I feel, I like to see the doctors comfortable, anyway.

BURROUGHS *(acting out what follows)*: In the evening see Walt for a moment. He presses my hand long and tenderly; we kiss and part, probably for the last time. I think he has in his own mind given up the fight, and awaits the end.

WHITMAN *(a sudden burst of vitality)*: The only critical doubt I ever have about John is that sometimes I feel as if I would like to poke him up with a stick, or something to get him mad; his writing sometimes seems to go to sleep.

BURROUGHS: Full of sad thoughts about Walt Whitman; expect each day to hear of his death, and trying to taste the bitter cup in advance, so as to be used to it when it really comes. How life will seem to me with Whitman gone, I cannot imagine. He is my larger, greater, earlier self. No man alive seems quite so near to me.

WHITMAN *(clutching his head in his hands)*: The trouble is sore and broken brain . . . Today my head *thicks* . . . *(He slumps forward, and freezes.)*

BURROUGHS: Black crepe on Walt's door-bell, shutters closed.

(BURROUGHS *slumps to his knees, grasps his head in his hands, his shoulders shaking.)*

(Blackout.)

Scene Five

(FIDRYCH *and* LUCIANO *sit with their backs to the audience,* WHITMAN *is slumped in his chair, and motionless. The* NARRATOR *and* BURROUGHS *are standing. Throughout the scene* BURROUGHS *is extremely agitated, flitting from one part of the stage to another like a scared rabbit.)*

BURROUGHS: To be in a house where there is a piano is torture to me. Strange how things came to be invented! My God, isn't it awful! The greatest players give me the shivers, and the greater they are, the more they claw and paw at it. It's the devil's own invention. *(Pause.)* I do not favor the typewriter. It would not do for me. The machine would get into the writing. They are part of our mechanical age and I hate 'em. Your writing will lose its freshness and individuality, if you compose on a machine. I can only think with a pen in my hand. *(Pause.)* I had a surprising letter. Mr. Ford, of automobile fame, is a great admirer of my books—says there are few persons in the world who have given him the pleasure I have. He wants to do something for me—he wants to present me with a Ford automobile all complete, and send a man to teach Julian how to run it. His sole motive is his admiration for me and my work—there shall be no publicity in connection with it. I am embarrassed by his offer. What shall I do? I want the machine, but how can I accept such a gift from a stranger, and keep my self-respect? *(Pause.)* I wrote back: "If it would please Mr. Ford to present me with one of his cars, it would please me to accept the car." *(Pause.)* Ran the car yesterday to Port Ewen, and then came home and ran it into the locust tree just outside our gates.

Never look back while driving your car! . . . the little beast sprang for that tree like a squirrel. Broke or bent his forward spring so we can't crank her. *(Pause.)* We have just taken a run of a few miles in the car. The blind, desperate thing still scares me. How ready it is to take to the ditch, or a tree or a fence! *(Pause.)* In driving the car in the old barn, I get rattled and let it run wild; it bursts through the side of the barn like an explosion. There is a great splintering and rattling of boards and timbers, and the car stops with its forward axle hanging out over a drop of fifteen feet. *(Pause.)* I barely missed ending my days last spring. My Ford overturned up here on our fine macadam road and came down on top of me. It broke the bone in my arm close to the shoulder. The weight of the car pressed against my chest, and I couldn't speak. It was very fortunate that the car was no heavier. If you are going to be wrecked in an automobile choose a Ford every time. *(Pause.)* August 29 came Edison and his party to take me with them on a motor-trip. They camped in my orchard, an unwonted sight—a camper's extemporized village under my old apple trees— four tents, a large dining-tent, and at night electric lights. *(Pause.)* I am writing this on my knee beside the camp fire at 7:30, while breakfast is being got ready. Mr. Ford is standing with his back to the fire on the other side, talking with a caller. Mr. Firestone is warming his hands over the coals. Edison is not up yet. *(Pause.)* We have two big cars, two Fords, and two trucks with supplies and camp equipage—too much of everything.

NARRATOR: A Japanese chef headed the kitchen staff. Even lunches under the trees were sumptuous repasts served on white linen with solid silverware. The tents were equipped with electric lights. Only flush toilets were lacking.

*(*BURROUGHS *scurries about, as though looking for an outhouse.)*

BURROUGHS: The luxuries of the Waldorf-Astoria on wheels . . .

NARRATOR: The caravan consisted of several cars: Harvey Firestone and his twenty-one year-old son in a Pierce-Arrow: Edison, who had a Cadillac, riding with Ford in his Cadillac touring car most of the time: a Ford fitted out as a kitchen; a Cadillac truck for camping equipment: two Packards, and an Edison Simplex. There were cooks, chauffeurs, and photographers, in the party. Each camper slept in his own ten-by-ten tent complete with floor, electricity, screens, folding cot, mattress, blankets, sheets, pillows, and name plate on the outside flap. There was a special kitchen tent with refrigerator and a dining tent with a table that seated twenty. Maybe because their equipment was so elaborate, no one wore casual clothes; each man appeared at breakfast every morning in shirt and tie.

BURROUGHS: Stay in Washington until 30th, see old friends, drive about in a car Mr. Ford provides. Meet President Wilson. Dine out nine days in succession. *(Pause.)* February 25 Here at Ft. Myers, Florida, with the Edisons and the Fords. *(Pause.)* Leave at noon with Mr. Ford on his private car for the Southern cruise.

NARRATOR: It was supposedly a time of quiet in the country, but every move the campers made was documented by newsmen and photographers. Almost every movie theatre in the country featured newsreels of Ford, Edison, Firestone, and Burroughs engaging in high-kicking, sprinting, tree-chopping, and tree-climbing contests. Newspaper headlines blazoned, "Million of Dollars Worth of Brains Off on a Vacation," or "Genius to Sleep Under the Stars."

BURROUGHS: The magazine writer has a new problem—how to address himself to the moving-picture brain—the brain that does not want to read or think, but only to use its eager shallow eyes—eyes that prefer the shadows and ghosts of people flitting around the stage than to see the real flesh and blood. How an audible dialogue would tire them—it might compel them to use their minds a little—horrible thought! For my own part, I am sure I cannot interest this moving-picture brain, and do not want to. It is the shallowest brain that has yet appeared in the world. What is to be the upshot of this craze over this mere wash of reality which the Movies (horrible word!) offer our young people? *(Pause.)* Mr. Ford attributes all evil to the Jews or the Jewish capitalists—the

Jews caused the war, the Jews caused the outbreak of thieving and robbery all over the country, the Jews caused the inefficiency of the Navy . . . *(Pause.)* His interest in birds is keen and his knowledge considerable. A lovable man.

(Blackout.)

Scene Six

*(*WHITMAN *faces front, but is slumped in his chair motionless.* BURROUGHS *has his back turned, in his chair.* LUCIANO *and* FIDRYCH *are seated, facing front.)*

LUCIANO: Although I was promoted to the major leagues with eleven other umpires, it did not take me long to become well-known to all the veteran umpires and many fans. I wasn't the best young umpire in the group, or the brightest, or even the most handsome.
*(*LUCIANO *rises, faces left, his eyes raised to the horizon.)*

LUCIANO: But I was the only bird-watcher.

*(*BURROUGHS *turns in his chair, faces* LUCIANO, *suddenly interested in him.)*

LUCIANO *(continuing)*: For some reason people find it strange that a man my size should enjoy watching birds. I suppose they think I should be crushing them instead, but as soon as I realized other people thought it was funny, I stopped telling anyone about it. I've hunted all my life. I started watching birds because I wanted to know what it was I had just missed with my gun. Actually the experiences are quite different. Hunting involves other people, or a dog, while birding is a solitary experience. I go by myself deep into the woods, and listen to the silence, and think, and watch the beauty of nature. Then I'm able to go back to the ballpark. I've been doing it for many years. In the minor leagues, if I had a rough game and needed to unwind, I'd get up at 4:00 A.M. and drive to the nearest woods and take a long walk. I'd usually be back in my hotel room and asleep before my partner was awake, but if he did wake up and ask me where I'd been, I'd just wink at him and he'd wink back knowingly and I never had to explain. I've charted over 275 different birds. The rarest is a monk parrot, a tropical bird never seen in the north. After I spotted it I went home to try to figure out what it was, and then had a representative of the Audubon Society come out and verify it for me. Frank Umont was the man who discovered my secret. We roomed together my first year in the majors. Early one morning, while we were in Washington, D.C., I got up and drove to Virginia for a long walk. By the time I got back Frank was out of the room and I made the incredible mistake of falling asleep without putting away my binoculars.

(FIDRYCH *suddenly comes to life, tossing the ball, grinning, leering.*)

LUCIANO: Binoculars were then popular with baseball players who used them for stealing opponent's signs during games and peering through hotel windows between games. Actually no one was ever known to steal a sign. So when Umont walked into our room and found my binoculars on the dresser he assumed he had caught me with the high-powered evidence. I tried to convince him I was not a Peeping Tom.

NARRATOR: Then what are these for?

LUCIANO (*standing proud, erect*): Bird Watching.

(*The* NARRATOR *almost doubles up in laughter. He falls into* LUCIANO'*s chair.* LUCIANO *gazes into the distance, his eyes ecstatic. He remains thus for the rest of the scene, and* BURROUGHS'*s attention remains fixed on him. The* NARRATOR *regains his composure, turns to* FIDRYCH.*)

NARRATOR: So what'd you think of the image that got created of you in the media by that book and all the other stuff people wrote?

Like some funny cartoon character—this flaky, nutty guy who talks to baseballs?

FIDRYCH (*rising*): I ain't flaky, nutty, I just—that's just the way I went through the game. Like I told you. I never knew anything about it, until they started mentionin' it. Y'know? Like—this guy's talkin' to baseballs. And then they say, Did you do it in Little League? I look back to Little League—did I do it? I seriously look back. And I say, Dad, did I do it? And he says, Yeah, you did it before. I go, Wow, I did? Y'know? Now they're startin' to make me think, What did I do? Y'know? But yet I was doin' it all along and didn't know it.

NARRATOR: Well, it isn't something you can consciously think about. Like saying, Today I'll go out and I'll talk to this baseball.

FIDRYCH: Hey, there's been many games that I've gone out and I haven't talked to the baseball. If you're gettin' down to talkin' to baseballs—in the beginning I was just pitchin', and I was feelin' good, and I was pitchin'. Y'know, it was just the first game I started in baseball. The second game, I was still talkin' to the base-ball, but maybe not as much. But still I was doin' it. And every game I do it. It just depends what kind of atmosphere I'm in when I'm pitchin' that game that you're gonna get into. It's just like, any kind of time you do work—if you're goin' good, you're gonna stay in that atmosphere, right? And then somethin' different comes up, and you're still doin' all right. Y'know? Some days you don't talk, some days you do. Like after you lose a game, they say, I don't think you talked to the baseball that much! Y'know? Whaddaya mean? I did the exact same things as I did when I went there the first time, as I did the second time. And you just—you just say, Well, maybe I should have talked more. And then you say, *Whoa*, wait a minute, this guy's tellin' me I didn't *do* it, now. Then you go, *Whoa*. You say, Wait, wait, I was out there. I did what I hadda do. I didn't win but I still did the same things I did the first time out, y'know? But just the breaks went the other way! That's normal! But just because this guy said, maybe in the third inning you didn't talk hard—you didn't say three words to the ball. Where you might not have talked to it, you might have just pitched and didn't say a thing—you just, y'know, walked around and didn't do nothin'. You were just thinkin' in your head. But then when it got down to the bare facts of bein' more explosive—y'know, to blow up a little bit more—*that's* when you started blowin' up at yourself—and *voom*, they started talkin' about the ball. But it's— hey, third inning, if I didn't give up any runs, they wouldn't have said it then. They say, you gave up two runs, but you weren't talkin' to the ball. If you were talkin' to the ball you wouldn't have gave up the runs. And then you start lookin' you start thinkin' about a person then, y'know?

NARRATOR (*rising, addressing audience*): On nights or days when he was pitching on the road, opposing players would scatter birdseed on the pitcher's mound.

(*The* NARRATOR *and all actors freeze—except* WHITMAN. WHITMAN *slowly comes to life, raising his head, shifting in his chair. He removes his false whiskers, painstakingly gets to his feet, ambles slowly downstage, and addresses the audience.*)

WHITMAN: I have always had a good deal to do with actors; met many, high and low; they are gassy; you'll have to beware of that.

(WHITMAN *winks.*)

(*Blackout.*)

Acknowledgments & Bibliography

ACKNOWLEDGMENTS

The text of *An American Chronicle* is excerpted from the following books by Paul Metcalf: *Will West*, *Genoa*, *Apalache*, and *Waters of Potowmack*.

Excerpts in *The Players* from Mark Fidrych and Tom Clark, *No Big Deal* (Lippincott Co., 1977) are reprinted with the permission of the authors.

Excerpts in *The Players* from Ron Luciano and David Fisher, *The Umpire Strikes Back* (Bantam, 1982) are reprinted with the permission of the authors under the following conditions:

1) credit must also be acknowledged in all programs of licensed performances of the play,

2) the material can be used only in full performances of the play and not in any other context, and

3) the rights include only the written text and staged performances of the play. Film, taped, or recorded versions of the play for which compensation is paid are specifically excluded, as are all forms other than those identified.

The Players was first published in the special Paul Metcalf edition of *SAGETRIEB*, Volume 5, No. 3 (Winter 1986).

BIBLIOGRAPHY

With the exception of some transitional lines given to the Narrator, all the words spoken in *The Players* were actually spoken or written by the characters to whom they are ascribed. Following are the sources:

Barrus, Clara. *The Life and Letters of John Burroughs.* Boston and New York, 1925.

———. *Whitman and Burroughs: Comrades.* Port Washington, New York, 1968.

Brough, James. *The Ford Dynasty.* Garden City, 1977.

Burroughs, John. *Accepting the Universe.* Boston and New York, 1920.

———. *Birds and Poets.* Boston and New York, 1904.

———. *Field and Study.* Boston and New York, 1919.

———. *Indoor Studies.* Boston and New York, 1904.

———. *Leaf and Tendril.* Boston and New York, 1908.

———. *Literary Values.* Boston and New York, 1904.

———. *Notes on Walt Whitman as Poet and Person.* New York, 1971.

———. *Riverby.* Boston and New York, 1904.

———. *The Summit of the Years.* Boston and New York, 1913.

———. *Time and Change.* Boston and New York, 1912.

———. *Under the Maples.* Boston and New York, 1921.

———. *Ways of Nature.* Boston and New York, 1905.

———. *Whitman: A Study.* Boston and New York, 1896.

Conot, Robert. *A Streak of Luck.* New York, 1979.

Fidrych, Mark, and Clark, Tom. *No Big Deal.* Philadelphia and New York, 1977.

Folsom, Lowell Edwin. "America's 'Hurrah Game': Baseball and Whitman." *Iowa Review* (Spring-Summer 1980).

Gelderman, Carol. *Henry Ford, the Wayward Capitalist.* New York, 1981.

Holloway, Emory, and Schwarz, Vernolian. *I Sit and Look Out: Editorials... by Walt Whitman.* New York, 1932.

Johnson, Clifton. *John Burroughs Talks.* Boston, 1922.

Josephson, Matthew. *Edison.* New York, 1959.

Kligerman, Jack, ed. *The Birds of John Burroughs.* New York, 1976.

Luciano, Ron, and Fisher, David. *The Umpire Strikes Back.* New York, 1982.

Nelson, Kevin. *Baseball's Greatest Quotes.* New York, 1982.

Nevins, Allan. *Ford: The Times, the Man, the Company.* New York, 1954.

Rodgers, Cleveland, and Black, John. eds. *Editorials, Essays . . . as Editor of the* Brooklyn Daily Eagle *in 1846 and 1847.* New York, 1920.

Swift, Hildegarde Hoyt. *The Edge of April.* New York, 1957.

Teller, Walter. *Walt Whitman's Camden Conversations.* New Brunswick, 1973.

Traubel, Horace. *With Walt Whitman in Camden.* New York, 1961; Philadelphia, 1953; and Carbondale, Illinois, 1964.

Traubel, Bucke, and Harned, eds. *In Re Walt Whitman.* Philadelphia, 1893.

Whitman, Walt. *Complete Prose Works.* Philadelphia, 1892.

Wiley, Farida A., ed. *John Burroughs' America.* New York, 1961.

MOUNTAINEERS
ARE ALWAYS
FREE!

MOUNTAINEERS ARE ALWAYS FREE!

"About the year 1749 there was in the county of Frederick [Virginia] a man subject to lunacy, and who, when laboring under the influence of this disease, would ramble a considerable distance into the neighboring wilderness. In one of these wanderings he came on some of the waters of Greenbrier River. Surprised to see them flowing in a westerly direction, on his return to Winchester he made known the fact . . ."

Jacob Marlin and Stephen Sewell—influenced by the account of the lunatic who had wandered across the Blue Ridge—settled in the Greenbrier country. However, one was Catholic, the other Protestant, and they argued and separated, the seceder taking up residence in a hollow tree in the yard. They greeted each other every morning, and spoke no more for the rest of the day.

John Brown: "I may be very insane, and I am so, if insane at all. But if that be so, insanity is like a very pleasant dream to me."

In 1763 the King of England issued a proclamation forbidding all persons to take possession of lands west of the Alleghenies. But there already were pioneers, including the most remote settlement at Loony's Creek.

* * *

. . . north of Pittsburgh, south of Roanoke, west of Cleveland, east of Savannah . . .

. . . the most northern of the southern, western of the eastern, southern of the northern, eastern of the western . . .

* * *

In 1674—long before the fabled lunatic—one Gabriel Arthur, illiterate indentured servant, was captured by Cherokees, and adopted by a Cherokee chief. He accompanied the chief on a raid against the Shawnees, crossing the Blue Ridge and the Alleghenies, working down the Kanawha River to the Shawnee village on the Ohio. Here he was wounded, separated from the chief, and captured by Shawnees. "And heare Gabriell received shott with two arrows, one of them in his thigh, which stopt his runing and soe was taken prisoner, for Indian vallour consists most in their heeles, for he that can run best is accounted ye best man. These Indians thought this Gabrill to be noe Tomahittan by ye length of his haire, for ye Tomahittans keepe their haire close cut to ye end an enime may not take an advantage to lay hold of them by it. They took Gabriell and scowered his skin with water and ashes, and when they perceived his skin to be white they made very much of him and admire att his knife gunn and hatchett they tooke with him. They gave those things to him againe. He made signes to them the gun was ye Tomahittons which He had a desire to take with him, but ye knife and hatchet he gave to ye king. They not knowing use of gunns, the king received it with great shewes of thankfulness for they had not any manner of iron instrument that hee saw amongst them whilst he was there they brought in a fatt beaver which they had newly killd . . ." Using sign language, young Gabriel promised to return with guns, knives, and iron tools, to be traded for beaver pelts . . . and the Shawnee let him go. Somehow he made his way back to Virginia.

* * *

1609: "JAMES, BY THE GRACE OF GOD, King of *England, Scotland, France and Ireland*, Defender of the Faith, &c." The Charter did "give grant and confirm" to the London Company "all that Space and Circuit of land, lying from the Sea Coast of the Precinct aforesaid, up into the land throughout from Sea to Sea, West and Northwest . . . Together with all the Soils, Grounds, Havens, and Ports, Mines, as well Royal Mines of Gold and Silver, as other Minerals, Pearls, and Precious Stones, Quarries, Woods, Rivers, Waters, Fishings, Commodities, Jurisdictions, Royalties, Priviledges, Franchises, and Preheminences . . ." So that the Colony of Virginia laid claim to land from the Atlantic to the Pacific. (Today, West Virginia's northern panhandle, varying in breadth from two to twelve miles, is all that remains of this western claim).

1734, "Orange County" was created, a more modest proposal, to include all of what is now West Virginia, Kentucky, Ohio, Indiana, Illinois, Michigan, and Wisconsin.

1773, a group of speculators proposed "Vandalia" (West Virginia and Kentucky), so named "in Compliment to the Queen," who took great pride in her alleged descent from the Vandals.

*   *   *

George Washington: "Any person . . . who neglects the present opportunity of hunting out good Lands and in some measure marking and distinguishing them for their own (in order to keep others from settling them) will never regain it." "By this time it may be easy for you to discover, that my Plan is to secure a good deal of Land . . ." "I would choose if it were practible to get pretty large Tracts together . . ." "I woud recommend it to you to keep this whole matter a profound Secret, or trust it only with those in whom you can confide and who can assist you in bringing it to bear by their discoveries of land and this advice proceeds from general very good Reasons and in the first place because I might be censured for the Opinion I have given in respect to the King's Proclamation and then if the scheme I am now proposing to you was known it might give the alarm to others and by putting them upon a Plan of the same nature (before we could lay a proper foundation for success ourselves) set the different Interests clashing and probably in the end overturn the whole all which may be avoided by a Silent management . . ." "I will have the lands immediately surveyed to keep others off . . ."

This process of claiming and surveying was known as "taking up land" . . . a term with which the Indians might have had difficulty. "Between April 26, 1743, and May 7, 1754, the council of Virginia granted to speculators more than 2,500,000 acres, most of it lying west of the Alleghenies." George Washington alone took up about 34,000.

Land titles were in a state of utter chaos.

* * *

"The Indians must have known something about West Virginia. They avoided it. Before the Europeans arrived with their glass beads, firewater, and gunpowder, the Indian nations had spread out and divided up the North American continent. Modern anthropologists have worked out maps of the Indian occupancy of pre-Columbian America according to the languages spoken. The Shawnee and Cherokee occupied areas to the south and southwest. The Monacan settled to the east, and the Erie and Conestogas claimed the areas north of West Virginia. Even the inhospitable deserts of the Far West were divided and occupied. There is only one spot on the map labeled 'Uninhabited': West Virginia."

Initial pioneer settlement into and across the Alleghenies largely bypassed West Virginia, following the major rivers instead to Kentucky and Tennessee. West Virginia dropped back in time, a pocket, a frontier, isolated.

"It seems very strange that any person should have settled there when the whole country was almost vacant."

* * *

But game was abundant, "deer, elk, and buffalo, so gentle as not to be frightened by the approach of man." Animal and human trails, crossing the mountains, were widened into rough roads (early fourwheel wagons were called shake-guts). Mountains fenced the settlers' cattle, and vegetables were added to hog and hominy.

*   *   *

Abraham Lincoln, grandfather of the president, passed through the territory. And the Hanks family paused at a cabin near Mike's Run for the birth of Nancy, the president's mother.

Daniel Boone trapped beaver up the Gauley River, to the Yew Pine Forest . . . hunted and trapped on the Great Kanawha, and surveyed 200,000 acres.

"Selim, the Algerine, of remarkable history, passed up the Kanawha Valley in search of the white settlements to the East. Selim was a wealthy and educated young Algerine; he was captured in the Mediterranean by Spanish pirates; was sold to a Louisiana planter, escaped, made his way up the Mississippi, and up the Ohio. Somewhere below the Kanawha he met with some white prisoners; and a woman among them told him, as best she could in sign language, to go toward the rising sun, and he would find white settlements . . . He turned up Kanawha, then Greenbrier, etc., and was finally discovered, nearly naked, and on the point of starvation, not far from Warm Springs, and kindly taken care of. Through a Greek Testament in possession of some minister who saw him, it was discovered that he was a good Greek scholar and thus communication was opened up between him and the minister who understood Greek. Selim studied English, became a Christian, returned to his home in Algiers, was repudiated by his parents because he had given up the Moslem for the Christian religion. He returned to America, heart-broken, and finally died in an insane hospital."

*   *   *

Slowly at first, and then more rapidly, the tide of settlement increased. But on the frontier and borders—especially along the Ohio—there were Indians, often in complex conflicts and connivances with British, French, and colonials.

1771, the Indians, for the first time, formed a confederacy: Shawnees, Delawares, Wyandot, Mingoes, Miamis, Ottawas, and Illinois—led by the Shawnee chieftain, Cornstalk. Indians traded across the river for whiskey, and gunplay became common.

October 10, 1774, an army of Virginians, gathered and deployed to attack the Indians, lay sleeping on the grounds at Shawane Town, an old Shawnee village on the banks of the Ohio, at Point Pleasant. During the night the Indians crept upon them, "through a heavy growth of timber with foliage so dense, as in many places to intercept, in a great measure, the light of the moon and the stars. Beneath lay many trunks of fallen trees strewed in different directions and in various stages of decay. The whole surface of the ground was covered with a luxurious growth of weeds interspersed with close-set thickets of spice-wood and other undergrowth. A journey through this in the night must have been tedious, tiresome, dark and dreary. The Indians, however, entered upon it promptly and pursued it until break of day." The frontier army would have been destroyed, had not two of their number risen early to go hunting. They were discovered by the Indians and fired upon; one was killed, the other escaped to return and spread the alarm. The Virginians were thus prepared for the Indians, and after day-long battle, the savages were repulsed. At night-fall, "all was quiet save the groans of the wounded, for only the dead could rest in such a night as that."

West Virginians to this day will claim that this—The Battle of Point Pleasant—was the first engagement of the American Revolution. There is good evidence that "the Indians were influenced by the British to commence the war to terrify and confound the people, before they commenced hostilities themselves the following year at Lexington." Lord Dunmore, Governor of the Virginia colony, apparently acted with duplicity. It may well have been his intention to sacrifice the colonial army at Point Pleasant, so that he could effect an alliance with what would have been a victorious Indian army to fight the rising tide of rebellion. The result, however, was the opposite: the colonial victory quieted the Indians on the Allegheny border, for the early, crucial years of the Revolution.

*　　*　　*

Chief Logan, of the Mingoes: "Col. Cresap, the last spring, in cold blood, and unprovoked, murdered all the relatives of Logan, not sparing even my women and children. There runs not a drop of my blood in the veins of any living creature."

Cornstalk: "Then let us kill all our women and children, and go and fight till we die. I can die but once, and it is all one to me, now or another time." An hour later, he was murdered.

1777, the year of the three sevens, was called the "bloody year." "Dark, mysterious clouds of malignant spirits hung upon the horizon, threatening every moment to overwhelm and exterminate the halfprotected pioneer in his wilderness home. At length the storm broke over them, and there was scarcely a settlement . . . that did not experience its fatal and terrible effect. The fury of the savages during this year seemed to have no bounds. The wretched inhabitants were massacred with every conceivable cruelty. Men, women and children were chosen objects of their revenge, and scarcely a settlement west of the Alleghenies escaped their visits and their fury."

Thefts, murders, rapes, burnings, scalpings, whole families massacred, tortured . . . "One of the Indians they flayed, and tanning the skin, manufactured it into shot pouches." . . . settlers beheaded by Indians, their heads mounted on poles, as a warning . . . "Desolation and murder heightened with all Barbarous Circumstances, and unheard of instances of Cruelty." . . . if the Indians spared the lives of young women, it was only to "Carry them away to gratify the Brutal passions of Lawless Savages." . . . Mrs. Draper tried to escape, with her baby, but she was captured, and "the child brained against the end of one of the house logs." . . . an early settler at the mouth of Paint Creek dreamed one night that he was bitten by a snake. He interpreted this to mean that he would be shot by an Indian. That very day he was, indeed, shot and killed by an Indian . . . "Bald Eagle, an old and friendly Delaware chief, was wantonly murdered by some straggling whites, set up in his canoe, with a pipe in his mouth, and sent floating down the Monongahela." . . . "Red Hawk claimed that he had once fired eleven well-aimed shots at George Washington, and had then desisted, believing Washington to be under the protection of the Great Spirit, as his gun never missed its mark before." . . . in 1820 the last wild elk was seen; the last buffalo, 1825.

*   *   *

1767, one Harman Blennerhassett was born in England. He claimed to be Irish, of "noble descent," and a biographer describes his parentage "as among the most distinguished of the gentry of Ireland, who could trace their lineage as far back as the English King John."

1797, wealthy and married, he went to Europe, supplied himself with a library, then shipped to New York, journeyed overland to Pittsburgh, barged down the Ohio to Parkersburg, where he bought an island in the river—Blennerhassett Island. Here on this "gem of nature" in the midst of the wilderness—an island that had once been coveted by George Washington—he bought slaves and *hired* hands to clear the land and began construction of his man-sion—a creation on which he eventually expended the outlandish sum of sixty thousand dollars.

The mansion's appearance, to a boatman floating down the river, generated emotions "not unlike those experienced in gazing on the Moorish palaces of Andalusia." "The ground rose gradually on all sides to its centre, and on this favorable spot was the house, erected in the style and splendor of a Parisian pavilion. It was but sixty feet square, consisting of two stories, connected with wings by a semi-circular veranda, luxuriantly covered with myrtle, and commanded an extensive range of one of the loveliest regions of the world . . . Everywhere were contrasts and surprises, evidencing an eye that had surveyed the best effects of Europe; and, to crown the whole, walks, lawns, and shrubberies were blooming with all the flowers and fruits, and vocal with all the melody a generous clime so literally dispenses to this Italy of the West. The effect of this contrast between the perfection of wild and cultivated loveliness, of this discovery of the triumph of Art in the very stronghold of Nature was perfectly entrancing." "On a nearer approach was observed the beautifully graded lawn, decked with tasteful shrubbery, and interspersed with showy flowers; while, a little in the distance, the elm threw its dark branches over a carpet of most beautiful green sward. Beyond these, the forest trees were intermingled with copse-wood, so closely as to exclude the noon-day sun; and, in other places, they formed those long sweeping vistas, in the intricacies of which the eye delights to lose itself; while the imagination conceives them as the paths of wilder scenes of sylvan solitude. The space immediately in the rear of the dwelling was assigned to fruits and flowers; of which the varieties were rare, excellent and beautiful and the manner in which they were disposed over the surface, unique, elegant and tasteful. Espaliers of peach, apricot, quince and pear trees, extended along the exterior, confined to a picket fence; while, in the middle space, wound labyrinthine walks, skirted with flowering shrubs and the eglantine and honey-suckle flung their melliferous blossoms over bowers of various forms." ". . . huge sycamores and other kingly forest trees guarded and graced the head of the isle, and the wild-grape, trumpet-vine and creepers, thick and matted, interlaced the shores and touched the willows that encircled the wilderness on every side." "Greeting the eye in front of this mansion . . . a graded lawn of several acres adorned with walks and dotted here and there with shrubbery and clusters of bright flowers and extending eastward to the rippling water's edge of the upper end of the island, with an opening in the reserved trees."

"The hall was a spacious room, its walls painted a sombre colour, with a beautiful cornice of plaster, bordered with gilded molding, running round the lofty ceiling; while its furniture was rich, heavy and grand. The furniture in the drawing-room was, in strong contrast with that of the hall, light, airy and elegant; with splendid mirrors, gay-coloured carpets, classic pictures, rich curtains, and ornaments to correspond, arranged, by Mrs. Blennerhassett, with nicest taste and harmonious effect. A large quantity of silver-plate ornamented the sideboards and decorated the tables. The whole establishment was chastened by the purest taste, and without that glare of tinsel finery, too common among the wealthy."

"Blennerhassett spent much time in his library reading, conducting 'philosophical experiments,' playing the violin and cello. He was reputedly able to repeat the whole of Homer's Iliad in the original Greek. Tall and stooping, and aristocratically near-sighted, he liked to hunt, but he was a poor shot, due to his eyesight. He was terrified of earthquakes and thunderstorms. He would go to bed if an electrical storm passed over."

"Lady Margaret . . . could read and fluently converse in Italian and French, and was endowed in mind and manner and educated to grace with ease any position in the courts of Europe. In figure she was tall and well proportioned . . . In dress her taste inclined to the showy and attractive, and she aimed to select and adapt her outfit to her well-shaped form . . . In the saddle she was an expert equestrienne . . . Often her cloth, scarlet riding robe, spangled with gold lace and glittering buttons and her flowing tresses waving beneath her ostritch-plumed hat, glimmered in the vine and leaftangled woods, as she freely rode along the river paths . . . It is said that a farmer's son rented and cultivated a field of corn on the island, near the avenue leading from house to river, for the sole purpose of stealing a look at her beautiful person . . ."

"This estate upon a lovely island . . . was indeed a rich dominion for cultivated minds, a picture of peace, repose, quietude, innocence and happiness."

*   *   *

JULY 12, 1804, Aaron Burr mortally wounded Alexander Hamilton in a duel at Weehawken, New Jersey. Some months later—finding it convenient to be at some remove from Weehawken—Burr shipped down the Ohio, and called upon the Blennerhassetts.

"At that time Mexico was trying to throw off the yoke of Spanish rule, and a war was also imminent between Spain and the United States; and Burr . . . conceived the idea of organizing and assembling a large force of armed men for the purpose of colonizing that region, with the ultimate object of conquering Mexico and establishing himself king or emperor, and then annexing to that usurped country all of the territory west of the Alleghenies . . . After having accomplished this much, it was then his purpose to march upon the capital of the United States, into the halls of Congress, overthrow the American republic over which he had recently served as vice president, and install himself as the central head of a great empire, extending from the Atlantic Ocean to the Rocky Mountains, and from the Great Lakes to the Gulf. But in order to carry out his designs, it was necessary to secure financial assistance. He knew that Blennerhassett was a person of considerable means, and decided to visit him."

Aaron Burr—the confidence man. And cultivated, stooping, near-sighted Harman Blennerhassett—the perfect mark.

DECEMBER 10, 1806: "With a small fleet of river boats and a company of young adventurers from the vicinity Blennerhassett started down the Ohio River under cover of darkness . . . planning to meet Burr at Natchez. Rumors of a treason plot had already spread over Virginia and had reached President Jefferson at Washington, and the next morning a body of Virginia militia came to the island to arrest the two conspirators. Both had gone but the mansion and the island were confiscated and many of the beautiful furnishings were damaged or destroyed. Mrs. Blennerhassett and the children fled."

Burr and Blennerhassett were arrested and tried for treason. Both were acquitted, but Blennerhassett was ruined. The estate was seized by creditors, the tailored grounds given over to slovenly farming . . . and, in 1811, the mansion burned.

Harman and lady Margaret wandered, tried their hands at this and that. Both died in penury.

*   *   *

Yew and Droop. Sinks of Gandy, Dolly Sods, Roughs of the Guyan. Colic Mountain, Lankey Mountain, Bible Knob. Rich, Cheat, and Shavers.

The town of Mountain was originally named Mole Hill.

*   *   *

On Calder's Knob, one William Calder, a native of South Carolina, built a mansion and a one hundred ft. tower. It was his intention to climb the tower and view his native state from the top—across two states—with the naked eye. He failed in this but the tower nonetheless afforded him a moment of glory: on the night he received news that Fort Sumter had been fired on and captured, he celebrated by burning the tower to the ground.

John Brown: "These mountains are the basis of my plan. God has given the strength of the hills to freedom; they were placed here for the emancipation of the negro race; they are full of natural forts, where one man for defense will be equal to a hundred for attack they are also full of good hiding places, where large numbers of brave men could be concealed, and baffle and elude pursuit for a long time. I know these mountains well, and could take a body of men into them and keep them there, despite of all the efforts of Virginia to dislodge them. God has established the Allegheny Mountains from the foundation of the world that they might one day be a refuge for fugitive slaves."

*   *   *

JULY 11,1861, Brig.-Gen. Jacob D. Cox, commanding a Union brigade on board a fleet of sternwheelers, steamed up the Great Kanawha. "Our first day's sail was thirteen miles up the river, and it was the very romance of campaigning . . . The afternoon was a lovely one. Summer clouds lazily drifted across the sky . . . The scenery was picturesque, the gently winding river making beautiful reaches that opened new scenes upon us at every turn . . . The landscape seemed more beautiful, the sunshine more bright, and the exhilaration of out-of-door life more joyous than any we had ever known."

With a hostile engagement at the mouth of Scary Creek, they steamed 70 miles upriver, to the head of navigation. Thereafter travel was overland.

"Bad weather and worse roads, uncertain communications, rugged terrain, and the presence of resistance and subversion in the rear of both armies: these conditions conspired to make the Civil War in West Virginia 'an affair of outcasts' . . ."

Confederate and Union forces, struggling in the broken and tangled Allegheny hills and gorges, often became separated, isolated, lost, at times mistaking one another for friend or enemy. Scouting became a mad confusion of misconception and rumor. In the cold rains and floods of winter, supply lines were a shambles, the movement of artillery a nightmare. "Looking at the map it seemed an easy thing to do; but the almost wilderness character of the intervening country with its poor and sparsely scattered people, the weary miles of steep mountain-roads becoming impassable in rainy weather, and the total absence of forage for animals, were elements of the problem. . . ." "He reported the country absolutely destitute of everything and the roads so broken up that he could not supply his troops."

"A driving summer rain turned fields and highways into muddy ponds; soggy clothing and squashing boots . . ."

"All the clouds seem to concentrate over this ridge of mountains, and by whatever wind they are driven, give us rain."

". . . the dome of the watersheds of northwestern Virginia, covered by a vast and dense forest of large evergreen trees, reaches an altitude of nearly 5,000 feet, so that, naturally, it is at all times a damp and chilly region having a large rainfall. During this particular season the precipitation was very much larger than usual . . . the whole country became saturated with moisture, and even the graded mountain roads, cut up by the constant passing of heavy army trains, were converted into streams of axle-deep mud . . . This continuous damp and chilly weather caused a great amount of sickness of every kind among the thousands of unseasoned troops . . . Nearly every house in this sparsely settled country was converted into a hospital . . . Supply trains could not reach the camps . . . an ordeal more trying than that of constant fighting . . ."

The Surgeons of a rebel regiment stationed at Huntersville requisitioned some ninety quarts of whiskey 'for medical purposes,' in a single week of November 1861.

*   *   *

". . . in West Virginia that conflict was a fratricidal struggle, in which brother was arrayed against brother, father against son, and neighbor against neighbor." Soldiers were recruited and enlisted in both armies.

The town of Romney changed hands 56 times. Order was presumably kept by the Home Guard, who "kept their headquarters at the courthouse, sat up nights, arrested each other and everybody else they found prowling about . . ."

Besides Union and Confederate recruiters, vying for support, there were bushwhackers and swamp dragons, raiding parties of mountain guerillas.

"One Union courier bushwhacked in the spring of 1862 was disemboweled and beheaded, his bloody head stuffed into the cavity in his trunk."

*　　*　　*

In the campaign in the Kanawha Valley, Wise and Floyd, Confederate "politico generals," shared command. (Both had been governors of Virginia, neither had military training). They spent the better part of the campaign sabotaging each other. Confederate efforts in the Valley were a dismal failure.

"The Lincoln administration found West Virginia a convenient place to install certain generals whose political influence was too great to pass over, but whose military talents were too limited to trust in a more important theatre of war."

*　　*　　*

1863, Confederate General William E. Jones conducted raids in the mountains. May 9, he marched to "'Oiltown,' in the newly opened Burning Springs field. There . . . he demolished equipment and burned crude oil estimated at 150,000 barrels. In his report to General Lee, Jones described the resulting scene: 'By dark the oil from the tanks on the burning creek had reached the river, and the whole stream became a sheet of fire. A burning river, carrying destruction to our merciless enemy . . .'"

Another general: "On the 20th of June we started for Martinsburg . . . . As we approached Martinsburg late in the afternoon we heard a strange singing and screaming in the air which resembled the notes of a gigantic Aeolian. These sounds grew more distinct and definite as we advanced, and still nearer the town we perceived immense columns of black smoke rolling up between us and the setting sun, and tinging the whole landscape with a coppery hue. As these clouds rose from the direction of the railroad shops it was easy to imagine their origin; but the accompanying sounds were unaccountable, until, turning into one of the lower streets of the town, a scene was suddenly presented to us which more resembled a dream of Dante's *Inferno* than an exhibition of real life. Jackson's brigade were performing a grand *auto da fe* upon the rolling stock of the Baltimore and Ohio Railroad. The foreground of the picture was occupied by a ruin of classic form and beauty—that of the pillared viaduct which had been destroyed some weeks before. On the open space in front of the work-shops stood, ranged upon the tracks, between forty and fifty locomotives roasting amidst the flames of a thousand cords of wood, distributed, refreshed and stirred up constantly by a brigade of wild Confederates. The rocks, hills, and houses which surrounded the place of execution were crowded by many hundred spectators, the old men, wives and children of those who had depended on the road for their subsistence. Twilight was approaching, and as the lurid light of the fires prevailed the aspect of the scene grew still more unearthly. The rebel soldiers, with their bronzed faces, raggedly picturesque ostumes, and fiendish activity, were not unworthy representatives of the familiars of Beelzebub. They worked in silence too, with the sullen and desperate look of men who were executing the work of Fate rather than their own will. Motionless and mute the groups of citizens looked on, terror-stricken, yet every pallid face lowering with dumb execration. The locomotives, as the flames licked their iron bodies, and the heated air rushed through the steam whistles impressed the spectator with the idea that they were living victims, who moaned and shrieked with an agony surpassing human comprehension . . .

June 21: The dawn of morning dispelled these distempered fancies, but brought with it no reviving cheerfulness. Between dreams and realities there was not so much difference after all. On the railroad we could see the wilted and discolored bodies of the locomotives lying amidst the smoke and ashes of their funeral pyres. Their wailings had ceased, and the general feeling of relief thereat was expressed by one of the Negroes, who thanked God they were 'out of their misery.'"

By the spring of '63, the lack of food, the depredations of war, the raids of the irregulars—bushwhackers and swamp dragons—pushed the mountain counties into a state of anarchy.

Earlier—January 1862—eleven of General Loring's officers addressed a letter to Jefferson Davis, begging to be transferred out of West Virginia.

And Brig.-Gen. Cox, who had served in West Virginia, was transferred to the Army of the Potomac, later was ordered back to the Kanawha country: "I acquiesced with reasonably good grace."

*   *   *

OCTOBER 24, 1861: "WHEREAS, it is represented to be the desire of the people inhabiting the Counties hereinafter mentioned, to be separated from this Commonwealth, and to be erected into a separate state, and admitted into the Union of States, and become a member of the Government of the United States: . . ."

The formation of West Virginia was an opportunistic military gesture: it was important that the Union army maintain connection between the eastern cities and the banks of the Ohio.

"The People of Virginia, by their delegates assembled in Convention at Wheeling, do ordain that a new State, to be called the State of Kenawha, be formed and erected . . ."

Other names proposed included Allegheny, Augusta, Potomac, Columbia, Western Virginia, New Virginia.

"My desire is to see West Virginia free from all the shackles that shackle man."

Montani semper liberi!

West Virginia boys are coming, from her
mountains, swift and strong—

> Thousands upon thousands marching,
>   you can hear their battle song;
>
> You can see their banners waving, O my
>   country, 'tis for thee
>
> That they lift their voices chanting:
>   "Mountaineers are always free!"

President Lincoln: "I believe the admission of West Virginia into the Union is expedient."

"WHEREAS, by the act of Congress, approved the 31st day of December last, the State of West Virginia was declared to be one of the United States of America, and was admitted into the Union on an equal footing with the original states in all respects whatsoever ... Now, therefore, be it known that I, Abraham Lincoln, President of the United States, do hereby, in pursuance of the act of Congress aforesaid, declare and proclaim ..."

The State of West Virginia was formally admitted at ceremonies conducted June 20, 1863. And thus became, under the banner of Union, the only state ever successfully to secede from the Union.

Virginia's gift to her new sister, at the time of separation, consisted of a few law books, and an insane asylum.

*   *   *

"My mother's husband, who was the stepfather of my brother John and myself, did not belong to the same owners as did my mother. In fact, he seldom came to our plantation. I remember seeing him there perhaps once a year, that being about Christmas time. In some way, during the war, by running away and following the Federal soldiers, it seems, he found his way into the new state of West Virginia. At that time a journey from Virginia over the mountains to

West Virginia was rather a tedious and in some cases a painful undertaking. What little clothing and few household goods we had were placed in a cart, but the children walked the greater portion of the distance, which was several hundred miles. I do not think any of us ever had been very far from the plantation, and the taking of a long journey into another state was quite an event. The parting from our former owners and the members of our own race on the plantation was a serious occasion. From the time of our parting till their death we kept up a correspondence with the older members of the family, and in later years we have kept in touch with those who were the younger members. We were several weeks making the trip, and most of the time we slept in the open air and did our cooking over a log fire out of doors. One night I recall that we camped near an abandoned log cabin, and my mother decided to build a fire in that for cooking, and afterward to make a 'pallet' on the floor for our sleeping. Just as the fire had gotten well started a large black snake fully a yard and a half long dropped down the chimney and ran out on the floor."   —Booker Taliaferro Washington

*   *   *

"The white man of this state and adjoining states is about the most contemptible person on the face of God's earth. He is unbearably ignorant and does not know it. He has generally been brought up on the mountains, hog fashion . . . He is a small, ferrety-eyed fellow, with hollow lanky cheeks, a thin pointed nose with about seventeen hairs on his chin . . ."

". . . a class of men who are noted for their ignorance, indolence, duplicity and dishonesty . . . a stolid, vicious-looking countenance, an ungainly figure, and an awkward, if not ungraceful, spinal curve in the dorsal region, acquired by laziness . . ."

*   *   *

"One day Confederate partisans, drawn by firing in the mountain wilds of Logan County, were surprised at what they found. The noise came from the depths of a ravine in which lay a large body of Union soldiers, spread out in attack formation. They were shooting from the shelter of rocks and aiming at a knob that towered above everything around it. Somebody back in history had dubbed this high point Devil's Backbone. It was an isolated crag reached by a single path up through the rocks. At the top, a bit of barren tableland, stretched like a floor between protecting ridges, offered the best in natural forts. Up toward this point the Union invaders spasmodically sent their bullets. Hour after hour the fighting went on. Guns sang out down in the bottom and their slugs whined upward to strike harmlessly against the face of rock. Pitted against this fusillade was a single rifle, its shiny black barrel pointed ominously from above. At first one crevice and then another it appeared, steadied, and belched its lead down into the ravine. As the exchange went on and on, spasmodic puffs of smoke broke with frenzied persistence from the guns in the bottom, and were answered with more measured delay by a single puff from above. At times a sudden fury speeded up the firing, and the partisans hiding in the trees knew it represented another casualty for the Union, another bull's-eye for the sharpshooter on the ridge. The sun sank and darkness began to blot out the crag; then the firing slackened and finally died away. For a while there was silence; then the Federals gave up and withdrew, laboriously lugging their wounded over the rocks. Later, in the black of night, the lone gunman came down. Once clear of the crag, he made his way along intricate trails and across impossible terrain with the ease of a forest animal. In military legend, the wisest think twice before fighting an enemy on his own ground, and the one-man army of the Devil's Backbone, the lanky Captain Devil Anse Hatfield, had proved the maxim true."

". . . a bearded six-footer, a Stonewall Jackson type, whose height was somewhat diminished by rounded shoulders and a slight stoop. His hair was thick, his eyes gray and deep-set below bushy eyebrows, and his nose was hooked like a scimitar. He wore a dark brown beard that swelled in size as it swung downward . . ."

But where did the trouble start? "The most prevalent name among adherents of the Union in the Kentucky border counties was McCoy. Just as predominant among the Confederate independents on the West Virginia side were the Hatfields . . . bullets from their guns occasionally made their way into places where they should not have been." Was the feud a heritage of the war? "Their troubles had been brewing for years, stirred by a combination of things, not the least of which was the discovery that a Hatfield youth, slipping across the Tug to lie with a McCoy girl, finally had got her pregnant." Was this the spark?

Or was it the case of the disputed hog? Long, lean razorbacks ranged at large in the mountains, possession to be claimed in the fall of the year by the distinctive notch the owner had cut in each creature's ear. 1873, at Floyd Hatfield's Stringtown sty, Randolph McCoy claimed one of Floyd's hogs, and hauled Hatfield into court. Guns were stacked outside, and the trussed-up hog lay on the court's dirt floor. Jurors voted predictably along clan lines; but one Bill Staton, sole eyewitness, swore that he had watched Floyd Hatfield notch the creature's ear. The hog was awarded to Hatfield. McCoy hurled a rock at Staton. The feud was on.

Later, election day, when, according to custom, the men were all armed and mostly drunk, Tolbert McCoy approached Ellison Hatfield. "I'm hell on earth!" he screamed; and repeated it, "I'm hell on earth!" To which Ellison replied, "You're a damn shit hog!" McCoy swung at Hatfield, struck him in the stomach and, with a hitherto unseen knife, gashed him open. Young Hatfields and McCoys charged in, and there was a melee.

A shot rang out. Ellison Hatfield slumped to the ground, hit in the back. The crowd, living a life of its own, fell dead silent; the fighters breathed heavily, and were otherwise still. Then a murmur began on the outskirts, grew as the crowd surged inward, swelled to wild shouting, as McCoys struggled to escape to the woods . . . and the gasps of Ellison Hatfield shook the leaves and grass scuffed at his mouth.

*   *   *

The railroad came to the hills, and the c&o dug a tunnel at Big Bend.

"John Henry was always singing or mumbling something when he was whipping steel. He would sing over and over the same thing sometimes. He'd sing

'My old hammer ringing in the mountains,

Nothing but my hammer falling down.'"

"John Henry was the best driver on the c&o. He was the only one that could drive steel with two hammers, one in each hand. People came from miles to see him use the two 20-lb. hammers he had to drive with."

"He often said his strength was brought from Africa."

". . . rawbony, and as black as he could be."

"John Henry was a coal-black man,
Chicken chocolate brown . . ."

"They said Big Bend Tunnel was a terrible-like place, and many men got killed there. Mules too. And they thronged the dead men and mules and all together there in that fill between the mountains."

"Kill a mule, buy another,
Kill a nigger, hire another."

Somebody invented a new-fangled steam drill, and the company sent one to Big Bend. It was supposed to drive steel faster than a man could. "John Henry wanted to drive against it. He took a lot of pride in his work and he hated to see a machine take the work of men like him."

"Well, they decided to hold a test to get an idea of how practical the steam drill was. The test went on all day and part of the next day."

> "Well, the man that invented the steam drill
> Thought he was mighty fine,
> John Henry sunk his fourteen feet
> And the steam drill made only nine,
> The steam drill made only nine."

> "Before I'd let the steamer beat me down,
> I'd die with my hammer in my hand, by God!
> I'd die with my hammer in my hand."

John Henry won. But he wouldn't rest. He took sick and died soon after that.

> "John Henry was hammering on the right side,
> The big steam drill on the left,
> Before that steam drill could beat him down,
> He hammered his fool self to death."

Some say "his death was caused from a busted blood vessel in his head." Others say

> "He broke a rib in his left-han' side,
> And his intrels fell on the groun'."

There is a legend that John Henry's ghost is still driving steel in Big Bend Tunnel.

> "Tomorrow at sunrise
> I am goin' to be a natural man."

*   *   *

"Most of the time I'm all right; I mean I figure we're better off here than in some big city, where you never lay your eyes on a piece of land, and you're lucky if you see a bird flying. I tell my kids that this is a good place to be born, and not to worry because somehow they'll make it through, like I did. But there will be a minute now and then that I don't believe myself, listening to myself talk, I just don't believe my own words. It's then that I figure it's real bad here . . ."

> *Mother Jones—a sweet-faced grandmotherly Irishwoman whose life span connected the presidencies of Andrew Jackson and Herbert Hoover—Mother Jones came into West Virginia: "Has anyone ever told you, my children, about the lives you are living here, so that you may understand how it is you pass your days on earth?"*

"I worry about my kids, I'll be honest and tell you. I'd like for them to have a better life than I ever had, but I don't believe they ever will, and it's too bad. That's why I tell my wife that we can't be too good to them; even when we do have something they want, we've got to let them know that here in West Virginia, in this county, it's not like they see on that television set."

> *"Medieval West Virginia! With its tent colonies on the bleak hills! With its grim men and women! When I get to the other side, I shall tell God Almighty about West Virginia!"*

"Sometimes when we're arguing I tell my brothers that they're wrong to keep on bragging how lucky a man is to pick his guitar and be living here . . ."

> *"Get your guns, you cowardly sons of bitches, and get into the woods!"*

"But it's a little strange about Daddy, our mother says: he begins to feel bad when the sun melts the snow and it's easier on us to leave the creek. He'll go to church and he'll say he's glad the weather is warming up, and we can leave the creek, but then he'll come home from church or the store over there, where we get the provisions, and he'll get real sad and down, and say he wishes we were back in January, and the whole state of West Virginia was covered with snow . . ."

". . . no where in the country could you find more brutality than you do here. Men have been shot down in cold blood. The children have been starved to death, some of them."

"We've been here so long, it's as long ago as when the country was started. My people came here and they followed the creek up to here and they named it Rocky Creek; they were the ones, that's right. In the Bible we have written down the names of our kin that came before us and when they were born and when they died, and my name is there and I'm not going to leave here, because there'd be no mention of me when I got married and no mention of my children, if I left the creek."

"We don't want Sunday schools. We've had enough of them. We want to fight."

"The minister says that all over the country people are moving and moving, and they don't know what to call their home, because they'll no sooner get to a place, when they'll be planning to leave because of some reason. But us—well, here we are and here we'll be."

"Don't give up your guns, and if you haven't got good guns, buy them."

"When I was a boy I recall my people burying their old people, right near where we lived. We had a little graveyard, and we used to know all our dead people pretty well. You know, we'd play near their graves and go ask our mother or daddy about who this one was and what he did, and like that."

"Pray for the dead and fight like hell for the living."

"The other way was through the Bible: everything was written down on pieces of paper inside the family Bible. There'd be births and marriages and deaths, going way back, I guess as far back as the beginning of the country. I'm not sure of the exact time, but a couple of hundred years, easy."

"If I pray I will have to wait until I am dead to get anything; but when I swear I get things here."

"We're *part* of this land; we were here to start and we'll probably see it die, me or my kids will, the way things are going. There will be no one left here and the strip miners will kill every good acre we have."

"There is never peace in West Virginia because there is never justice."

"I thought of that at the funeral. I thought maybe it's just as well to die now, if everything's headed in that direction. I guess that's what happens at a funeral. You get to thinking."

"Arm yourselves, return home and kill every goddamned mine guard on the creeks, blow up the mines, and drive the damned scabs out of the valleys!"

"I could curl up and go to sleep down there in that mine and it would never bother me in the least. It's something like your own house. You get used to it."

"Men who live up those lonely creeks have only the mine owners' Y.M.C.A.s, the mine owners' preachers and teachers, the mine owners' doctors and newspapers to look to for their ideas. So they don't get many."

"Who could go down in the mines in peace? If you really thought about it you wouldn't work in it, would you?"

"Damn you, you are not fit to live! Of every ton of coal so much was taken out to hire professional murderers to keep you in

*subjection, and you paid for it. You stood there like a lot of cow-
ards, going along chewing scab tobacco and you let yourself be
robbed by the mine owners—and then you go about shaking
your rotten head. Not a thing inside."*

"A fellow gets attached to a job like that. He don't like to leave it.
He wants nothing else."

*"You can expect no help from such a goddamned dirty coward
[Gov. Glasscock], whom, for modesty's sake, we shall call
'Crystal Peter.' But I warn this little Governor that unless he
rids Paint Creek and Cabin Creek of these goddamned Baldwin
Felts mine guard thugs, there is going to be one hell of a lot of
bloodletting in these hills. Talk about a few guards getting
bullets in their skulls, the whole damn lot of them ought to get
bullets in their skulls."*

"Thought I heard a sea-gull, / 'Way down in the ground; / Thought
I heard a sea-gull, 'Way down in the ground. / Must've been those
miners / A-turnin' that coal around."

*   *   *

"Blueville, a suburb of Grafton, is the birthplace of Ann Jarvis, who
in 1907 asked a small group of friends . . . to observe with her the first
anniversary of her mother's death, by wearing white carnations."

Thus was born: Mother's Day.

An International shrine to Motherhood has been erected in
Grafton.

Abraham Lincoln: "All I am or ever hope to be I owe to my angel
mother."

*   *   *

In the early days of the coal mines, labor was scarce, and company agents recruited blacks in the Deep South, ethnics in mid-Europe, jailbirds from everywhere, the recruits trundled in sealed trains to the mining camps where they went underground. The jailbirds soon surfaced, reverted to type, became moonshiners, hit men, gamblers, and pimps. Cinder Bottom in Keystone, McDowell County, became the "International Whorehouse District of the Coal Fields."

"The only difference between Keystone and hell is Keystone has a small stream of black polluted water running through it."

The whorehouses were wide open, to keep the miners happy. And—an off-pocket in the south—they were fully integrated: blacks, whites, ethnics, freely cross-fucking.

*   *   *

The union came in. (The blacks liked "joining the union," it resonated well with memories of the Civil War, "joining the Union" army.)

1912, the miners at Paint Creek went on strike. Thrown out of their company owned shacks, they set up a tent colony in nearby Holly Grove. Company gunmen hid in the surrounding hills, regularly peppered the tents with gunfire. But the miners—prime marksmen—returned fire, sniping expertly at guards and scabs. The C&O Railroad constructed an armor-plated, bulletproof train, sporting machine guns and rifles. Late one night, when miners and families were sleeping, the train passed slowly through Holly Grove, on C&O tracks, machine guns blasting.

The strike was finally settled by Gov. Hatfield, nephew of Devil Anse, who forced a settlement on both sides.

*   *   *

Early 1920, the union opened a drive in the open shop mines of Logan and Mingo counties, where the gunplay of Hatfields and McCoys still echoed. Mingo and Logan teemed with private gunmen, mine guards illegally deputized. At Matewan they met all trains, "to advise all passengers not to take the air on the platforms of Mingo County." Organizers were beaten and executed. The formula was "Kill 'em with one gun, and hand 'em another"—so the killing would look like self-defense.

Suspected of joining the union, miners and their families were evicted: gangs of blacks breaking down doors at dawn, setting out furniture in all weather, the guards reminding the miners that they were being set out by niggers. The Y.M.C.A. would not help, preferring to avoid controversial issues, and the Red Cross backed off, as the evictions were not an act of God.

Chief of Police of Matewan was Sid Hatfield, the "Terror of the Tug," who smiled more, the angrier he became. Hatfield sided with the miners, against the agents: "We'll kill those sons of bitches before they get out of Matewan."

MAY 19, 1920, Albert Felts, leader of the agents, approached Sid Hatfield on the main street of Matewan, tried to arrest him with a false warrant. No one knows who fired the first shot, but it started a fusillade of bullets that developed into a full-scale battle. In five minutes, there were eleven dead bodies.

The train from Bluefield pulled in. The engineers took one look down the street, and backed the train out of town.

Guerilla warfare broke out throughout the territory. Finally, an army of 6,000 miners and sympathizers marched to Blair Mountain and engaged 2,000 scabs, detectives, and thugs. "It bloomed into a full-fledged war that was covered by the press with their ace war correspondents." But it was in many ways a "comic opera war," the miners "wasting thousands and thousands of rounds of ammunition and hitting no one." "When U.S. Army Major

Thompson talked with Colonel Eubanks about arrangements for relieving the Logan army, Eubanks's conversation impressed him as muddled. Upon arrival in Logan, Thompson discovered why: he found Eubanks and his staff so intoxicated as to render them unfit—they had been on a drunk for at least twenty-four hours." "Boys fourteen and fifteen years old manned positions with high-powered rifles. Frequently men fired off cartridges for no apparent reason."

When the army moved in, they were supported by Billy Mitchell's 88th Light Bombing Squadron. The planes became mired in the mud, had to be jacked up. One crashed on takeoff, had to be dismantled and shipped out. One was forced down by engine trouble, broke an axle on landing. Another was blown off course, missed Charleston, then hit a fence on landing. Two more were lost in fog, wound up in Tennessee, one hitting a ditch on landing, the other a fence. A few made it to Charleston, were immediately ordered back home, as being useless. One crashed into a mountain on the return.

Nevertheless, the army cowed and subdued the miners. They surrendered their guns, went back to open shop mines.

"John L. Lewis no longer had a problem in West Virginia. He had nothing."

Much later, when a nationwide coal strike was threatened, Lewis was cornered by reporters, who found him reading the *Iliad* and the *Odyssey*. "Amazed to discover a labor leader reading classical literature, the journalists probed for an explanation. Lewis responded: 'The world is about the same now as it was then.'"

*　*　*

"High explosives were manufactured in Point Pleasant during World War II. Seven miles outside of town, part of the 2,500-acre McClintic Wildlife Station and animal preserve and bird sanctuary was ripped up. Miles of underground tunnels were dug, linking camouflaged buildings and factories. One hundred 'igloos' were scattered across the fields and woods—huge concrete domes with heavy steel doors where the finished explosives could be safely stored. Dirt and grass covered the domes so that from the air the whole area had a harmless, pastoral appearance. A few scattered buildings linked by unimproved roads with no suggestion of all the activity going on below ground. It looked like nothing more than it was supposed to be, a haven for birds and animals . . ." This was the TNT area.

Coal mine at Everettville, 1927: "The great force of the explosion was through the main entry toward the mine mouth. With clothes burned away and charred beyond recognition, many bodies were found in this passageway. They were hanging from the mine ribs, draped around support pillars, pressed against mine walls, buried under wreckage, and mangled beyond all belief—eyeballs blown from sockets, abdomens torn open and bowels strewn over the mine floor, heads smashed like overripe fruit, collapsed lungs, crushed chests, arms and legs torn from bodies . . ."

Farmington, 1968: "A series of explosions sparked fierce fires deep below the earth in a soft coal mine early today, trapping 78 of 99 miners who were at work. Efforts to reach the men, who were trapped 600 feet below the ground, were put off . . ." "After the last blast, flames roared anew from the wrecked portals hundreds of feet into the night sky, casting an orange glow that could be seen for miles against the low-hanging clouds." "Dwindling hopes for the survival of 78 men trapped since dawn Wednesday by explosions and fires in a gas-filled soft coal mine were depressed still further today by a new explosion in the 600-foot deep tunnels." "Two rescue teams penetrated into the shafts of the Consol No. 9 coal mine tonight and found clear air but no trace of the 78 men missing for nearly five days." "Air samples today showed that lethal levels of carbon monoxide and a potentially explosive concentration of methane gas were still present in the Consol No. 9 coal mine. Hope was all but given up for 78 missing miners." "The big coal mine where 78 men have been missing for nearly a week throbbed with another explosion today soon after a mine official said the search would continue no matter how remote the possibility of success." "There has been no contact with any of the 78 since the first explosion ripped through the mine . . ." "Sealing the mine would shut off air flow through its portals and would extinguish the fire. But it would also cut off any air supply to the missing men." "Relatives of 78 missing miners pleaded with officials today not to seal the mine. 'Even if just one man comes out it would be worthwhile . . .'" "Workers searched for some evidence of life through a sensitive listening device lowered into the mine tunnel, but heard nothing." "Company officials and Government and union representatives ordered a fiery coal mine sealed tonight, making it a tomb for 78 men trapped in the mine for nine days. The Consolidation Coal Company president, John Corcoran, told a news conference . . . that 'work on sealing the mine will begin at once.'" "Officials of the Consolidation Coal Company said that the hazardous job of sealing No. 9 mine, where 78 men have been trapped for more than a week, was completed early today. There were no incidents . . ."

Logan County: "A huge coal-slag heap serving as a dam burst under the pressure of three days of torrential rains early this morning, sending a wall of water through a narrow valley dotted with small impoverished mining towns. At least 37 persons were killed and it was feared that the figure might rise to 90."

"The dust was as thick as fog behind the drills. You came out of there after working a shift, and you were white all over. You could squeeze your nose, and it was like toothpaste coming out." This was the construction of Hawk's Nest Tunnel, drilled and blasted through the almost pure white silica of Cauley Mountain, early 1930s. The men worked 10- to 12-hour shifts, six days a week. Those who fell ill were quickly replaced by other job seekers who had hopped freight trains, hitchhiked, or walked to Fayette County in search of steady jobs. "The whole driving of the tunnel was begun, continued and completed with grave and inhuman disregard of all consideration for the health, lives and future of the employees." "Doc Harless had a man's lungs there after an autopsy. They was so solid, you couldn't stick a penknife in 'em." ". . . a local undertaker was hired to cart the bodies away and bury them in shallow trenches . . . The Congressional report said 169 men were buried there 'with cornstalks as their only gravestones.'" "They buried them like they were burying hogs, putting two or three of them in a hole." In 1939, Gov. Homer "Rocky" Holt refused to sanction a Federal Writers' Project guide to West Virginia until a lengthy and graphic discussion of the Hawk's Nest project was toned down.

Point Pleasant, December, 1967: "A towering suspension bridge collapsed during rush hour and Christmas shopping traffic today, sending an estimated 75 cars and trucks 80 feet down into the Ohio River." "Suddenly the whole bridge convulsed. Steel screamed. The seven-hundred-foot suspension bridge twisted and the main span split from its moorings at either end. Electric cables strung across the bridge snapped in a blaze of sparks. Fifty vehicles crashed into the black waters of the Ohio, tons of steel smashing down on top of them." "The bridge just keeled over, starting slowly on the Ohio side, then following like a deck of cards to the West Virginia side. There was a big flash and a puff of smoke when the last of the bridge caved in, I guess the power line snapped."

A group of miners, trapped for days following an explosion, ran out of water, and took to drinking their own urine. "It gagged me, you know." "It came up at first." "Your mouth gets so dry and you rinse your mouth out—quite bitter. Well, you just force yourself; you got to take it." "You rinse your mouth several times first, and then eventually you would take a little swallow, and after a while it wasn't as bad as you thought it was." It was "improvised water." "Eventually I drank as much as I wanted." "One fellow down there—I thought he was drinking beer. He seemed to be at the can all the time." The men referred to it as "lime rickey."

*   *   *

". . . it was common in some churches for worshipers to handle snakes. Authority for this practice was cited in the sixteenth chapter of St. Mark in which Christ is quoted as saying, 'These signs shall follow them that believe: in my name shall they cast out dev-ils; they shall speak with new tongues; they shall take up serpents.'"

To handle snakes without being bitten is to have "perfect victory" over them. "When you are in the anointing, you are perfect."

"It's tremendous. It came over me in such a fantastic way. I felt it through my whole body. I just went plumb out in under the power. . . . God was telling me to take up the serpent." "I feel kind of warm all over, like a warm covering." ". . . it was like a heavy warm rain coming down upon him." "You just feel like it. A tingling-like. All over my body. My hands feel numb-like. Sometimes I've had them to just draw up, to draw up because of more anointing."

"God pours it out so fast that I'm doing it before I have time to say, 'Should I or shouldn't I?' Whenever you have time to let your mind do any thinking, you don't have the strongest anointing."

"Sometimes I'll get a serpent so fiery, I'll have to wait for perfect victory. It takes away *all fear*. Then I can handle even the real fiery serpents."

"A big gold rattlesnake struck at him, and hit his hand. But it didn't actually bite him because it closed its mouth too fast. Brother Enos said, 'In Jesus name, don't you do that no more.' And that serpent settled down right then and there."

"I just unbuttoned my shirt and stuck the cobra inside. It crawled around on the inside, all the way around. Then I pulled it back out. I was just getting step-by-step instructions from the Lord."

"Today, when the anointing comes, it slowly starts in Danny's chest and makes him breathe hard. He then feels a numbing process beginning in the bones of his fingers and arms. Next, it flows to his face and legs. Lastly, it spreads through his belly and envelops his entire being. 'Then it bursts out from inside my flesh to the very outside, and it seems like every cell in my fingers comes alive,' explained Danny. 'And as it increases, it's like a fire. It starts to draw.' When the power becomes stronger, Danny feels chilled. His flesh gets cold. He says, 'It doesn't make any difference how hot it is out, my hands get cold. I've had them get almost like ice.' Once he's anointed completely, it runs from his head to his toes, like an electric current sweeping up and down him."

"Oh Lord, I long to see the day when they quit calling me a low-down Jesus snake handler."

*　　*　　*

"My podner and I were hunting on the Buckhannon, and camped at Indian Camp. One evening, just after nightfall, while reclining near our fire, we were startled by hearing from the canopy of laurel which crowned the brow of the overhanging rock, the soft notes of a melody, strange, weird, and entrancing. As the music floated down through the darkness, I was enthralled. Never had I heard cadence of such mingled sadness and joy. It was the voice of a woman, but not of earth; the carol of a bird, from Paradise. It seemed everywhere; it filled the recesses of the cavern, it stole through the thickets and flooded the forest with melody sweet and unreal. I was enraptured, transported, lost. I laughed, I wept. My comrade, unable to control his feelings, sprang upon the large rock in the entrance of the cavern and danced in mad abandonment. How long the song lasted, I never knew. It died away as mysteriously as it came, and left us wondering what it could be."

"200 years ago, a Mr. and Mrs. Livingstone of Middleway, West Virginia, gave accommodation to a stranger for the night. In the morning the stranger was dead. He bore no identification, and they gave him a simple burial. 'No sooner had the Livingstones come home from the burial than the logs in the fireplace began to writhe and cry out in pain. One by one, they sailed out of the hearth and around the room, comets trailing tails of fire. The Livingstones scrambled after them, terrified that their house would go up in smoke, but as fast as they replaced a log on the fire, it would hurl itself back into the room.' Later: '. . . holes appeared in the Living-stones' linens and clothes, all of them neat crescent moons.' A young boy 'swaggered into the house, began taunting the ghost, but cowered and fled the instant the wizard reached down unseen and snipped out the seat of his pants.'"

"Point Pleasant! Does our world begin and end there? The New River—one of the world's oldest, geologically—joins the Gauley to form the Great Kanawha, which emptied into the Ohio at Point Pleasant. Here the Frenchman Celeron de Blainville (usually misspelled de Bienville) buried a lead plate August 18, 1749, to claim the area for France. Here George Washington found his Eldorado, the spot—as one Washington biographer has said—he loved more than any other on earth. In 1774 occurred the Battle of Point Pleasant. Then in the 1960s Point Pleasant was the center of a UFO-monster 'invasion' . . ."

"Of interest here is the 'Green Bank Formula' established by eleven of the world's leading scientists at a secret meeting at Green Bank (site of the Green Bank National Radio Astronomy Observatory)." ". . . here the astrophysicists have been swinging the huge disk of their receiver to intercept possible signals from other sentient beings in outer space."

"Connie Carpenter, a shy, sensitive eighteen year old, was driving home from church . . . when she suddenly saw a huge gray figure. It was shaped like a man, she said, but was much larger. It was at least seven feet tall and very broad. The thing that attracted her attention was not its size, but its eyes. It had, she said, large, round, fiercely glowing red eyes that focused on her with hypnotic effect. As she slowed, her eyes fixed on the apparition, a pair of wings unfolded from its back. They seemed to have a span of about ten feet. It was definitely not an ordinary bird, but a man-shaped thing which rose slowly off the ground, straight up, like a helicopter, silently. Its wings did not flap in flight. It headed straight toward Connie's car, its horrible eyes fixed to her face, then it swooped low over her head as she shoved the accelerator to the floorboards in utter hysteria."

"A huge, bird-like creature, with glowing red eyes, had suddenly dropped like a heavy wet sack upon the sand of the yard. It made a flapping, gurgling sound as it righted itself and stood up."

"There, blocking the road, crouched a huge, black *thing*. Ape-like in appearance, it straightened up and stood about eight feet tall. It seemed to be watching them with curiosity and remained in the middle of the road for about 30 seconds while the two youths, now near panic, wondered what to do. Then the creature waddled off into the woods and they gunned the car out of there."

"No one noticed a nose or mouth, only eyes, or eye-like openings, from which projected 'greenish-orange beams of light.' These light beams pierced through the haze pervading the scene . . . No one is sure whether the shape rested on the ground or was floating . . . there was a strange, nauseous odor resembling burning metal, or burning sulfur."

". . . they saw two red eyes glaring at them; a huge monster, ten feet tall, breathing fire, with a bright-green body and a blood-red face, waddled toward them, and they turned and ran."

"He wore a silvery skin-tight costume and had very long silvery hair."

"It didn't seem to be walking exactly. It was almost gliding . . . faster than any man could run."

". . . an overpowering odor, 'like metal,' that so sickened them they vomited for hours afterward."

"Its head, all the witnesses agreed later, was shaped like an 'ace of spades.'"

"It loved to chase cars, and frighten menstruating women."

". . . the pop-eyed pterodactyl . . ."

"... his car began to falter again. Sparks flew from under the hood ... as if it had a bad short ... he saw the strange animal standing by the road staring at him with huge, luminous eyes ... 'The points were completely burned out of my car ...'"

"The year of the Garuda was at hand. A dark force was closing over a little town I had never even heard of: Point Pleasant, West Virginia."

"... many UFOs were seen regularly in the area. So many people were congregating at the best sighting areas that the police and firemen had trouble regulating traffic. People were actually coming from hundreds of miles around to spend entire nights watching ..."

"A man of dark complexion came out of the strange flying machine and approached him. The man was dressed in a blue shirt and blue trousers, and gave the witness a message saying he came from another world called *Lanulos*."

"... on a population basis recorded UFO sightings in West Virginia far exceed those of any other state."

"Since that sighting on November 2, 1967, Mrs. Thomas had been plagued by bad dreams. 'I saw a lot of strange people around the river,' she explained. 'It's like some kind of invasion or something. They come over the bridge in trucks and they pour into the TNT area. We grab the kids and run. I can't figure out what it means ...' 'Just before I got your letter ... had a nightmare. There were a lot of people drowning in the river and Christmas packages were floating everywhere in the water.'"

And the next day, the suspension bridge at Point Pleasant writhed, convulsed, and collapsed, drowning commuters and Christmas shoppers.

*   *   *

A West Virginian can spit tobacco juice 19 feet into a head wind. Levi Morgan, frontier Indian fighter, "was the only man known who could at full speed leap between the first and second bars of a split rail fence and land on his feet."

An early hunter on the Cheat River reported seeing a rattlesnake with the body of a small fawn between its jaws.

"West Virginia—the Switzerland of America."

"In 1794, Dr. Jesse Bennett, of Wheeling, performed the first recorded Caesarean operation in America."

"1857, box cars on the Northwestern Virginia RR carried enough staves to barrel the Mississippi or to coop all the whiskey which floats down the Father of Waters."

1933, the largest shipment of matches ever assembled—twenty carloads—was sent from Wheeling to Memphis.

"Iaeger . . . was the starting point of the longest, heaviest train ever assembled . . . consisting of five hundred coal cars and three diesel engines pulling with three more three hundred cars back, it weighed more than forty-seven thousand tons" and "was more than four miles long."

West Virginia was the first state to institute a sales tax.

". . . West Virginia children are still expected to believe that James Rumsey, not Robert Fulton, invented the steamboat; that Amos Dolbear, not Alexander Graham Bell, invented the telephone . . . and so on. They are also taught to memorize the West Virginia locations of such items as the world's largest clothespin factory, the world's largest ashtray . . ."

"The 24-mile-long nylon fence that the artist Christo draped across the California mountains was sewn by the good folks of Smithville, West Virginia."

* * *

On the night of November 8, 1805, one Abel Clemmons, of Clarksburg, killed his wife and eight children with an axe.

"At Jaco Inn, on Jaco Hill, run by old man Jaco, many travelers are reputed to have disappeared. Their reputed bones were found many years later, in a nearby cave."

John Powers murdered five women in Quiet Dell.

* * *

"THE GREENBRIER. For more than two centuries The Greenbrier has been ladies and gentlemen being served by ladies and gentlemen . . . it still is. The Legend Continues. The Greenbrier derives its splendor from the panoramic elegance of the Allegheny Mountains themselves. The exclusive vista of 6,500 acres spanning an upland valley is yours to enjoy as is the pleasure of being our welcomed guest. The Greenbrier's proven ability to anticipate your special needs and to serve them with courtesy and efficiency is legendary. We're proud of our heritage at the Greenbrier . . . Many of our staff proudly claim two and even three generations of family service with the Greenbrier . . . beautifully appointed rooms and suites in the Hotel, spacious Guest Houses and Cottages . . . a large reception area and meeting rooms with patios, terraces, and rooftop gardens . . . jogging, hiking, horseback riding . . . crosscountry skiing . . . fishing . . . trap and skeet . . . formal gardens . . . Creative Arts Colony . . . shops, boutiques . . . three 18-hole championship golf courses . . . 20 championship tennis courts . . . indoor and outdoor swimming pools . . . bowling alley . . . game room . . . sauna and Fitness Center . . . Everywhere you turn at the Greenbrier another rich experience awaits you. From the foyers filled with magnificent paintings and art treasures to the stately Georgian architecture and gracious service, everything speaks of time-honored tradition. *At the Greenbrier, the legend continues.*"

The Hale House, a hotel built in Charleston in 1871, had a hundred bedrooms—and one bathroom.

*   *   *

Frank and Jesse James refused to rob a bank in Princeton: "The bank was so insignificant that to rob it would be a reflection on their prowess."

*   *   *

"About Indian Camp there hovers an interesting tradition of a 'Lost Mine,' and buried treasure of fabulous richness. Its origin antedates the Revolution, with some apparent foundation of truth; although the region is not alone in its claim to the scene of original operations . . . The mine was worked by a party of Spanish and English adventurers, who were subsequently nearly exterminated by their Indian allies . . . It is believed by some investigators that straggling bands of the early Spanish explorers of the Southern tidewater, penetrated the Virginia and Kentucky wilderness. It would have been in keeping with the traditions of these insatiable gold seekers to have done so . . . Near Indian Camp in 1883, I was shown the ruins of the 'ancient mine' . . ."

Bibliography

Alvord, Clarence W., and Bidgood, Lee. *The First Explorations of the Trans Allegheny Region by the Virginians, 1650-1694.* Cleveland, 1912.

Anderson, Jean. *The Haunting of America.* New York, 1975.

Barker, Gray. *They Knew Too Much About Flying Saucers.* New York, 1956.

The Berkshire Eagle. [Pittsfield, Mass.], May 2, 1986.

Brooks, Maurice. *The Appalachians.* Boston, 1965.

Chappell, Louis W. *John Henry: A Folk-Lore Story.* Fort Washington, 1968.

Coleman, McAlister. *Men and Coal.* New York, 1943.

Coles, Robert. *The Children of Crisis.* Boston, 1970.

Cometti, Elizabeth, and Summers, Festus P., eds. *The Thirty-Fifth State: A Documentary History of West Virginia.* Morgantown, 1966.

Cox, Jacob D. *Military Reminiscences of the Civil War.* New York, 1900.

Downes, Randolph C. "Dunmore's War: An Interpretation." *Mississippi Valley Historical Review* (1934).

Dubofsky, Melvin, and Van Tine, Warren. *John L. Lewis.* New York, 1977.

Egan, Michael. *The Flying, Gray-Haired Yank.* Philadelphia, 1888.

Fetherling, Dale. *Mother Jones, The Miners' Angel: A Portrait.* Carbondale, 1974.

Fitzpatrick, John C., ed. *The Diaries of George Washington.* Boston, 1923.

__________, ed. *The Writings of George Washington.* Washington, 1931.

Gibbens, Alvaro F. *Historic Blennerhassett.* Chillicothe, 1850.

The Greenbrier. [Publicity Literature]. White Sulphur Springs, 1985.

Hale, John Peter. *Daniel Boone.* Wheeling, 188?.

__________. *Trans-Allegheny Pioneers.* Charleston, 1886.

Hall, Granville. *The Rending of Virginia.* Chicago, 1902.

Hume, Brit. *Death and the Mines: Rebellion and Murder in the United Mine Workers.* New York, 1971.

Johnson, Guy Benton. *John Henry.* Chapel Hill, 1929.

Jones, Mary H. *The Autobiography of Mother Jones.* Chicago, 1972.

Jones, Virgil C. *The Hatfields and the McCoys.* Chapel Hill, 1948.

Keel, John A. *The Mothman Prophecies* New York, 1975.

__________. *The Eighth Tower.* New York, 1975.

Korson, George. *Coal Dust on the Fiddle.* Philadelphia, 1943.

Lee, Howard B. *Bloodletting in Appalachia.* Morgantown, 1969.

Lewis, Virgil. *History of the Battle of Point Pleasant.* Charleston, 1909.

Lucas, Rex A. *Men in Crisis: A Study of a Mine Disaster.* New York, 1969.

McWhorter, Lucullus Virgil. *The Border Settlers of Northwestern Virginia from 1768 to 1795.* Hamilton, Ohio, 1915.

Menzel, Donald H., and Boyd, Lyle G. *The World of Flying Saucers.* New York, 1963.

Metcalf, Paul. *Waters of Potowmack.* San Francisco, 1982.

Moore, George E. *A Banner in the Hills.* New York, 1963.

Myers, Sylvester. *Myers' History of West Virginia.* Wheeling, 1915.

New York Times, December 17, 1967.

__________, November 21-December 1, 1968.

North, E. Lee. *Redcoats, Redskins, and Red-Eyed Monsters.* South Brunswick and New York, 1979.

Pelton, Robert W., and Cardon, Karen W. *Snake Handlers: God-Fearers? Or Fanatics?* Nashville and New York, 1974.

Potomac Basin Reporter. [Interstate Commission on the Potomac River Basin], Rockville, Maryland, February, 1986.

Rice, Otis K. *The Allegheny Frontier.* Lexington, 1970.

Ross, Malcolm W. *Machine Age in the Hills.* New York, 1933.

Safford, William H. *Life of Harman Blennerhassett.* Chillicothe, 1850.

Siviter, Anna Pierpont. *Recollections of War and Peace, 1861-1868.* New York, 1938.

The Springfield Republican. [Springfield, Mass]., October 26, 1986.

Summers, Festus B., and Ambler, C.H. *West Virginia: The Mountain State.* New York, 1958.

Taylor, Walter H. *General Lee, His Campaigns in Virginia, 1861-1865.* Norfolk, 1906.

Washington, Booker T. *Up from Slavery.* Boston, 1965.

Williams, John Alexander. *West Virginia.* New York, 1976.

Withers, A.S. *Chronicles of Border Warfare.* Cincinnati, 1895.

Writers' Program, Works Progress Administration. *West Virginia: A Guide to the Mountain State.* New York, 1941.

"... and nobody objected."

"And there I found very many islands filled with people without number, and of them all I have taken possession for their Highnesses, by proclamation and with the royal standard displayed, and nobody objected."

—CHRISTOPHER COLUMBUS,
reporting on his First Voyage

ONE

Who was he? Where was he born? When was he born? Where did he come from? Where had he traveled? What had he done? Where did he study? What did he know? What was his name?

He was described as "a man from the land of Genoa, a merchant of books of print who traded in them . . ." Yet he bragged to Ferdinand and Isabella that he had gone to sea at fourteen, and that he had "been twenty-three years upon the sea without quitting it for any time long enough to be counted . . ."

Was his hair white, or was it red? Was he the son of a poor weaver who neglected his loom, ran a tavern, had to be bailed out of a Genoese jail where he had been locked up for debt?

Was Genoa a jail to Christopher, with the Mediterranean Sea at his feet, spreading outward, beckoning?

Why could his son Ferdinand, returning to Genoa years later, find no trace of the family?

Why did Christopher speak Spanish with a Portuguese accent? Why did he write in Spanish, even before he arrived in Spain? Or in Latin, with errors that a Spaniard would make?

Las Casas reported that: "In the matters of the Christian religion, no doubt he was a Catholic and of much devotion."

But was he protesting too much, laboring doubly hard to prove his Christian fervor? Was his family, in fact, Spanish Jews who had fled Spain and the Inquisition a generation or two earlier? Why did he write that "the holy spirit works in Christians, Jews, Moors . . ." and "All people received their astronomy from the Jews"?

There were name changes: Colombo . . . Colomo . . . Colom . . . Colón . . .

It was in Portugal, before going to Spain, that he married Doña Felipa, and engendered his first son, Diego. But "wanting to go on sailing, he left his wife there."

Why does he seem so much the preincarnation of Don Quixote, who also believed in islands, who had to adventure, and who set such great store by the titles and trappings of his status? (Columbus: "... that he should be honored and armed a Knight with golden spurs.")

He would discover islands where he would be secure against the threat that his uncertain heritage might come to light.

Or was he—for all the mysteries, the obfuscations, the clouds of black ink that, like the squid, he oozed out around the facts of his life—simply put, an outrageous, wholesale liar?

TWO

It was said that Isabella "meant to finance the expedition herself by drawing on the royal treasury." Her funds, generally depleted, were perhaps enriched now by Moorish plunder, and by property and money confiscated by the Inquisition.

There was also a substantial loan (over a million *maravedis*), secured by one Luis de Santángel, keeper of accounts of the royal household, who borrowed from the *Santa Hermandad*, the Secret Police.

De Santangel imposed a fine on the citizens of the town of Palos, ordering them to build, equip, and man two caravels, at their own expense.

The fine, perhaps, was for smuggling.

THREE

Who was he? Where did he come from? What went on in his head?
   Was he, in truth, Don Quixote?
   "He saw visions and he heard voices." And he wrote that "St. Peter, when he jumped into the sea, walked on it as long as his faith was firm."

"The [Portuguese] King, as he observed this *Christovoa Colom* to be a big talker and boastful in setting forth his accomplishments, and full of fancy and imagination with his Isle Cypango than certain whereof he spoke, gave him small credit."
   "... they all considered the words of *Christovoa Colom* as vain, simply founded on imagination ..."
   The Spanish cosmographers "judged his promises and offers were impossible and vain ... and that it was all air and there was no reason in it ..."
   "... the said Admiral always went beyond the bounds of truth ..."
   But Isabella—with insanity touching both her mother and her daughter—was just strange enough to listen ...
   On the several voyages, he deceived his crews, hoarded the charts, misled even the sovereigns as to where and how far he was sailing. He claimed to have developed a "mode of reckoning derived from astronomy which ... resembles a prophetic vision."

When Ovando set sail, against Columbus's advice, and all but three or four of his twenty-eight ships went down in a storm, Columbus was accused of raising the tempest himself, by magic act ...

Columbus:
"St. Augustine says that the end of this world is to come in the

seventh millenary of years from its creation . . . there are only lacking 155 years to complete the 7000, in which year the world must end."

. . . condoning and justifying all brutalities against the Indians, as extreme haste must be made to convert the heathen . . .

Did he once chop the paws off a wild monkey, and throw him to a wild pig, to enjoy the battle between the two?

FOUR

When the flotilla set sail on the first voyage the ships were manned largely by experienced seamen, with a lesser number of jailbirds.

There were no women. Women were bad luck on the ocean.

And no priests.

On later voyages, the more extensive use of jailbirds was proposed—when it was determined that the Indians could not be made to work. Convicted criminals would be reprieved if they agreed to settle in Española. Excluded from this opportunity were those found guilty of:

> heresy
> lèse majesté
> treason
> counterfeiting of coinage
> and sodomy

FIVE

Columbus:

"The Paradise on Earth is a pleasant place, situated in certain regions of the Orient, at a long distance by land and by sea from our inherited world. It rises so high that it touches the lunar sphere . . ."

"I always read that the world, land and water, was spherical . . . Now I observed so much divergence, that I began to hold different views about the world and I found that it was not round . . . but pear-shaped, round except where it has a nipple, for there it is taller, as if one had a round ball and, on one side, it should be like a woman's breast, and this nipple part is the highest and closest to heaven . . ."

"There is a spring in Paradise which waters the Garden of Delights and which splays into four rivers."

"We reached the latter island near a large mountain which seemed almost to reach heaven, and in the centre of that mountain there was a peak which was much higher than all the rest of the mountain, and from which many streams flowed in different directions, especially toward the direction in which we lay. At a distance of three leagues a waterfall appeared . . . which precipitated from such a high point that it seemed to fall from heaven."

"I think the earthly paradise lies here, which no one can enter but by God's permission."

On the first voyage, early in the return, Columbus set out to discover the island of Matinino, inhabited, as the Indians told him, only by women.

"In Cariay and the neighboring country there are great enchanters of a very fearful character . . . When I arrived they sent me immediately two girls very showily dressed; the oldest could not be more than eleven years of age, and the other seven, and both exhibited so much immodesty that more could not be expected from public women . . ."

". . . the women have very pretty bodies, and they were the first to bring what they had . . ."

"On the previous day . . . he saw three mermaids, which rose well out of the sea."

In the Gulf of Paria, he observed the tiny oysters clinging to the mangrove roots, the oyster shells open, to catch from the leaves above, dewdrops that engender pearls.

SIX

Pope Alexander VI:

"Alexander, bishop, servant of the servants of God, to the illustrious sovereigns, our very dear son in Christ, Ferdinand, king, and our very dear daughter in Christ, Isabella, queen, of Castile, Leon, Aragon, and Granada, health and apostolic benediction. Among other works well pleasing to the Divine Majesty and cherished of our heart, this assuredly ranks highest, that in our times especially the Catholic faith and the Christian religion be exalted and everywhere increased and spread, that the health of souls be cared for and that barbarous nations be overthrown and brought to the faith itself."

Father Ascensión:

"This will be discovering here another world, to the end that in all of it may be preached the Holy Gospel, and the conversion undertaken of many souls throughout its whole extent who live without religion or knowledge of the true God or of his most sacred law. Since all have been ransomed by the most precious blood of Our Redeemer and Lord Jesus Christ, it is a very great pity that they should be condemned for want of this light and the knowledge of the truth. May His Most Holy Majesty, for He created them and died for them, grant that to so many and various nations of lands so remote and as yet undiscovered, knowledge be given of His most holy law, that they may receive and believe it, and that by means of holy baptism their souls may be saved, and that they may enjoy it."

". . . the Spaniards can go on settling other districts and places suitable for effecting the conversion of souls, and affording them profits and advantages; for if the Spaniard does not see any advantage he will not be moved to do good, and these souls will perish without remedy if it is understood that no profit will be drawn from going there. But if they are lured by self-interest they will go on discovering new lands every day, so much, indeed, that it will be necessary to keep them in check..."

Columbus:

"There are many spices, and great mines of gold and other metals."

"Thus the eternal God, our Lord, gives victory to those who follow His way over apparent impossibilities."

On the Indians: "Christendom shall make good business with them."

Las Casas:

"What good tidings all over the land, and such a good show of Christian gentility and goodness."

SEVEN

Columbus's mission was "to reduce to the obedience of their Highnesses savage and warlike peoples who live in mountains and in the wilderness."

And yet the Sovereigns' express command, for the second voyage, was that the Indians were to be treated "well and lovingly."

He found the natives to be "well-built, with good bodies and handsome features . . . They do not bear arms, and do not know them . . ."

". . . the lands of the country cannot be more beautiful . . . nor the men more cowardly . . ."

"I did not find, as some of us had expected, any cannibals among them, but on the contrary, men of great deference and kindness."

". . . wonderfully timorous . . ."

". . . timid beyond cure . . ."

"With fifty men we could subjugate them all . . ."

"As soon as I arrived in the Indies, on the first island which I found, I took some of the natives by force . . ."

> (Las Casas: ". . . as if indeed it was necessary to instill hatred before preaching the Gospel!")

Isabella issued a slave-raiding license: "To take Indian men and women for slaves, without harming them . . . to take them as nearly as possible with their consent; and in the same manner he may take monsters and animals of any kind . . ."

Columbus sent five hundred slaves to Castile, "a cargo of human cattle." Many of them died of cold.

Las Casas:

". . . our work was to exasperate, ravage, kill, mangle and destroy . . ."

". . . each generation of men has a time appointed for its calling."

"It was a general rule among Spaniards to be cruel; not just cruel, but extraordinarily cruel so that harsh and bitter treatment would prevent Indians from daring to think of themselves as human beings or having a minute to think at all. So they would cut an Indian's hands and leave them dangling by a shred of skin and they would send them on, saying, 'Go now, spread your news to your chiefs.' They would test their swords and their manly strength on captured Indians and place bets on their slicing off of heads or the cutting of bodies in half with one blow."

In Haiti, every Indian, fourteen or older, was ordered to bring in a certain amount of gold every three months. But there were no gold fields, no mines, only dust to be gathered in the streams. Natives who failed to fill their quota had their hands cut off, or they were hunted down with dogs and killed.

Later, mines were opened: ". . . mountains are stripped from top to bottom and bottom to top a thousand times; they dig, split rocks, move stones, and carry dirt on their backs to wash it in the rivers . . ."

After six or eight months in the mines, the men were sent home, where their wives had continued to work the soil alone. Husbands and wives—both—were too tired to procreate.

The naked Indians fought back, "with no other shields than their bellies."

Las Casas:

"The Spaniards found pleasure in inventing all kinds of odd cruelties, the more cruel the better, with which to spill human blood. They built a long gibbet, low enough for the toes to touch the ground and prevent strangling, and hanged thirteen of them at a time in honor of Christ Our Savior and the twelve Apostles.

(". . . each generation has a time appointed for its calling.")

"When the Indians were thus still alive and hanging, the Spaniards tested their strength and their blades against them, ripping chests open with one blow and exposing entrails . . ."

(". . . each generation . . .")

"Then, straw was wrapped around their torn bodies and they were burned alive . . . My eyes have seen these acts so foreign to human nature, and now I tremble as I write, not believing them myself, afraid that I was dreaming."

> (One, being burned at the stake, refused baptism for fear that in heaven he would find more Christians there.)

Las Casas, on Columbus:

"His was a crafty ignorance, if indeed it was ignorance and not greed."

The Indians "fled to avoid . . . the ferocious and wild condition of the Spaniards . . ."

". . . they rushed in all directions like lunatics, women dropping and abandoning infants in the rush, running for miles without stopping, fleeing across mountains and rivers."

Masses of the natives created their own final mode of escape: ingestions of casava poison.

Bibliography

Berkhofer, Robert F., Jr. *The White Man's Indian: Images of the American Indian from Columbus to the Present.* New York, 1978.

Bolton, Herbert Eugene, ed. *Spanish Exploration in the Southwest. 1542-1706—Original Narratives of Early American History.* New York, 1908.

Brandon, William. *The Last Americans: The Indian in American Culture.* New York, 1974

Collier, John. *Indians of the Americas.* New York, 1947.

Davenport, Francis Gardiner. *European Treaties Bearing on the History of the United States and Dependencies.* Carnegie Institutions of Washington, 1917.

de las Casas, Bartolomé. *History of the Indies.* New York, 1971.

de Madriaga, Salvador. *Christopher Columbus.* London, 1949.

Ford, P.L., ed. *The Writings of Christopher Columbus.* New York, 1982.

Jennings, Francis. *The Invasion of America: Indians, Colonialism, and the Cant of Conquest.* Chapel Hill, 1975.

Konig, Hans. *Columbus: His Enterprise.* New York, 1976.

Metcalf, Paul. *Genoa.* Highlands, N.C., 1965.

Morison, Samuel Eliot. *Christopher Columbus, Mariner.* Boston, 1955.

__________. ed. *Journals and Other Documents on the Life and Voyage of Christopher Columbus.* New York, 1963.

Nash, Gary B. *Red, White, and Black: The Peoples of Early America.* Englewood Cliffs, 1970.

Sauer, Carl Ortwin. *Early Spanish Main.* Berkeley, 1969.

Vogel, Virgil, ed. *This Country Was Ours.* New York, 1972.

ARAMINTA
AND
THE COYOTES

ARAMINTA
AND THE COYOTES

1820, or thereabouts, on the Brodas plantation, Maryland, near
Bucktown:

One Araminta Ross came into being. Name later changed to
Harriet. She was one of eleven children.

According to legend she was "one of those Ashantis": courageous,
rebellious . . .

> (for four centuries the Ashantis on the West Coast of
> Africa fought off British invasion, colonial possession,
> bondage)

Araminta grew to be five feet tall, her skin the very blackest of blackness,
her eyes sullen, hooded with heavy lids, her lower lip protruding . . .

> . . . she was, indeed, the utmost niggerish of niggers,
> superbly designed to engender her owner's antipathy.

Araminta sang . . . her voice had a husky timbre, the result of child-
hood bronchitis. She loved to sing!

and she loved to run! to run! to run!

Later, as she developed her theatrical skills, she could, when it
became useful to her, let her face go slack . . . so as to appear unbe-
lievably stupid.

*   *   *

Age thirteen—or perhaps it was later, she might have been fifteen or sixteen—Araminta worked one day in the cornfield. The young slave next to her, laboring in desultory fashion, suddenly rose and slipped away. The overseer caught sight of him, and ordered him back. But the slave ran on, and the overseer took off in pursuit.

Araminta's heart began to flutter . . . a fluttering she would experience again and again, life-long, whenever she felt trouble. She followed the two men.

Out of the cornfield, down the old rolling road, to the crossroads . . . the male slave, the overseer, and the young girl. The slave ducked into the country store, the overseer cornered him . . . but the man was young, big and strong, and the overseer ordered Araminta to help tie him up.

She did not move. She stood in the doorway, and did not move. The slave ducked past her, slipped out, and the overseer, furious, picked up a two-pound iron weight and hurled it after him.

By miscalculation—or was it?—the aim was faulty. The iron struck the motionless girl full in the brow, a straight blow. Her skull cracked and crushed, she slumped to the floor. Blood poured from the gash.

*   *   *

She was taken, unconscious, to the slave quarter, deposited in the corner of the cabin on a bundle of rags—rags that became her home for weeks to come. Fellow slaves looked in on her, and all predicted she would die—such a great dent in her head, the blood that had poured out. She lay still, sleeping, sleeping . . . breathing. When she came awake, she looked at the world silently, through dulled eyes. She endured headaches quietly . . . but at night she could be heard to moan and whimper.

Brodas, the owner, looked in upon her, with dismay. He put her up for sale, and brought a succession of buyers to the cabin. They would look at her—at the great hole in the brow, the wasted flesh, the dulled eyes. No offer was made. Rumor reached the cabins that she might be sold south.

*   *   *

Slowly, she began to come back. She would emerge from time to time from the cabin. But she remained uncommunicative. Brodas —initially angered, for she had defied the overseer—finally decided that the blow to the head had knocked her senseless.

At any moment, and without warning, she would drop to the ground and fall into a coma—a brief and unpredictable sleep. Narcolepsy. Paroxysmal trance. A heavy and wearying rest. When she awoke she would appear unaware of what had happened, continuing as before. The children of the quarter, with the cruelty natural to children, taunted her, called her lazy—with her dazed look, her head hanging to one side. She kept her thoughts to herself.

> (These narcotic episodes remained with her to the end of her life.)

*   *   *

Even as a child, Araminta had hated housework, preferred to be in the fields alongside the men. After the accident, when her strength began to return, Brodas finally sold her, as a housemaid. Here she was regularly whipped, declared to be "not worth a sixpence." The new owner returned her, and Brodas, as a last resort, put her to work in the fields.

Her strength not only returned, but developed at an extraordinary pace. With her long skirts dragging the ground, the signature bandana wrapped around her head, she could be seen hoeing corn, hauling wood, splitting rails. Her arms became fibrous, her hands strong and calloused.

Her father was hired out as a timber inspector, superintending the cutting of timber for the Baltimore shipyards. Araminta worked with him, cutting and hauling the logs. "Her usual stint was half a cord of wood a day."

Powerful men watched in astonishment, as she lifted barrels of flour and other heavy weights.

Brodas became proud of her, would show her off to his guests, drawing "a loaded stone boat like an ox."

*   *   *

In 1844, with the consent of her owner, she married another slave, one John Tubman. The name Araminta, and its diminutives Minta and Minty, disappeared. She became, as she was known for the rest of her life: Harriet Tubman.

*   *   *

Later, many years later, when she met the legendary John Brown, he referred to her as General Tubman, and said of her, she "is the most of a man naturally that I ever met with."

*   *   *

Her sleep remained troubled, filled with intense three-dimensional dreams, events appearing more sharply to her than in her waking moments. She dreamed of real places, places she had never seen, and later in life, when she did see these places, she recognized them, from her dreams.

She dreamed of "flying over fields and towns, and rivers and mountains, looking down upon them 'like a bird,' and reaching at last a great fence or sometimes a river over which she would try to fly . . ." She believed in her dreams, and in omens, and at times "she would break forth into wild and strange rhapsodies."

> (She always knew when there was danger near, by the fluttering of her heart. "They may say 'Peace, Peace,' as much as they like, *I know it's going to be war.*")

In her fantasy she saw a line, and on the northern side were white women, stretching hands across the boundary to welcome her.

*   *   *

She prayed that her face would be washed clean, and her heart purified of sin. And she prayed for her owner, Brodas: "Oh Lord, convert Ole Master. Oh, dear Lord, change that man's heart . . ."

Later, as she became hardened, her prayer changed: "Lord, if you're never going to change that man's heart—*Kill him,* Lord, and take him out of the way." And she said it over and over again. *"Kill him,* Lord. *Kill him."*

It was not long after that Brodas became ill, and the doctor told the family that he would surely die. One morning, suddenly, the master was dead.

*   *   *

The year was 1849. Brodas was gone, and rumor spread through the quarter that the slaves would be dispersed. Two of Harriet's brothers had already been sold to the chain gang, and it was thought that the two remaining, together with Harriet, would follow.

Years earlier, Harriet had been befriended by a white woman in the neighborhood, who had told Harriet she would help her if she ever wished to escape.

Harriet spoke to her brothers, persuaded them to join her. But on the night of departure, the men cowered, and returned home. Harriet went on alone.

She headed for the white woman's house, taking with her a treasured quilt, as a gift. The woman accepted the quilt, and gave Harriet a slip of paper, with directions to the first sympathetic house, north. Unable to read, Harriet nonetheless followed the directions—and the North Star—and arrived safely.

Thus she traveled for the first time, self-conducted, along the rails of the Underground Railroad. Destination: Philadelphia.

*   *   *

From Africa, on the slave ships, to labor on the plantations . . . the new slaves, newly arrived, were called "saltbacks."

And then, to escape . . .

Like many a slave, Araminta, as a child, had believed that there was a *real* Underground Railroad, a steam train that ran through a tunnel from South to North, carrying slaves to freedom, leaving a trail of smoke and cinders . . .

*   *   *

Throughout her life, she held daily conversations with God, and her every move was under His direction.

If there was danger, there was the heart fluttering . . .

"They may say, 'Peace, Peace,' as much as they like, *I know it's going to be war.*"

*   *   *

On the Mexican side
of the Rio Grande:
"I wonder how many
have drowned in this?"
"No one knows what happens
to the ones trying to cross.
In the river, we're neither here nor there . . .
so no one counts."

"The banks of the river harbored a world different from that of the dusty shacks behind us—one of greenery, cool breezes, and dancing shadows. Somehow, though, the murky waters of the Rio Grande beyond did not exude the epic quality that I had expected . . . it looked too tame and weedy, too mundane to serve as the great symbol of division between two cultures, two economies. Though apparently deep, it could not have been more than fifty yards across. And the u.s. side, grassy and treeless with a couple of junked cars visible: this is the promised land?"

Preparing to cross: ". . . they could see the boat—two automobile hoods welded together . . ."

or perhaps a leaky rubber raft: ". . . a rapid stream of big bubbles emerging from underneath . . ."

"The river can go wild when flash floods hit it. It is a river that heeds no boundaries between nations, is in fact so unpredictable and has shifted courses so often that new agreements had to be made to determine the boundary between the u.s. and Mexico. Its currents can be swift. It can offer surprise eddies and undertows, all of which can kill. The discovery of bodies is so routine that local newspapers make little, if any, note of them. No one really knows how many men and women have started to cross the river and drowned before reaching the other side . . ."

"No one knows how many bodies have floated down the river and into the Gulf of Mexico, never to be found."

Sin papeles, without papers, he engages with a coyote to guide him across the border and into the States. Crossing, he becomes a mojado, a wetback.

The coyote may be simply a passador, passing the mojado on, or he may be an engachador, contracting the wetback's labor to a u.s. employer.

To the coyote, the mojado is a pollo—chicken—hence the coyote is a pollero.

Among the mojados there may be an alambrista—a wire-cutter to cut a way through fences.

To the u.s. Border Patrol—la migra—they are all wets, mojados, pollos . . . and sometimes tonks, a remnant of jargon from confrontation with Chinese Tongs.

Crossing over, the wetback may be subject to robbery and rape by fellow wetbacks who have been robbed by gangs of anglo, chicano or Mexicans—by Mexican police who follow them across—and by their own coyotes: polleros turned pistoleros.

"Another coyote?" Sí. "And I will be his pollo. And over there"—he gestured to the Border Patrol—"they are cabrones—goats" (but in slang, cuckolds or bastards).

"We are all animals of one sort or another, verdad?"

* * *

"The Underground Railroad was a risky venture, and Harriet became adept at subterfuges and disguises. She would have been a great actress, her friends said, for she could hollow out her cheeks and cause her body to shrink, and totter about impersonating a very old woman."

"On one of her expeditions . . . she had the incredible nerve to enter a village where lived one of her former masters . . . Her only disguise was a bodily assumption of age. To reinforce this her subtle foresight prompted her to buy some live chickens, which she carried suspended by the legs from a cord. As she turned a corner she saw coming toward her none other than her old master . . . to make an excuse for flight, she loosed the cord that held the fowls and gave chase to them as they flew squawking over a nearby fence."

". . . wild and strange rhapsodies . . ." and the ability to appear stupid . . .

*   *   *

You are strapped to the underside of the coyote's car . . . or you are braced by your legs across the rods, close to the brake line, on the underside of a freight car . . . you ride atop a 12′ truck and come to a bridge with 13′ clearance . . . frozen in a refrigerator truck . . . crushed behind crates in a boxcar . . . the coyote's junk car catches fire, the passengers escape, but you are locked in the trunk . . . your coyote hires an empty cement truck, you and the other pollos are loaded into the mixing tank, and as the coyote drives across the bridge, he throws the switch, to activate the mixer . . .

A sophisticated ring of coyotes, mostly women, became known as Las Hueras—The Blondes. Two of them had dyed their hair.

Across the border from San Diego lies sprawling Tijuana. Fully a fourth of Tijuana's population is transient—making it the largest of the wetback ciudades trampolines.

Tijuana and San Diego were once one, and they are still linked by tubes, ditches, and shared water sources. Some of the tubes are large enough to stand in, others are a mere three feet high.

Half of the houses in Tijuana have no sanitation, and the tubes are used for public toilets—as well as tunnels for wetbacks—crawling on hands and knees, through unspeakable filth and stench . . .

Across the border, you sleep during the day, and walk at night, guided, not by the North Star, but by the red lights on the radio towers.

> ("We . . . continued through orange fields, when a dog began barking. We then changed direction, and Juan said, 'This is too bad, that dog was barking at people.' I asked him what he meant and he said 'Don't you know that dogs bark differently depending on what they are barking at? Now the people in the house know . . . that we are here.'")

> (If you are lucky you will discover a discarded road map, a map, say, of California and Arizona. Unable to read it, you will nevertheless study it, the names of all those cities and places . . .)

1974: ". . . a group of wetbacks inadvertently wandered onto the Marine base at Camp Pendleton while the troops were having night maneuvers. The wetbacks triggered signal flares and one group of marines thought they were the 'opposing army.' The marines attacked, their automatic weapons filled with blanks. The Mexicans stood there, amazed, as the marines advanced on them, firing away. As they were being taken away, the Mexicans were heard to remark that they were rather surprised that the Americans reacted so strongly to their intrusion and one said he could not understand how the marines could have fired so much and not hit anybody."

> echarsela de mojado
> —to go as a wetback—
> valio madre
> —was worth mother—
> i.e.,
> weren't worth nothin'

*　　*　　*

Arriving in Philadelphia, Harriet established the pattern of taking a menial job, saving her money, and then returning south, to bring other slaves northward to freedom. Traveling in winter, for the long dark nights—wearing her long, full skirts—she would start north on a Saturday night, so the slaves would not be missed until Monday.

Abductor, conductor, her tracks passed through Camden, Dover, Blackbird, Laurel, Millsborough, Concord, Seaford, Georgetown, Lewes, Milford, Frederica, Smyrna, Delaware City, Middletown, New Castle, and Wilmington—to Philadelphia.

If she encountered a white person, she turned, so she would be seen facing south. Once, fearing pursuit, she placed her group of slaves on a southbound train. She would ride the cars herself, to eavesdrop on her pursuers. She was nicknamed Moses, and it was years before her pursuers discovered Moses was a woman. Searches for her were fruitless.

Infants who traveled with her were silenced with paregoric.

On her first trip north, her brothers, who had agreed to go with her, backed down. (Her husband also refused.) Never again did a slave, once committed, leave her group. There might be one who would lose heart, but she would win him with persuasion or threaten him with the revolver that she carried. "You go with me or you die." Or, as in one case: "I told the boys to get their guns ready and shoot him. They'd have done it in a minute; but when he heard that, he jumped right up and went on as well as anybody."

The slave owners put up posters advertising the runaways—and Harriet paid a slave to follow them, and tear down the posters.

On one hurrying trip, fearing pursuers, she made her way, danger-ously, along the road, instead of through the woods. She developed a headache, and, fighting against it, she nevertheless fell to the ground and was instantly asleep. Paroxysmal trance. When she awakened, it was daylight, under a bright sun. Her slaves were squatting or standing around her. They knew of her sleeps, knew it was useless to disturb her. She was instantly on her feet, her heart, not fluttering, but pounding. Ordering the group to follow her, she plunged into the woods, almost running. She followed a zigzag course, and some of the slaves thought she was tricking them, taking them back to the plantation. But they continued to follow. They came to a river, and Harriet announced that while asleep she had dreamed of this river, and the Lord had told her to cross it. It was mid-winter, and the water was icy and deep. The slaves stood on the bank, while Harriet walked in. They watched. The water came to her waist, her breasts, her shoulders, her chin. Then it receded, slowly. She crossed, and emerged on the other side. The slaves followed. Cold and wet, they walked through the woods, until coming to a cabin, in a clearing. Harriet had seen this cabin in her dreams, and she knew they would be safe there. They were indeed welcomed, by a family of free Negroes. They were fed, their wet clothing dried before the open fire. Starting out the next day, they followed Harriet's mysterious routing through the woods, and came again to the spot where she had gone to sleep, by the side of the road. The grass had been trampled by horses' feet; the ground was littered with the stubs of half-smoked cigars. The patrollers— "patter-rollers"—had been there. A poster had been nailed to one of the trees. Harriet tore it down.

*   *   *

With the passage of the Fugitive Slave Act (1850), it was no longer enough to deliver the slaves north of Mason and Dixon. To be safe, they must cross into Canada.

"We had heard of Canada . . . simply as a country to which the wild goose and the swan repaired at the end of winter, to escape the heat of summer . . ."

"I could not forget all the horrid stories slaveholders tell about Canada. They assure the slave that, when they get hold of slaves in Canada, they make various uses of them. Sometimes they *skin* the *head,* and wear the wool on their coat collars—put them into the lead-mines, with both eyes out—the young slaves they eat . . ."

The first group to cross with Harriet Tubman "earned their bread by chopping wood in the snows of a Canadian forest—they were frost-bitten, hungry and naked."

* * *

1857, she wanted to bring her aging parents out—but she needed money. She went to the Abolitionist office in New York: "I'm not going to eat or drink till I get enough money to take me down after the old people." She demanded twenty dollars—money that they said they didn't have. So she sat down on the floor and went to sleep. She slept all morning, and into the afternoon. Word got around, and when she awoke, sixty dollars had been raised.

She brought out her parents.

* * *

To cross the desert at night, where the temperature may reach 150° . . . and on to days of stoop labor:

". . . he can always get a job because he can weed a 1,000-foot furrow without once straightening up."

'ILLEGAL ALIENS FARM CITRUS FOR

GOLDWATER COMPANY'

"A mammoth Arizona citrus farm partly owned by the brother of Sen. Barry Goldwater has profited for more than a decade from the sweat of illegal Mexican aliens."

"[Aliens] paid $100 or more a head to 'coyotes' . . . one of whom callously left a boy with an injured leg in the desert to face 120-degree heat with only a gallon of water and a bit of marijuana."

"Lived amid their excrement and garbage in orange-crate shelters . . ."

Deductions in pay were made for Social Security, the numbers issued all beginning with 000—numbers that do not exist.

". . . tuberculosis, lice, scabies, impetigo, influenza . . ."

"The father was naked, trying to bathe as best he could in a shallow irrigation ditch."

On a ranch near El Paso, the "men, and often the women, slept under the long wagons, under trees, in trucks, or in the open fields. The flies, valley mosquitos, and other insects of the southwestern summer, crawled over the workers by night. They welcomed sunrise each morning as an escape to the fields."

In August 1978, the Immigration and Naturalization Service staged a raid on a tomato and cucumber farm in Maryland: ". . . dozens of illegal aliens were suddenly in flight. Some were reportedly jumping out of windows, sprinting from the dilapidated buildings that had once been a World War II prisoner of-war-camp through the mired roads toward the woods . . ."

. . . woods through which, perhaps, Harriet Tubman had led her charges.

*　　*　　*

A price of $40,000 was placed on Harriet Tubman's head—on the one the slave holders called Moses, convinced she was a man.

In all she made a total of 19 trips, freeing some 300 slaves.

"I never ran my train off the track, and I never lost a passenger."

She was the Skipper, the Brains, the Captain. She was also the Throttle Artist, the Drum, the Grunt, the King Snipe, the

Rawhider. Gathering her freight in the Garden, she presided over her Circus. There were no Cushions, no Harness, no Glass Car, Grass Wagon, or Drone Cage, and her railroad had no Herald. There was no Rust, so she was never known to Hoptoad. She might have to Fly Light, and there was no Lizard Scorcher. If pursued, she could Horse Over. Traveling at night, there was no Window Music. But she might dream of the Indian Valley Railroad. She was the Grabber, the Big Ox.

*　*　*

It is a silent invasion, a network, stretching to the continental limits.

> 26 Mexicans jammed in a motor home, en route LA to Chicago.
>
> 7 in a sedan, 3 crammed in the trunk.
>
> 20 in a 6 x 10 truck, doors locked and rubber-sealed, in the desert daytime heat.
>
> 15 3 days in a van, LA to South Dakota, 2 packs of luncheon meat, 1 loaf of bread.
>
> 22 asphyxiated in a tank truck.
>
> 37 locked in a truck, 3 days, 3 nights, San Diego to Brooklyn.
>
> 21 in a camper, LA to the nation's capital. One sandwich each day, each.

Two became janitors at the Immigration and Naturalization Service offices in Washington. Two were employed at O'Hare Airport in Chicago. Two were security guards, FBI offices, Newark, New Jersey. And two were found painting the Statue of Liberty!

Glossary of Railroad Terms
(in order of appearance)

Skipper	conductor
Brains	conductor
Captain	conductor
Throttle Artist	engineer
Drum	a hard-shelled conductor
Grunt	locomotive driver
King Snipe	foreman of a track gang
Rawhider	executive or superior who is hard on his workmen
Garden	freight yard
Circus	railroad
Cushions	passenger coaches
Harness	dress uniform of a passenger conductor
Glass Car	passenger car
Grass Wagon	tourist car
Drone Cage	private or business car
Herald	the device, monogram, or symbol of a railroad company
Rust	tracks
Hoptoad	to derail
Fly Light	to go on duty after missing a meal
Lizard Scorcher	dining car chef
Horse Over	to throw the mechanism of a locomotive into reverse
Window Music	scenery
Indian Valley Railroad	equivalent of Big Rock Candy Mountain
Grabber	Conductor of a passenger train
Big Ox	conductor

Bibliography

Beebe, Lucius. *High Iron, a Book of Trains.* New York, 1938.

__________. *Mixed Train Daily.* Berkeley, 1961.

Blockson, Charles L. *The Underground Railroad.* New York, 1987.

Bradford, Sarah H. *Harriet, the Moses of her People.* New York, 1901.

Buckmaster, Henrietta. *Let My People Go.* New York, 1941.

Clarke, Lewis, and Clarke, Milton. *Narrative of the Sufferings of Lewis and Milton Clarke.* New York, 1969.

Commonwealth. July 17, 1863.

Conrad, Earl. *Harriet Tubman.* Washington, 1942.

Douglass, Frederick. *My Bondage and my Freedom.* New York and Auburn, 1855.

Marlow, Joan. *The Great Women.* New York, 1979.

Petry, Ann. *Harriet Tubman.* New York, 1955.

Siebert, Wilbur H. *The Underground Railroad: From Slavery to Freedom.* New York, 1898.

Wyman, Lillie B.C. "Harriet Tubman." *New England Magazine* (March 1896).

*　　*　　*

Arizona Daily Star. March 20, 1977.

Common Ground. Autumn, 1949.

Cruz, Pablo. *Pablo Cruz and the American Dream.* Salt Lake City, 1975.

Davidson, John. *The Long Road North.* Garden City, 1979.

Ehrlich, Paul R., Bilderback, Loy, and Ehrlich, Anne H. *The Golden Door.* New York, 1979.

Halsell, Grace. *The Illegals.* New York, 1978.

Johnson, Kenneth F., and Ogle, Nina M. *Illegal Mexican Aliens in the United States.* Washington, 1978.

Kiser and Kiser. *Mexican Workers in the United States.* Albuquerque, 1979.

Lewis, Sasha Gregory. *Slave Trade Today.* Boston, 1979.

Life. March 21, 1951.

McWilliams, Carey. *North from Mexico.* New York, 1960.

Miller, Tom. *On the Border.* Tucson, 1985.

New York Times. July 10, 1973, and March 10, 1974.

Reavis, Dick J. *Without Documents.* New York, 1978.

Samora, Julian. *Los Mojados: The Wetback Story.* South Bend, 1971.

Washington Post. March 4, 1975, November 20, 1976, August 7, 1978, and
    April 2, 1979.

HUASCARÁN

Huascarán (Woss-ca RON) was inspired by my reading of Barbara Bode's *No Bells to Toll* (Charles Scribner's Sons, 1989), an account of the great Peruvian earthquake of 1970. So vast in magnitude and yet too little remembered by the world today, this earthquake and its aftermath exposed the people's extreme vulnerabilities. The poem highlights events from the disaster, drawing on the words of the survivors, as quoted by Bode, as well as from her own words in depicting the trauma and desolation the earthquake engendered.

ONE

I

The Incas are said to have encouraged Pizzaro
to found Lima   as their revenge

It is "the strangest, saddest city in the world"

*   *   *

From Lima, on the Pan-American Highway,
northwestward along the coast,
sand dunes drift across the pavement,
a landscape of desert, lizards, and worm-like snakes,
of winter fog and shimmering summer currents

A right turn, and northeastward,
climbing   climbing,
up the slopes of the *Cordillera Negra,*
bulrushes, palmetto, papaya climbing
to the Andean tableland, the *puna:*
alder, cactus, eucalyptus   climbing
to the *Callejón de Huaylas*   the valley, the alley
between the Andean ranges: the *Cordilleras Negra*
and *Blanca*   the peaks of *Blanca*
capped in snow

Across the *Negra,* and into the *Callejón,*
        one is contained in the valley, the alley
                        the door

back, the door down, the door below

closed

This is another world!

There are the villages:
Recuay, Carhuaz, Huaraz, Yungay, Caraz, Huallanca
—and the city, Huaraz
Settlements as nowhere else in the world
at the foot of such steep mountains:
the *Cordillera Blanca,*
crested by *Huascarán*

The air is clear—
not the wet and fetid of the jungle, nor
coastal smoke and fog—

The parks of Huaraz are the lungs of Peru!

*   *   *

The valley floor still pitch black,
the morning sun slips through the *Blanca,*
around *Huascarán,* the light shifting,
peak to jagged peak, the clouds,
white and pink, shifting

At twilight, the winds are cold and still,
the sky smolders,
the sun lowers
                and the *Negra* is muted

The sun drops, like a settling bull,
beyond the *Negra*

The valley floor is black,
the stars are close

In the *Blanca,* giant needles of rock pierce the sky,
and the moon scrapes them,
sprinkling astral snow,
millions of ice crystals shimmering

*   *   *

Climbing   climbing,
out of Yungay,
up the slopes of *Huascarán,* of the *Blanca,*
all is vertical, all is Indian

The mountains disquieting and attracting,
the disquietude enticing

*   *   *

In their depths live invisible spirits,
and the mountains themselves are spirits,
the tallest, *Huascarán,* the most powerful

Above *Huascarán,* the celestial community:
sun, moon, and stars

Huascarán is alive, breathing, suffering,
Huascarán is magnetic,
Huascarán draws one's blood,
there are rocks on *Huascarán* that break open,
grow and sprout, blossom,
like a flower blooming
Huascarán is linked by tunnel to Cuzco,
to Cuzco: the magnetic center of the universe!

All people are united on the mountains

And yet one is silent. Alone
Silencio   Soledad

Climbing   climbing
Keep *Huascarán* before you. Don't turn your back

In Lima one cannot see *Huascarán*—

But *Huascarán* can be seen from Europe!

II

Of the two mountain ranges, the *Cordillera Negra* is the most ancient; it is worn and eroded. By contrast, the *Blanca* is young, jagged and steep.

Prevailing jungle winds climb the *Blanca*'s eastern slopes. Their moisture chills to snow and falls in layers upon glaciers and ice cornices. At more than 20,000 feet, the *Blanca* is the highest tropical range in the world.

It is so close to the equator that night turns to day, and day to night, with unsettling abruptness.

III

The guinea pigs rustle
in the kitchen yards in Huaraz

They make a whispering sound,
like the wind in the wild grasses

tstsu–tstsu   *tstsu–tstsu*

IV

Many strangers appeared in the valley,
and spirits were seen

Black butterflies fell to the ground,
bats entered the houses,
cocks crowed at night,
dogs barked too loudly

Cats fought on rooftops—
or coupled in strange ways

There was the smell of skunk—
or rotting cadavers

The screech owl increased in numbers:

E-tooo-tu-ooca   *E-tooo-tu-ooca*

TWO

I

3.23 P.M., Sunday, May 31, 1970,
old priest-archaeologist Padre Soriano,
on the terrace of his
little museum in Huaraz,

watched the doves suddenly take flight

Then the *huacas*, the Indian icons
that Soriano
had carefully collected,

began to wobble   to shake   to dance

II

There was no thought

Time stopped, locked

"I felt unbalanced, as if
five people were tugging me in different directions"

(And yet one felt stable,
an unwobbling pivot)

Birds rose   fell   rose

A man was killed by a sheep flying through the air

Lovers, surprised in an embrace,
were catapulted from their room,
impaled on a flagpole

In forty-five seconds, Huaraz foundered,
shattered by the shaking

The snow at *Huascarán's* summit
burst into a cascade of crystals,
like a white rose,
scattering its petals in the air

Hurtling downward, over half a mile wide,
a hundred feet deep,
a mile long,
the avalanche raced, at times, at
a quarter of a thousand miles an hour,
"as if on the wings of a condor"

Boulders hurtled back and forth
across the valley,
colliding, setting off sparks, like lightning

In four minutes—
save only for the tops of four palm tree—
Yungay was smothered:
a viscous mass of snow crystals,
blocks of black ice,
pulverized adobe bricks,
mud,
morainal matter

III

Seventy-five thousand
—more or less—
were dead
          or missing
in the *Callejón de Huaylas*

IV

"Tell me, Lord, what were you doing
the thirty-first of May of 1970
at 3:23 in the afternoon?"

The temperature dropped to near freezing,
a dust cloud rose to 18,000 feet,
shrouding the *Callejón*

Survivors huddled in the moonless night;
men stood in one spot, trembling

The ice melted, cadavers emerged

Survivors donned the clothes of the dead

For three days and three nights,
on the flagpole, the lovers remained,
impaled

(The Sun God punishes lovers)

"Tell me, Lord, what were you doing . . ."

V

Fifteen miles
beneath the floor of the peaceful ocean,
a section of the earth had moved eastward,
sliding like a block of ice

For millions of years, dead organic matter—
seashells, plant and animal carcasses—
had rained and weighed on the ocean floor,
warming it, lubricating the motion of the plates

The earth's crust had fractured,
and
a slab of the peaceful ocean floor
slid beneath the South American continent

VI

The epicenter was at 9° 24′ south latitude, 79° 18′ west longitude, some 15 miles west of the steel and fish meal center of Chimbote. Registration on the Richter scale was 7.7.

In the process of the disturbance, the young snowcapped peaks of the *Cordillera Blanca* gained some several feet in altitude.

VII

Since 1966, on the atoll of Mururoa
in the peaceful ocean,
the government of France
had conducted tests of the atom bomb

This was due west of Peruvian shores

Despite international protest,
bomb tests continued

"To drop a bomb is to disturb
the underpinnings of the earth,
to leave a hole which must be filled"

The last of these tests were
May 1   15   22,
and May 30   1970

*   *   *

"It was the bomb!
The bomb that caused the *terremoto!*"

"Vapors of contamination!"

*   *   *

"Or did a gringo drop a bomb
On *Huascarán?*"

*   *   *

"Or was it the man landing on the moon,
a provocation?"

VIII

There is only a thin layer of earth:

Beneath the earth's crust
all within is water

> (Water is possessed of life and meaning,
> water is inhabited by fantastic creatures.
> The *ichiqolqo*, an alluring blond being
> who beckons and entices one
> into bubbling brooks)

The *terremoto*, the earthquake,
was caused by winds entering the earth
at the poles

The winds clashed,
stirred the internal waters,
and *Huascarán*,
the mightiest volcano of water,

exploded!

IX

The whole earth is overripe, and rotting,
it is like an orange, an avocado, a banana,
rotting

and as the *Callejón*
is at the center of the universe,
it is destined to suffer first and most

"Shall we pardon God for the earthquake?"

THREE

I

Sixty-four aftershocks
shook the valley,
during the first night

Survivors huddled in the cold,
or men stood in one spot trembling

Or walked across the rubble of Huaraz,
over the bones of brothers

It was moonless, quiet,
save only for the creaking of the eucalyptus
and the hushed fall of snow masses from the summits

Silence   Solitude

Silencio   *Soledad*

II

Beneath three miles of dust cloud—
the sky blackened with pulverized adobes—
the *Callejón de Huaylas*
was cut off,
the air strip, the highway, the railroad
blocked with debris

The world
turned on its axis,
revolved around the sun,
but the *Callejón* remained poised and still,
awaiting reentry to the workings of the universe

"We are unhinged"

"Does anyone know what has happened?"

III

After forty-eight hours,
the first helicopter penetrated
the dust cloud, and
landed at Caraz

Cachi cachi the 'copter was called,
the noise like the noise of the wings
of an insect, *cachi cachi*
          (or the guinea pigs in the *ichu:*
          tstsu–tstsu)

Four days passed,
and 'copters dropped the first supplies,
medicine and food,

much of it crashing—
and never retrieved—
on the cordilleran slopes

          (the 'copters afraid to come too near,
          lest the vibrations
          engender landslides)

Ninety-six hours, and now the full scope
of quake and avalanche—
terremoto y aluvión—
became known,

even in Lima

IV

Ask a native, What is nature?
and he will name the names of the mountains

They have suffered,
as they are mineral they cannot talk,
but they are alive and they breathe

The birds were suffering,
the rocks, the mountains,
the sun, the wind, the desolate peaks,
all were sharing our sorrow

"The mountains make me afraid,
but I would never want to leave"

V

The shaking of the layered earth
stirred up the past,
stone with stone

Like the outer bark of the *quinual,*
the day is translucent,
a clear window,

a palimpsest:
one polychrome pushing through another,

the layers of daybreak light,
the planted fields,
the straw huts,

the piles of stone,

the *huacas,*

the crucifixes,

the tape decks

VI

Dogs ate the dead,
and cadavers were burned,
in fear of epidemic

"Huaraz is naked"

"I ask pardon for this nakedness"

*   *   *

The Mayor of Huaraz survived—
and fled the valley

Within several days,
the few of the medical staff who lived,
left

The peasants, the *campesinos,*
came down from the uplands,
helping to dig out the dead,
and looting:
typewriters, adding machines, telephones,
gas pumps from service stations,
all such things as they could never use

A dentist wandered the ruins,
begging for someone to kill him

At night, across what once was Yungay,
could be heard the screams of the crazy one

*   *   *

"*Huascarán*, you are a traitor, a villain!"
"*Huascarán*, you are a murderer!"

*   *   *

A man in black coat and tie,
with stiff white collar,
peered over a remaining standing wall,
on which was painted, in black letters,
Funeral Parlor

FOUR

I

Forty-five seconds
the earth shook

and the *Callejón*
stood still,
      unhinged

Forty-eight hours,
      ninety-six hours,

then the world imploded,
the *terremoto* a hole
that must be filled:

Parachutists jumped to the valley with provisions,
Argentine medics and nurses landed
at a tiny strip in Anta,
there were mercy missions from California and Russia,
the OAS sent in tin and pasteboard dwellings,
the Russians dropped a giant
inflatable geodesic dome,
the Germans sent black igloos
of hardened foam plastic

Gradually, the center of Huaraz was abandoned,
survivors setting up camps in the foothills

(At Nicrupampa the water spigots didn't work,
there were six privies for five thousand,
and typhoid broke out)

The bureaucrats in Lima concluded that,
with so much foreign assistance pouring in,
the survivors must be doing nicely

*   *   *

The dead are living corpses,
to be seen and heard
hovering over the ruins of Huaraz
at night

Souls not absolved will remain,
restless and vexed,
for a year

A native guard,
watching over the ruins at night,
saw a man approaching,
his face hidden by a scarf

The guard touched him,
found he was all bone

Two guards heard and saw a religious procession,
the band playing,
drums, flutes, and trumpets,
musicians and instruments luminous

Reaching the plaza,
the mass turned into a lone man,
wearing a poncho

The guards went mad.

II

The valley was invaded, too,
by keepers of the soul

"... and there shall be ... earthquakes ..."

"There shall not be left here
one stone upon another ..."

All the foreigners were to blame!

The reform Catholics,
with a secular theology of liberation,
were shaking the Church,

acting like Protestants

The wounded, medieval Christ
became—in the universal leveling—
    a risen triumphant Christ

who would demand
—this Marxist Jesus—
the final extirpation
of the ancient Indian rites

The Protestants, the Evangelicals—
already in the valley
before the quake—

a few are said to have shouted,
"Punish more! Punish more!"
as the pagan Catholic earth
shuddered beneath their feet

Twenty Evangelicals, in Yungay,
lay buried beneath the aluvión,

but in Huaraz,
not a single evangelical perished

It was a sign

The Catholics stoned the Evangelicals,
said to 'em,
you are kissing the ass of the devil!

But the Protestants,
bringing food and aid from the north,
and treading upon the old and broken
icons and images,
grew luxuriantly

Evangelism—*el culto*—
Was climbing the mountains!

*　　*　　*

The more one knows the more one doubts

But there is the doubt that ignites faith

*　　*　　*

In Huaraz,
the Assembly of God
occupied a temple
that had withstood the quake

Far into the night—night after night—
the faithful could be heard
singing the familiar hymns,

and speaking in tongues

Glossolalia!

the strange incoherencies
vanishing into the air
of the valley

III

A group of men, survivors,
spent their days drinking,
walking up and down the road

"We wake, we drink, we dream"

"It doesn't matter if another day comes or not"

"At times one does not know how to go on living"

"Tell me what I can do *now*":

the very next moment

*   *   *

Desprendimiento,

         detached

FIVE

I

The shaking of the layered earth
stirred up the past,
stone with stone

The survivors became *bricoleurs,*
handymen,
arranging and rearranging the odd materials,
practicing the art of *bricolage:*

the older shining through,
a palimpsest

II

Chapels that survived
were used as granaries

New granaries,
built by reformists,
were quickly turned into chapels

and numberless libations of corn beer
were poured on the ground

III

Survivors—
so few with those who perished—
felt the pain of their guilt

Some fled to Lima,
only to return,
unable to abandon
bruised and injured Huaraz

"If I go away,
Huaraz is going to suffer a little more"

"Huaraz is like a mother,
tender and wounded
We must be at her side
Until she is well"

"I have pain for this region
I shall never leave it"

IV

The camps became hated places

"How painful it is to live in a house
that does not belong to one!"

To live *en casa ajena,*
an alien house,
the house of another

The families chose to rebuild
on the precise sites
where their homes had fallen,
to live with the dead

"Here there is life!"

"We want to be here,
to die where we were born"

"One's own being makes him stay,
returning for the night to the same place"

Terruño: one's place, one's land

One was released by the *terremoto*
from all but the land

Huaraz must be rebuilt, entire,
"in its place"

V

The bureaucrats in Lima suddenly
woke up!

Huaraz, Yungay,
had been wiped out!

The entire *Callejón* is a
tabula rasa!

What an opportunity!

The Revolutionary Military Government would now take command, the *Callejón* would be rebuilt in conformity with modern technologies, and all decisions would emanate from Lima.
    The Commission for the Reconstruction and Rehabilitation of the Affected Zone came into being.

CRYRZA!   CRYRZA!

"The earthquake of the 31st of May 1970 confirmed the unequal and unjust socioeconomic and politial order existing in the Affected Zone, a situation that as Revolutionary Peruvians have the obligation to change through the tasks of Reconstruction and Rehabilitation."
    The first act of CRYRZA was to place a moratorium on all transactions pertaining to real estate.

So that the survivor,
poised in his hated camp,
could not lay a hand on his own land

So far, so remote,
this distracted Andean valley,

and all eyes of the world
focused upon it

"The things announced by the government are bad,
because it is thinking very high . . .
Even the skin of the potato they are controlling"

A great map was unveiled,
with the "new" city of Huaraz

Census takers—statistics stalkers—
woke survivors at night,
to be counted

But night after night,
a crippled old woman
hobbled to the ruins,

slept in a tent
in her *terruño*,
her place.

VI

CRYRZA!

Near the quake's anniversary
a brigade of bulldozers
crawled up the mountain road
from Pativilca

attacked the ruins
at Huaraz

CRYRZA paid the contractors
for the rubble   by the cubic meter

so they dug and dug,
lit torches to work around the clock,

unearthed a microbus
with twenty-nine cadavers,

dug and leveled,

leveled,

and then trundled back,
back down the mountain road,

with the rubble

If the camps,
the cardboard houses dropped from the sky,
had been a bombing, *un bombardeo,*
CRYRZA's dozers
were a second quake

CRYRZA was earthquaking! *Terremoteando!*

Huaraz lay still   leveled
for more than another year

SIX

I

Spain's greatest bullfighters
offered a *corrida* in Madrid,
to benefit the survivors

After sixteen months,
nothing moved at Huaraz

There was a rumor that the *Callejón*
would be abandoned,
everyone would be moved to the coast!

But then, after twenty months,
CRYRZA arrived again, in force,
with bulldozers and shiny new jeeps

Modern offices were set up

Huaraz—what was left—became an occupied city

"We must create a metamorphosis in the valley . . ."

"Upon the ruins of the cities
and the dust of the earth today faded,
we will construct a part of the New Peru
of our children"

To reject the "new Huaraz,"
to reconstruct the "old reality,"
would be "antijustice" and "antitechnology"

Instead, a "human revolution" must take place

II

From time to time
a straggler came down from the camps
in search of *terruño*

He marked out in chalk lines
on the leveled landscape
what had been "his" land

He wrote his name in the dust,
Planted a tiny Peruvian flag,
and started to rebuild

And overnight his work was dismantled by
CRYRZA

III

The peasants were told they must become responsible,
they must handle their own land transactions

"You must learn how to use a typewriter"

"Huaraz must take on the physiognomy of a city, which
means uniformity"

Trenches for sewer and water were dug by CRYRZA

They were deep, and for months
remained empty

A peasant, wandering at night,
would fall in,
become lost

IV

CRYRZA built model concrete houses

"We want to bring a better life
to the people up here
We don't want them to die
in the huts they could build for themselves"

"But these people are so strange . . ."

The natives felt the concrete houses held no sense of what a
room is,

what a window is

Worst of all,
the windows did not face *Huascarán*

V

The Indian must be "humanized,"
he must be "culturized"

All will be equal

The earthquake leveled the landscape,
now humankind will be leveled,

each family to receive an allotment
of 300 square meters

in the new Huaraz

VI

"The priests will make candles
from our body fat,
the landowner will use it
to grease his tractor"

But the new priests
—The Reform Catholic priests—
went into the fields in shirt-sleeves,

explained exploitation

"Now you will be equal . . ."

VII

At once,
in the midst of food, drink, and merriment,
everyone would suddenly burst into tears

"This is what we are really living
Do you see how we are"

"Our story must be told,
the world must know,
so that we do not live like shadows without footprints"

"You must remember not to forget"

The tears flowing . . .

VIII

"This landscape softens our character
We do not explode so easily
when we live in this paradise
We endure like water
dripping slowly into a gourd"

"Then suddenly we explode"

When the world comes to an end,
all will be flat

There will be no mountains

VIII

"This landscape softens our character
We do not explode so easily
when we live in this paradise
We endure like water
dripping slowly into a gourd"

"Then suddenly we explode"

When the world comes to an end,
all will be flat

There will be no mountains

SEVEN

I

Were the two mountain ranges at war?
the *Cordilleras Negra y Blanca*
trying to destroy each other?

*   *   *

The Sun God punishes lovers
(the couple impaled on the flagpole)

"But why am I alive, among so many dead?"

"What were you doing, God, at 3:23 P.M. . . . ?"

"Shall we pardon God, for the earthquake?"

> *(El loco*, the crazy one,
>   claimed to have buried 6,892 cadavers)

"It was the Will of God, the Punishment"
Castigo de Dios

We are naked   We are guilty   Forgive us

    the whole earth is overripe, and rotting . . .

II

The priests of the Church,
those with an ear to Marx, to Peking,
plunged into social mobilization
and agrarian reform

"Theology of liberation"

"Political hermeneutics of the Gospel"

Siding with the oppressed,
the men of cloth became pragmatic,

while the Revolutionary Military Government
in Lima
spoke of its mission with messianic zeal,

Church become secular,
Government sacred

and between the two,
the *campesino*

III

In all the valley
there was not a church bell in its belfry

The Soledad bell—
from the church sacred to
the *Señor de la Soledad*—
lay on the ground

"We have to put our bell in place.
This bell is the most renowned and important bell
from before. It is from before!"

The *campesinos* came down the mountainsides
with candles, flowers, drums, flutes, and trumpets,

a tiny wrinkled old woman
directed the work—

She called for ropes to hoist the bell,
stones to hammer into the ground
a frame of logs from which the bell would hang

"Straighter, straighter, straighter!"
"No, farther back, back, back"

For want of a ladder
a man stood on a donkey
to raise the bell

"No, pull, pull, pull!"

"Let us have some *chicha!*"

The liquor was poured,
the band played,
the bell was hoisted
from the donkey's back

"Ring the bell!"

But there was no clapper

So they hit the bell with a stone,
and the band played,
drums, trumpets,
a *huayno,*
and the *chicha* flowed

"It has another sound,
I don't know how to say it,
but lovely, lovely,
not like other bells"

IV

All the ancient Indian customs—
the dances and bands,
processions and fireworks—
held the Indian backward and superstitious,

and must be extirpated

"To uproot the *huacas* from their hearts,
a second and third plowing will be required"

The *huacas,* the primitive idols,
had the faces of men and women,

some the Indians called sons, wives, or brothers

But "some of the *huacas*
are hills and high places,
which time cannot consume"

A second and third plowing . . .

V

And after the *huacas,*
there were the Catholic icons,

which the reform priests
disparaged as assemblages of wood or gypsum

But to the native, they were flesh and blood

"A statue is a person
that enters through the eyes"

Like the *huacas,*
the icons
may have brothers and sisters,
many blood relatives

VI

Statues of saints had been shattered,
church bells lay on the ground

And then the bulldozers . . .

But some few of the icons survived,
and they were human:

wounded, but not dead,
to be saved,
to become once again healthy

"This is *San José*"
—the woman carefully disrobing the statue,
placing each garment in a pile on the ground—
"He was wounded in the earthquake
He has lost an arm"

"I had a dream last night
in which *San José* appeared to me
and said, 'Have you forgotten me?
How long are you going to allow me
to be put aside in a corner?
You must see to it that I am fixed up.'"

VII

Holy Week,
nearly two years after the quake,
the *campesinos* marched through the rubble,
carrying their wounded images

Easter Sunday,
the roads to the coast were open,
the sweet smell of gasoline filled the air,

and a driver slipped a cassette into his tape deck:

The valley,
the *Callejon de Huaylas*,
came alive with

"Jesus Christ Superstar"

EIGHT

I

In February, during carnival time,
the Indians from the countryside
would bring down into the valley towns
their great mountain crosses
which during the year stood on hilltops
defending their crops against hail and landslides

"The cross moves by itself through the air,
as if it had wings"
"We are carrying it,
and it is as if it weighed nothing"

                    "But if it is angry,
                    and doesn't want to move,
                    it weighs a ton"

The crosses would be taken to the churches
for a special Mass, during which
they would be blessed by the priest,
and would then make their return journey,
back up the mountains.

For 400 years it had been this way in the valley

The reform priests
turned against the practice

Such superstitious worship of crosses
—like the worship of primitive *huacas*—
must be extirpated

"But we continue dancing
and getting drunk with the crosses"

Dancing, perhaps fighting,
hurling flour and talcum on one another,
with paper streamers wrapped around their necks,
becoming stumbling drunk

> (The cross is human,
> it lacks only a mouth to speak)

> (In dreams,
> the cross is standing at your side,
> it speaks to you as a man speaks to you)

> (The mountains are mineral,
> they cannot talk,
> but they suffer)

II

The tin slab door at the entrance to the church
was flung open
and three *campesinos* struggled inside
with a cross so huge
they could barely get it through the doorway

Staggering under its weight,
they let it fall with a thump,
so that it lay propped on a wooden bench

The decorative *machitu,* the silvered leaves,
glistened in a ray of sun
that entered the open door

The exhausted men faced Padre Espinoza

The congregation,
between the *campesinos* by the fallen cross
and the priest by the altar,
looked from one to the other

in silence

"It will be damaged," the priest finally said,
softly

He whispered to two altar boys,
who walked to the back of the church
and whispered to the *campesinos*

Together, with great effort,
they stood the cross up,
resting it against a wooden beam

Again, *silencio*

At last Padre Espinoza raised the chalice,
extended it toward the cross, and began to sing:
"I adore you, Holy Cross"

and the congregation exhaled

Other crosses were shoved under the lintel

Padre Espinoza walked to the entrance
"You know that this was prohibited"

"Little father, we know, we know . . .
but please bless them"

"With affection, I do it"

and with holy water
he sprinkled the blessing
on the crosses

III

Staggering under their burdens
the Indians
ascended the steep mountain slopes,
not walking but running!

as if the crosses were flying of their own accord!

NINE

I

Years ago,
a lady went into the swampy countryside,
on the edge of Huaraz,
to pick grasses for her guinea pigs

(tstsu–tstsu)   *(tstsu–tstsu)*

A bleeding crucifix appeared to her

She rushed back to town,
gathered friends,
they bore the new Christ in procession,
installed the figure in the cathedral,
in a special glass case

The next morning he was not there

He had returned to the marsh

Every morning the people brought the figure
to the cathedral,
and every night he returned

He did not like the cathedral,
it was *casa ajena,* a foreign house,
the remote marsh was his place, his *terruño*

The Christ of Solitude:
El Señor de la Soledad

*   *   *

In another tale,
the image was carved in secrecy
by a bearded sculptor,
who never touched the food
that people left for him

and the people thereby knew
that the bearded man was Christ himself,
who would care for Huaraz and the countryside

The sculptor then became the image:
The *Señor de la Soledad* is Christ himself!
Christ himself lives in Huaraz!

Only through this image
are we able to know death!

He has appeared for the salvation
and protection of Huaraz,
he must never be taken to the countryside,

he must remain forever in Huaraz

Soledad means tranquility, to be alone

Here in Huaraz *El Señor* holds back the glacial lakes,
the volcanoes of water

He could make the whole world disappear,
if he wished

*   *   *

There was a fire (1965)
El Señor was damaged . . . wounded

The charred image lay in the church
prepared as for a wake

It was like burned flesh, not wood

El Señor de la Soledad is indeed Christ himself!

The bishop sent to Spain for a sculptor,
to Lima for an artisan
(The figure must not leave Huaraz!)

The two craftsmen restored the image
as it lay on a table in the open plaza,
in full view of the populace

*   *   *

There was a rumor
that the figure was not *El Señor,*

that the bishop had
sold the original in Spain,

and this was a duplicate

People had dreams
in which *El Señor de la Soledad* revealed himself,
begging to be rescued from Spain,

lest there be a catastrophe in the valley

(the absence of the image from Huaraz
could mean God's absence)

3:23 P.M., Sunday, May 31, 1970 . . .

   * * *

When *El Señor* was found,

dug out from under the rubble of the church,
the image was torn apart,
the feet crushed,
in the heat of the earth the paint had peeled

". . . pounded and beaten by fallen timbers,
suffering cold and heat . . ."

They covered him with flowers,
laid him on a table in a little hut,
put sweet-smelling herbs and lillies on him

Later he was moved to a makeshift cane-and-mud church,
wrapped in plastic
to protect against inclemencies

The people said his face was not right,
and since the earthquake, he was really poor:
"He hardly has any clothes left"

   * * *

Elsewhere—distant from the Soledad sanctuary—
the Evangelicals gathered,
singing the familiar hymns

speaking in tongues!

Glossolalia!

the strange incoherencies
vanishing into the air
of the valley

*   *   *

And yet, *El Señor*—
The Lord of Solitude—

"Do not look too long into his eyes—
—they are real!"

The Christ abandoned and forgotten,
naked in the face of solitude

*   *   *

Every night a deranged woman,
babbling and haranguing incoherently,
lay until dawn beside the wounded figure

EPILOGUE

In the *Blanca,* giant needles of rock pierce the sky
and the moon scrapes them,
sprinkling astral snow

E-tooo-tu-ooca   *E-tooo-tu-ooca*

Huascarán is alive, breathing, suffering

"Does anyone know what has happened?"

Cachi   *Cachi*

The more one knows, the more one doubts

       *　　*　　*

"To uproot the *huacas* from their hearts,
a second and third plowing will be required"

                (The mountains are mineral,
they cannot talk,
but they suffer)

"I have pain for this region
I shall not leave it."

"Tell me, Lord, what were you doing . . ."

"Huascarán, you are a murderer!"

CRYRZA! CRYRZA!

Terremoteando!

"It was the will of God, the Punishment"

"Punish more! Punish more!"

*   *   *

"Jesus Christ Superstar"

". . . dancing
and getting drunk with the crosses"

"Huaraz is naked"

"It doesn't matter if another day comes or not"

Silence   Solitude

Silencio   *Soledad*

"You must remember not to forget"

Bibliography

Blank, J.P. "Earthquake! The horror that hit Peru." *Reader's Digest,* Vol. 97, (October 1970).
Bode, Barbara. *No Bells to Toll.* New York, 1989.
Bonner, Raymond. "Peru's War." *The New Yorker* (January 4, 1988).
"Environmental Disaster-Acts of Nature and Man, The Peru Earthquake: A Special Study." *Bulletin of the Atomic Scientists* (October 1970).
Joseph, Lawrence E. *Gaia, The Growth of an Idea.* New York, 1990.

THE WONDERFUL WHITE WHALE OF KANSAS

The Wonderful White Whale
of Kansas

"From the far north they heard a low wail of the wind, and Uncle Henry and Dorothy could see where the long grass bowed in waves before the coming storm. There now came a sharp whistling in the air from the south, and as they turned their eyes that way, they saw ripples in the grass coming from that direction also."

> (Olson: "The fulcrum of America is the Plains, half sea, half land . . ."

> (Dorothy's last name is Gale

"The house whirled around two or three times and rose slowly through the air. Dorothy felt as if she were going up in a balloon."

*　　*　　*

"It was very dark, and the wind howled horribly around her, but Dorothy found she was riding quite easily. After the first whirls around, and one other time when the house tipped badly, she felt as if she were being rocked gently, like a baby in a cradle."

> "And now concentric circles seized the lone boat, and all of its crew, and each floating oar, and every lance-pole, and spinning, animate and inanimate, all round and round in one vortex, carried the smallest chip of the *Pequod* out of sight."

"In spite of the swaying of the house and the wailing of the wind, Dorothy soon closed her eyes and fell fast asleep."

". . . and the great shroud of the sea rolled on as it rolled five thousand years ago."

*   *   *

"Dorothy lived in the midst of the great Kansas prairies, with Uncle Henry, who was a farmer, and Aunt Em, who was the farmer's wife. Their house was small, for the lumber to build it had to be carried by wagon many miles. There were four walls, a floor and a roof, which made one room; and this room contained a rusty-looking cooking stove, a cupboard for the dishes, a table, three or four chairs, and the beds. Uncle Henry and Aunt Em had a big bed in one corner, and Dorothy a little bed in another corner. There was no garret at all, and no cellar—except a small hole, dug in the ground, a cyclone cellar, where the family could go in case one of those great whirlwinds arose, mighty enough to crush any building in its path. It was reached by a trap-door in the middle of the floor, from which a ladder led down into the small, dark hole.

When Dorothy stood in the doorway and looked around, she could see nothing but the great gray prairie on every side. Not a tree nor a house broke the broad sweep of flat country that reached the edge of the sky in all directions. The sun had baked the plowed land into a gray mass, with little cracks running through it. Even the grass was not green, for the sun had burned the tops of the long blades until they were the same gray color to be seen everywhere. Once the house had been painted, but the sun blistered the paint and the rains washed it away, and now the house was as dull and gray as everything else.

When Aunt Em came there to live she was a young, pretty wife. The sun and wind had changed her, too. They had taken the sparkle from her eyes and left them a sober gray; they had taken the red from her cheeks and lips, and they were gray also. She was thin and gaunt, and never smiled, now."

*   *   *

The young lives of both authors—Herman Melville and L. Frank Baum—were crossed by national depressions: Melville in 1837, Baum in 1893. Both men failed at earlier enterprises, before turning to writing.

In both novels—*Moby Dick* and *The Wizard of Oz*—the protagonist is an outcast, or an orphan. Biblical Ishmael was illegitimate, a "wild ass of a man," driven from the tribe, living in the desert.

> (Perhaps Kansas is the grim desert of the Old Testament, where Ishmael wandered, and Dorothy was so content)

Dorothy is specifically an orphan, with no mention of her parents.

In Melville's final novel, *Billy Budd,* the Handsome Sailor is once more a foundling: time, place, and circumstances of birth, unknown.

> "On the second day, a sail drew near, nearer, and picked me up at last. It was the devious-cruising *Rachel*, that in her retracing search for her missing children, only found another orphan" —ISHMAEL.

*   *   *

Children's librarians, critics, parents generally disapproved of *The Wizard of Oz.* It lacked literary quality; the writing was sometimes sloppy. The first edition was in fact published by a small press (with some of Baum's own money behind it); they could not afford a good editor. And how many times have we heard from the literary purists that Melville could have used a good editor! Look at *Pierre!*

Many an American poet has misfired on Melville. I know of no mention of him by Eliot; Williams mentions him once, obliquely ("Flossie is now reading *Moby-Dick*"); and Pound referred to Olson's Melville book, *Call Me Ishmael*, as "a labor-saving device: you don't have to read Melville."

Adults disapproved of *Oz*, but the children demanded it!

With the publication of *Moby-Dick*, one critic described it as "so much trash belonging to the worst school of Bedlam literature."

*   *   *

"The cyclone had set the house down, very gently—for a cyclone—in the midst of a country of marvelous beauty. There were lovely patches of green sward all about, with stately trees bearing rich and luscious fruits. Banks of gorgeous flowers were on every hand, and birds with rare and brilliant plumages sang and fluttered in the trees and bushes. A little way off was a small brook, rushing and sparkling along between green banks, and murmuring in a voice very grateful to a little girl who had lived so long on the dry, gray prairies."

Arrived at the Emerald City, Dorothy and friends were fitted with dark glasses, to filter the glitter and glare of it all, which otherwise would have blinded them. The Emerald City is Hollywood itself —theater!—manipulating us, with a dishonesty comparable to a politician's, through our eager suspension of disbelief.

How many American artists and writers have fled their barren Kansas or its equivalent, for a glittering Emerald City: Pound from Idaho, Eliot from Missouri, Crane from Chagrin Falls—the list is endless. And wherever they find themselves—Greenwich Village, London, the Left Bank, Bolinas—it is the Emerald City . . . and the green spectacles continue to protect their aging eyes.

*   *   *

But Dorothy was different. A child-woman, mature beyond her years, she adopted and cared for her damaged friends—the Scarecrow, the Tin Man, the Cowardly Lion; she accepted this responsibility cheerfully. But much deeper in her heart and mind was her responsibility to Aunt Em and Uncle Henry, and the grim, hardscrabble farm in Kansas. To return there is her constantly repeated wish.

"'Where is Kansas?' asked the man in surprise.

'I don't know,' replied Dorothy, sorrowfully, 'but it is my home, and I'm sure it's somewhere.'"

*   *   *

Melville's first book was *Typee* and the final work was *Billy Budd.* Within these brackets lies the body of his work.

Writing in Melville Society *Extracts* (September 1995), Elizabeth Renker points out that whereas *Typee* purports to be autobiographical, made up entirely of first-hand accounts, much of it was, in fact, lifted from the books of others; this was plagiarism, which Melville disguised by mutilating the texts so that they could not be traced. She suggests that while committing these acts, he was nonetheless disturbed by them; and she further suggests that this practice "shapes the terms of the text," particularly in his descriptions of the natives' facial tattoos. The natives become actors, their faces masked, or "made up"; and Melville is both playwright and director of this stagey performance.

In *Billy Budd,* written late in life, Melville presents us with Captain the Honorable Edward Fairfax Vere, Master of His Majesty's ship *Bellipotent,* faced with the dilemma of Billy, who had accidentally killed one of Vere's officers. Aware that the crew's sympathies (as well as, to some extent, his own) lay with Billy, Vere was nonetheless convinced that Billy must be hanged. Following procedure, he convened a Drumhead Court, and Captain the Honorable Vere—the Politician, the Performer—set about to swing its views to his:

> "But the exceptional in the matter moves the hearts within you. Even so too is mine moved. But let not warm hearts betray heads that should be cool . . . Well, the heart here, sometimes the feminine in man . . . must here be ruled out."

The Court convicted, and the Handsome Sailor was duly hanged.

*   *   *

"You see, Oz is a great wizard, and can take on any form he wishes. So that some say he looks like a bird; and some say he looks like an elephant; and some say he looks like a cat. To others he appears as a beautiful fairy, or a brownie, or in any other form that pleases him. But who the real Oz is, when he is in his own form, no living person can tell."

But as it turns out, there is no real Wizard. He is a trickster, a charlatan, a fraud—an actor: A creature of no self and all selves. He is a ventriloquist, and with this and other tricks he keeps the populace of the Emerald City happy. Fool 'em, convince 'em that what you're telling 'em is what they want to hear, feed on their eager suspension of disbelief. (If you live in Hollywood, and believe in Hollywood, how can you not be happy?)

Later, after the Wizard has revealed himself to Dorothy and her friends, the Scarecrow suggests that he should be ashamed of himself, and he quite readily agrees, indeed he should be. And yet, knowing him for what he is, the Scarecrow, the Tin Man, and the Lion willingly comply with his ruses, accepting and believing in the brains, the heart, and the courage that he doles out.

Dorothy is right: Better Kansas!

*　　*　　*

Melville's Star Performer, of course, was Captain Ahab.

Ahab, working the crew into a frenzy:

> "'What do ye do when ye see a whale, men?'
> 'Sing out for him!'
> 'And what do ye do next, men?'
> 'Lower away, and after him!'
> 'And what tune is it ye pull to, men?'
> 'A dead whale or a stove boat!'
>
> More and more strangely and fiercely glad and approving, grew the countenance of the old man at every shout; while the mariners began to gaze curiously at each other, as if marveling how it was that they themselves became so excited at such seemingly purposeless questions.
>
> 'Aye, aye!' shouted the harpooneers and seamen, running closer to the excited old man. 'A sharp eye for the white whale; a sharp eye for Moby-Dick!'"

All are swept along; all, that is, except pragmatic Starbuck, the business man:

> "'Vengeance on a dumb brute!' cried Starbuck . . . 'To be enraged with a dumb thing, Captain Ahab, seems blasphemous.'"

Ahab:

> "'Hark ye yet again,—the little lower layer.'"

Ah, yes, Ahab, that's the one that gets 'em, gets 'em every time: "the little lower layer." I am in touch with something deeper, something of which you, Starbuck, have only the dimmest intimations. The lower layer! The deeper wisdom! Wisdom of the East! Wisdom of God! Wisdom of the Ages! The Great All!
  Ahab, the Wonderful Wizard!

> "'All visible objects, man, are but as pasteboard masks. . . . there, some unknown but still reasoning thing puts forth the mouldings of its features from behind the unreasoning mask.'"

> "'So, so; thou reddenest and palest; my heat has melted thee to anger-glow.'"

Again, invoking the crew:

> "'The crew, man, the crew! Are they not one and all with Ahab?'"

Finally, Ahab, aside:

> "'Something shot from my dilated nostrils, he has inhaled it in his lungs. Starbuck now is mine . . .'"

Starbuck:

> "'God keep me!—keep us all!'"

*   *   *

The Scarecrow and Dorothy:

"'I cannot understand why you would want to leave this beautiful country and go back to the dry, gray place you call Kansas.'

'That is because you have no brains,' answered the girl. 'No matter how dreary and gray our homes are, we people of flesh and blood would rather live there than in any other country, be it ever so beautiful . . .'

The Scarecrow sighed.

'Of course I cannot understand it,' he said. 'If your heads were stuffed with straw, like mine, you would probably all live in the beautiful places, and then Kansas would have no people at all. It is fortunate for Kansas that you have brains.'"

> (Melville: "Who in the rainbow can draw the line where the violet tint ends and the orange tint begins? Distinctly we see the difference of the color, but where exactly does the first one visibly enter into the other? So with sanity and insanity."
>
> (. . . "he who has never felt, momentarily, what madness is has but a mouthful of brains."

* * *

The 1939 MGM movie, *The Wizard of Oz*, has been shown on television more frequently than any other movie ever made.

The book, published first in 1900, has sold more than 7,000,000 copies.

The silver shoes (ruby, in the movie) that carried Dorothy back to Aunt Em were lost in the flight. Their magic gone, Oz was presumably separated forever from Kansas. But with the publication of the book, almost at once there was a demand for sequels, and from 1900 until his death in 1919, L. Frank Baum turned out a new *Oz* book every year. He once tried to produce a final, terminal *Oz*, but the market wouldn't let it happen. After his death, ghost writers continued to turn them out, one a year. (For the purposes of this essay, I have consulted none of these sequels.)

Two years after Baum's death the revival of Melville's reputation began. It had slumbered for seventy years, since the publication of *Moby-Dick.* The book has now become a "classic," in the sense defined by Mark Twain, i.e., a book everybody wants to have read but nobody wants to read. Scholars become slightly funny in the head as they identify with Melville, with his "genius," his "insanity." Brow-beaten students, slave-driven through *Moby-Dick,* may react as follows:

"There are no women in it."

"What does this have to do with ME?"

Or one coed, bless her, who said to her professor: "I'm so glad you made me read it."

*   *   *

If there have been so many sequels to *Oz,* why not *Moby-Dick?* Perhaps that's an omission begging for correction:

Let's see, now. Ahab, officers, and crew went down with the *Pequod,* while Ishmael survived on Queequeg's coffin (Dorothy's magic shoes).

But perhaps they didn't all go down. Perhaps, through some meteorological or oceanic phenomenon, ship, boats, and men all floated to the surface, drifted to the nearby Marquesas, where the men settled and intermarried with the natives, and eventually scattered into the world.

> (There is a woman now living in Nuka-hiva who claims descent from Melville through his affair with the girl whom he identifies as Fayaway, in *Typee.* The natives honor her claim and she has become something of a celebrity.

A great-grandson of Ahab becomes a dentist in Peoria. A descendent of Queequeg is now the first female mixed-race mayor of a major American city. Starbuck's lineage leads to a hippie, a flower child, last seen in a cloud of marijuana smoke in a Vermont commune. (He heats his cabin with wood, and is an expert on the burning qualities of New England hardwoods: oak is excellent, but requires extensive seasoning; white birch is pretty, but burns too fast; ash is desirable, as it is light and requires little seasoning, due to low moisture content.)

A descendent of Tashtego now runs a computer-operated reservation service for tourists in New Bedford. He also has an interest in a whale-watching enterprise. One of Stubbs' great-grandsons married into an old Boston family, is now a corporate lawyer, and along the way has acquired an obscene amount of money. He vacations in the exotic places of the world: the Galápagos, the Antarctic, the Marquesas, or floating down the Seine in a barge ("we did our own cooking!") Still another descendent married a young gentleman from the South (forbears going back to the Confederacy). They live now in the Berkshires, near Melville's old home, and she writes popular novels. Etc.

*　　*　　*

"Dorothy lived in the midst of the great Kansas prairies, with Uncle Henry, who was a farmer, and Aunt Em, who was the farmer's wife. Their house was small, for the lumber to build it had to be carried by wagon many miles. There were four walls, a floor and a roof, which made one room; and this room contained a rusty-looking cooking stove, a cupboard for the dishes, a table, three or four chairs . . ."

"'And oh, Aunt Em! I'm so glad to be at home again!'"